COMING INTO PLAY

MY LIFE IN TEST CRICKET

Andrew Strauss

HODDER &
STOUGHTON

Copyright © 2006 by Andrew Strauss

First published in Great Britain in 2006 by Hodder & Stoughton
A division of Hodder Headline

The right of Andrew Strauss to be identified as the Author of
the Work has been asserted by him in accordance with the
Copyright, Designs and Patents Act 1988.

A Hodder and Stoughton Book

2

A CIP catalogue record for this title is available from the British Library

ISBN-13: 978 0 340 84066 5
ISBN-10: 0 340 84066 8

Typeset in Nexus Serif by
Rowland Phototypesetting Ltd
Bury St Edmunds, Suffolk

Printed and bound in Great Britain by
Mackays of Chatham Ltd, Chatham, Kent

Hodder Headline's policy is to use papers that are natural,
renewable and recyclable products and made from wood grown
in sustainable forests. The logging and manufacturing processes are expected
to conform to the environmental regulations of the country of origin.

Hodder & Stoughton Ltd
A division of Hodder Headline
338 Euston Road
London NW1 3BH

For Ruth and Sam

CONTENTS

CONTENTS

ACKNOWLEDGEMENTS

I am determined for this section of the book not to sound like an Oscars acceptance speech, but there are a number of people who have spent precious time and energy trying to get the best out of a very stubborn author.

Nothing would have been possible without my parents, and sisters, who have always been there to offer help and encouragement, during good times and bad. In helping me out with the text Angus Fraser showed the endless dedication that characterised his career, and I definitely owe him a decent bottle of wine.

Thanks, too, to Roddy Bloomfield and everyone at Hodder for giving me this opportunity. They showed great patience and appreciation of the various demands placed on Test cricketers. I would also like to thank the *Sunday Telegraph* for allowing me to use extracts from my column.

Finally, and most importantly, thanks have to go to my wife Ruth. She has been a tower of strength throughout my career, and has had to put up with me stomping round the house searching for the right words and phrases throughout the writing of this book.

There are many others, too. You know who you are.

Photographic Acknowledgements

The author and publisher would like to thank the following for permission to reproduce photographs:

AFP/Getty Images, Africa Visuals/Empics, AP/Empics, Philip Brown, Patrick Eagar, Empics, Getty Images.

1
ON THE OUTSIDE

There are many ways in which England cricketers learn of their selection. Some have received congratulatory phone calls from a selector, others are tipped off by an indiscreet journalist. Most, however, have realised their fate via the radio or television. I became aware of my selection for the one-day legs of the 2003/04 winter tours of Bangladesh and Sri Lanka during the morning session of Middlesex's final championship match of the season against Nottinghamshire.

Middlesex had secured their place in the following season's first division and the game was drifting along when suddenly the Test and one-day squads appeared on each of the electronic scoreboards at Lord's. I was aware of the imminent announcement, and felt I had a good chance of being selected, but it still came as a huge shock when I saw my name on the list. I was overwhelmed with excitement, and I found it ridiculously difficult to concentrate on the game I was playing in. My team-mates congratulated me and the members complimented me on my selection as I walked off the field and through the Long Room for lunch. It was a strange feeling. I felt that I was ready and had done enough to be selected but it was still unbelievably rewarding to gain recognition, and to realise all the years of hard work had been worthwhile.

Hearing of your selection is obviously a very special moment but it is only when your England kit begins to arrive that the enormity of what you have achieved starts to sink in. Once selected you move into the 'England bubble' and there is a constant supply of goods being delivered to your house. Mobile phones, blazers, bags – it was like being a kid at Christmas all over again. Best of all was receiving my England shirts. When I opened the parcel containing them I could not stop smiling. There they were, authentic England shirts with STRAUSS, 14, ENGLAND on the back. I could not take my eyes off them. It was brilliant. I had arrived.

My parents were absolutely thrilled. When I was at school they had never seriously believed that I would make a career out of cricket. They initially considered it to be a bit of fun and something I would drift away from before getting a job in the City. As I made my way at Middlesex, however, they gradually warmed to the idea of their son being a professional cricketer. They were understandably proud and pleased that I had stuck at my cricket and worked diligently. The progress to where I was now had not always been smooth and there had been times when I had found cricket a little tedious. But in all our eyes my choice of career had seemed worthwhile.

At Radley College I enjoyed all sport and, like any kid, preferred playing it to doing my history revision. You name it, I played it. Cricket, rugby, tennis, squash, golf – I gave them all a go, but I was never particularly focused on cricket. I treated sport as a recreation, something that helped me switch off from my schoolwork. We had superb facilities at Radley but the public school system is very much tailored towards getting good academic results, heading off to university and then migrating to the City. It is a well-worn conveyor belt which is surprisingly difficult to get off.

My parents were professional people and they encouraged me

to focus on my studies. Sport was there to be enjoyed, but only really to provide a much-needed distraction from the serious stuff. Mind you, if I was forking out that much money to send my child to a private school, I would probably feel similarly. What the school and my parents both did give me, however, was the opportunity to try anything and everything. From rock-climbing to rock music, we were encouraged to do it all, but making a career as a sportsman still seemed a slightly strange direction to be going in.

I was quite good at cricket at school but there seemed to be hundreds of others around the country who were much better than me. I scored a few runs opening the batting but I never felt I was anything special. What I did love, however, was the game. I would spend hours, either in front of the bowling machine, or playing stump cricket with my mates during breaks in lessons. I have always had a pretty good work ethic but I could only do this with support and I was very lucky to have Andy Wagner as my cricket coach. He is a great guy and has a great talent in under-standing what makes a player tick. We spent hour after hour in the nets at Radley working on grooving my shots. It was here where I established a technique that worked for me. Wagner and Bert Robinson, a Radley stalwart who had been at the school long enough to have coached the great Ted Dexter, taught me the fundamentals of batting. They kept their coaching simple and showed me the importance of playing straight and being balanced at the crease. Above all, however, they encouraged me to enjoy the game, go out there and express myself, and not get too down if things didn't go my way.

Although the majority of the cricket I played was for the school, I also represented Oxfordshire Under-19s, and during the long summer holidays I turned out for Gerrards Cross Cricket Club every now and then. It was all good fun, but hardly the sort of regime that was going to register on the radars of England age-group selectors. Quite frankly, though, I didn't care. I was playing the game for the right reasons, because I loved it and enjoyed it.

It was only when I went to Durham University in September 1995 to read Economics that I began to consider pursuing cricket as a career. It helped that Ben Hutton and Robin Martin-Jenkins, with their impeccable cricketing family credentials, were thinking of doing the same. I gained confidence from the fact that I was not the only person who was prepared to take the risk of jumping off the City-bound conveyor belt. But what I soon realised was that I was the only guy in the university side who did not have a summer contract with a county. I was a bit peeved about this and thought, if I am good enough to get into this side, why haven't I got one too? So I decided to do something about it and spoke to Andy Wagner, who has a number of contacts in the county game. I asked him if he could get me trials during the 1996 summer break because I had reached the stage where I now wanted to give cricket a go. Fortunately, he was able to arrange a net session with Middlesex and off I went in search of fame and fortune.

My preparation for the trial could not have been worse. I caught the train to Marylebone but I did not have a clue where Lord's was when I left the station. I wandered around the streets aimlessly for about 30 minutes before finally asking for directions. When I arrived at the Grace Gates I shyly explained the reason for my visit and was told by a gateman to go to the dressing-room in the Pavilion. At this stage I was not aware there was a changing-room at the back of the Pavilion and walked straight into the main Middlesex dressing-room, where the first team were in the middle of playing a first-class game against Warwickshire. Phil

Tufnell and Angus Fraser were sitting in one corner chatting and I remember Mark Ramprakash, who was the next batsman in, standing there in his pads and mentally preparing himself for another long innings. Shaun Pollock was bowling for Warwickshire and I just stood there thinking, bloody hell, this is a different world. What have I stepped into here? I was gobsmacked. Everything looked so different to what I had seen at a cricket ground before.

I felt like an idiot standing in the doorway because everybody turned round and looked at me as I came crashing in with my kit. Ramprakash, not famed for his politeness towards guys he doesn't know, gave me a scowl before walking off in the other direction. I eventually plucked up the courage to ask if anybody knew where Ian Gould, the 2nd XI coach was, and I was directed to what turned out to be the 2nd XI dressing-room. I nervously introduced myself to a few of the 2nd XI players and we wandered over to the Nursery ground for a net.

Walking behind the stands at Lord's, I had plenty of time to think about what I was doing. I did not know anyone, I did not know whether I was good enough to be there and I felt pretty insecure about the whole situation. I knew that it was down to me to make an impression. Nobody would help me and if I didn't grab this chance I would soon be following the route of hundreds of other players into the largely amateur game of minor county cricket.

The net session did not go particularly well and at the end of it most of the guys seemed to think that I was a left-arm seamer. Jamie Hewitt, who had played a bit of 1st XI cricket, was bowling at me and he gave me a torrid time. I couldn't get a bat on him and he was making me look like the novice I was. After a few minutes of playing and missing and getting rapped on the thigh, Gould waddled down the net and told me not to be nervous and to play my natural game. The problem was that I felt I *was* playing my natural game. Despite this inauspicious start, Gould placated me with the news that either he or Don Bennett, the Middlesex 1st XI coach, would come and watch me perform for Oxford U-19s against Middlesex the following week. This set in motion an incredible month that saw me go from an aspiring hopeful to a fully fledged contracted county player.

A quick 80 in that game, followed by a fifty, 98 and an 80 in my first three second-team matches, managed to impress the powers that be enough for them to offer me a two-year contract which I signed immediately. I played three more games for the 2nd XI before strutting back to Durham feeling very happy with myself. When I look back now I realise that everything had come to me too easily. I returned to Durham in September thinking that cricket would be a doddle, and I did not train or work hard at my game during the winter. I slipped into the student lifestyle of lots of late nights and not a lot of training, and I really paid for it the following season.

My return to Middlesex for the 1997 season could not have got off to a worse start. Ben Hutton and I made the journey down from Durham to Birmingham in my clapped-out Ford Fiesta. Having spent most of the last four weeks celebrating the end of exams, we had both reached our overdraft limits and had one tank of petrol to get us to the game. How we were going to feed ourselves was something we had not considered. We barely made it there without running out of petrol and were then forced to ask Ian Gould, the coach, to fund our meals. He was less than thrilled, and was beginning to build a picture of us as a couple of soft public school idiots, and he was absolutely right. Neither of us had any idea of what it meant to be a professional cricketer.

After preparation like that, it was inevitable that the cricket was unlikely to go well, and I had an absolutely shocking season, where my highest score in 12 innings was 40. It was the first time in my life that I had struggled for form and I did not know how to get out of it. I wasn't experienced enough to know what I was doing wrong and my play against spin was awful. Years of flat wickets against gentle schoolboy attacks just hadn't prepared me technically to play against top-quality spin bowlers, and I had no means of scoring unless they bowled badly. The world of professional cricket was not all about travelling around and having a great time. At some stage I had to learn how to improve my game, and I could only do that if I invested time and effort. It is definitely possible to learn more from your mistakes than from your successes, and if one good thing came out of the horrific summer, it was the realisation that, if I wanted to succeed in professional cricket, I had to treat it seriously.

Off the field, too, there were difficulties to contend with. Ben Hutton and I were getting ripped to shreds by the rest of the squad, who licked their lips when two public school 'jazz hats' walked through the door. We were easy targets. Everyone has a characteristic that allows people to take the piss out of them and for Ben and me it was our public-school upbringing. Keith Dutch, a salt of the earth sort of bloke, was remorseless. He pounced on our stupid mistakes, like running out of petrol on the way to games and turning up with the wrong kit, and ribbed us constantly. Occasionally the banter wore a bit thin but the fact that we were getting stick actually showed we had been accepted.

There were huge cultural divides in the dressing-room and

I will never forget Ricky Fay, a young fast bowler, taking me to his home one afternoon. We went to this intimidating council estate in Brondesbury Park and I was amazed. At public school you lead a pretty blinkered existence and this was a world I had never seen before. It was a massive learning curve for me and one for which I will always be grateful. Cricket can bring together people from all different backgrounds and bring them together like no other sport. If nothing else, I have been incredibly fortunate to get to know so many fantastic people purely through this great game.

I returned to Durham in October with a few quid in the bank account, a full tank of petrol and a great deal of motivation to improve myself after my horror season. The ECB had begun setting up a University Centre of Excellence over the summer, and Graeme Fowler, the former Lancashire, Durham and England opener, was put in charge of cricket. It was just what I needed in my final year. It gave me the chance to take my cricket seriously, which is not easy at university because of the distractions, like getting a degree, and suddenly there was a structure in place that allowed and encouraged me to do this.

We were all given fitness programmes and technical work to do. I quit playing rugby for Durham in order to concentrate on my cricket and I was in the gym every day. It was amazing how quickly your perceptions change of what being fit means. I used to think I was making an effort if I went for a 20-minute run, but now I was running for 45 minutes and doing an hour-and-a-half weights session. It was the first time I had paid attention to fitness. I had always played a lot of sport and that kept me in shape but I was really feeling the benefits. It toughened me up mentally and I started the 1998 season thinking that I deserved to go out and score a lot of runs.

Don Bennett, who had been Middlesex's coach since 1969, had retired and, in an attempt to revive the club's fortunes, they had employed John Buchanan, now the coach of Australia. Buchanan's approach surprised me because I had this image of him coming in and barking orders in a broad Aussie accent. But he didn't. He organised the net sessions but then just spent the rest of the time making notes and saying very little. We wondered what the hell was going on. After three or four days Buchanan sat us all down and explained the way he worked. He is a very analytical man. He watched you play, made notes and then chose the right moment to talk to you about it. His style is very similar to that of Duncan Fletcher, the current England coach. Fletcher is not the sort of coach who walks down the net and tells you what you are doing wrong in front of everyone. That style of coaching rarely works well. Fletcher, like Buchanan, treats you like an adult. He knows you know you are doing something wrong and has a quiet word with you at the end of a net where he will suggest you go away and work on something. He will then watch you and come back to you and ask you how it went.

The approach was very foreign to a Middlesex dressing-room where the person who shouted the loudest normally won an argument. The sad thing was that when Buchanan left at the end of the season he was beginning to realise what county cricket was like, and the players were starting to appreciate what he was about. Middlesex will always regret getting rid of him.

1998 proved to be a disastrous year for Middlesex but personally it went quite well. After a winter of hard training at Durham I felt confident that runs would come when I returned to Middlesex. And they did. This was a massive relief because during the winter I had at times doubted that I was good enough to make it. After a poor season in 1997 I knew I was under pressure. My contract was up at the end of 1998 and I wanted a new one. Once again it was do or die time. I showed far greater consistency than previously in the 2nd XI and I averaged just under 50 in the nine matches I played. The season finished with me making my first-class debut against Hampshire and playing in Middlesex's last three matches of the summer.

Unlike when playing my first senior one-day match, against Kent in 1997, I was not nervous before the Hampshire game. I felt I was ready for the challenge. I had scored heavily in the 2nd XI, I was now more comfortable amongst the guys in the 1st XI and I was generally feeling good about life. I went out with the attitude that I was going to enjoy myself and I did, scoring 83. The pitch at the old Hampshire ground in Southampton was good and the only bowler of note in their side was the former West Indian paceman, Nixon McLean. During the innings I had the pleasure of batting with Mike Gatting who scored 77. I am yet to meet anyone who has a greater love for the game of cricket or Middlesex County Cricket Club than Mike Gatting. His enthusiasm for the game, even at the back end of his career, amazed me. He was always perky at every training session. Even at the age of 41 he was like an 18-year-old. He is larger than life in so many ways and he gave so much to Middlesex. I never played under him as captain but he always supported me and was instrumental in getting me in the 1st XI. The two years he had as club coach did not work out but it was a shame to see his involvement with Middlesex end as it did in 2000.

I still have a vivid recollection of the day he was sacked. Middlesex, under Gatting and Gould's supervision, were training at Richmond Cricket Club when they were summoned to Lord's.

When Gatting and Gould were out of sight Justin Langer, the club captain, sat us all down and told us what a very sad day this was for Middlesex CCC. He informed us that Gatting and Gould were about to be sacked and that we, as players, were partly to blame for it. The coaching style of Gatting and Gould had not been universally popular and it was not working, but Langer was absolutely right. We had underperformed and by doing so we had undermined both of them. It was good that Langer said this and I have always felt some guilt over the way Gatting left. To his immense credit, though, he has never shown any bitterness to any of those who were involved in the decision to sack him.

I finished the summer of 1998 with a new two-year contract from Middlesex in one pocket, and an offer from Price Waterhouse, the City accountancy firm, in the other. By now, however, my mind was focused on the former, and the thought of resorting to the latter was becoming a more and more depressing proposition.

I realised that I had to improve my game considerably if I was to establish myself as a first-class cricketer. In an effort to achieve this I packed my bags and headed off to Sydney, Australia, with the financial help of the Middlesex Members' Club, where I sampled the delights of the southern hemisphere summer for the first time. There was plenty of sun, Bondi Beach was right on my doorstep, and along the way I gained my first experience of playing grade cricket. I loved Sydney and I enjoyed training with the guys at Sydney University but the cricket frustrated me. James Ormond, the Surrey fast bowler, was the club's principal overseas player and I spent most of the winter playing third-grade cricket. Third grade is of a similar standard to 1st XI club cricket in England and I scored plenty of runs, but the second-grade captain did not want to change his side and I remained where I was. The cricket may not have been fulfilling but the whole experience helped me grow up. I also met Ruth, my wife, whilst I was there.

On my return from Australia the omens for 1999 did not appear particularly good. My cricket had not advanced as much as I would have liked it to and Middlesex had re-signed Mike Roseberry, an experienced batsman, from Durham. I had finished 1998 on a high and with great intentions and here I was, in my first full season as a professional, back in the 2nd XI. I did not handle matters particularly well and my season was drifting along aimlessly before Justin Langer selected me in the first team on a hunch. No one was getting any runs in the first team, and it was his judgment that if the first-team guys weren't doing it, then he had to try someone else. I was the lucky beneficiary and repaid his faith by scoring 61 against Derbyshire at Lord's and played in Middlesex's final eight games of the summer.

When I first met Justin Langer in 1998, he was recognised as a run machine in first-class cricket in Australia, but had yet to convince the Australian selectors that he could successfully translate those runs into the Test arena. He had played for Australia, but his gutsy, largely defensive play seemed to be swimming against the tide of the domineering type of cricket that the Australians had become renowned for. His answer was to follow a well-trodden path, used by Australians and others, into county cricket, aimed at expanding their games, while at the same time impressing national selectors with the consistency of their scoring in England.

It was during the 1999 season, when I graduated rather tentatively into the first team, that I really got to know Langer the man, rather than the player who seemed to have held the Middlesex batting together single-handedly the season before. I must say that

I did find him fairly intimidating to start with. His reputation for being extremely intense about his cricket, both on and off the field, had preceded him somewhat, and there was definitely something in his steely blue eyes which demanded respect. In the intervening 12 months he had forced his way back into the Australian Test side, and had reinforced both his place, and his reputation as a courageous performer by getting a valuable hundred in Pakistan, helping the Aussies to a series victory. Still, he had his doubters both at home and abroad, most of whom were concerned about his 'limited' play.

Regardless of his style of play, he had already become a legendary figure within the Middlesex dressing-room, both for his sheer hunger for runs and his ability to send his team-mates scurrying in all directions as he vented his anger when dismissed. I was not totally surprised, therefore, to find, after being selected for my first game of the season, that the only spare place in the dressing-room was right next to our overseas pro. Everyone else had long since realised the potential danger to both man and equipment.

The advantage of sitting next to him, of course, was that I was able to get to know him more quickly than otherwise would have been the case. He is without doubt the most disciplined cricketer I have ever seen. It was as if he had to know that he had done more than everyone else before he batted in order to feel mentally prepared. Almost every day after play he could be seen sprinting shuttles long after everyone else had retired to the hotel or the bar. It seemed to be a mission of his to be the first at practice and the last to leave, and when the caterers at Lord's supplied us with some mouth-watering cakes for tea, he promptly threw them all in the bin both to lead us not into temptation, and to berate us for another awful batting effort!

His dedication, however, was not solely for himself. He was a tireless servant of Middlesex County Cricket Club by working with the junior players like myself on his days off, and challenging the coaches to try other methods than those that had been accepted as the norm in country cricket. For this reason, more than any other, he has my complete respect. I am not sure how much of what he said rubbed off on me subconsciously, but the fact that he tried so hard with me and others is a great testament to his character. The fact that his captaincy stint was ultimately unsuccessful was more a reflection on the age and inexperience of those playing for the team, rather than his leadership skills. His intensity, and demand for the highest standards, may not necessarily have brought out the best in young players, short on confidence, who didn't have the experience to churn out hundreds like he did, but his heart was always in the right place. There is no doubt that he found it particularly frustrating that others didn't share his drive and ambition, and he became so exasperated at our inability to bowl, field and bat as well as other sides, that he even resorted to bowling himself in critical stages of one-day games in a if-you-can't-do-it-I'll-show-you type of way. Unfortunately, his bowling talents didn't match his batting, and the opposing batsmen tucked into him as though all their Christmases had come at once!

English cricket was pretty much at an all-time low by the end of the summer. England had failed to make the second round of the World Cup and Nasser Hussain, the new captain, had been booed off the balcony at The Oval following his team's 2–1 Test series defeat by New Zealand. The England side looked in need of fresh faces but playing Test cricket still seemed an insurmountable distance away from me. It looked a completely different game from the one I was playing. Everyone seemed stressed out and the bowlers were either winging the ball down at 90 mph or turning it about three feet off the pitch. At the time I was still struggling to keep out the likes of Mark Illot and Tony Penberthy.

A lot of county cricketers say that the only reason they play the game is because they want to play for England. For me it was slightly different. To play Test cricket was always an ambition of mine but it seemed so far away whilst I was playing at Radley College, Durham University and for Middlesex 2nd XI. The fact that putting on an England cap and walking out to play was so far away made it difficult for me to channel my efforts into achieving it. So, instead, I set myself achievable goals and took one step at a time. I just tried to get over the next barrier that was placed in front of me. At Middlesex it was to get into the first team on a permanent basis and if I wanted to do that I knew I needed to improve my play against spin and also my fielding. Only then, having established myself in the side, did I start turning my attention towards England.

A prerequisite for getting into the England side was to improve both my play against spin and my ability to turn promising starts into match-winning contributions. With these priorities in mind, I returned to Sydney to play for Mosman at the end of the 1999 season and was picked in their first-grade side. Brett and Shane Lee were in the team. Shane had been playing one-day cricket for Australia for four years and Brett was on the verge of breaking into the team. The standard of cricket was unbelievable. This was not club cricket in any shape or form. Brett Lee was bowling 95 mph thunderbolts at some poor bloke from Bankstown who wasn't wearing a helmet and I was standing at third slip petrified that a catch would come my way.

There was a great intensity to the cricket and as a Pom I got a sackload of stick. In Australia you have to earn respect. The fact that you have a county contract and play first-class cricket in England means nothing at all. At my first practice session with Mosman I remember vividly being asked to bat against a giant left-arm fast bowler called Phil Alley. Alley had played first-class cricket for South Australia and New South Wales and his 6 foot 10 inch frame cut a menacing figure as he approached the wicket. I was trying desperately to negotiate his vicious bounce when I suddenly became aware of Warwick Adlam, one of the first-grade batsmen, standing close to me behind the netting. I looked at him for encouragement but all he said was: 'Now listen here, Pom. Everyone at the club is watching you to see how good you are. Don't shit yourself.' All I could do was turn round and give him a nervous laugh. It was a great example of having to prove to your team-mates and the opposition that you are good enough to be playing in that side. Opponents constantly remind you of this but, fortunately, I scored 80 and 60 in my first two innings and this eased the pressure.

Unlike the previous winter, I benefited enormously from the trip. The cricket was outstanding. The pitches had pace and bounce in them, everyone was highly competitive and practice was always full-on. Your game is being tested all the time because most Australian teams contain a leg-spinner and at least one fast bowler of some repute. It was easy to see why Australia were dominating world cricket when you looked at the system they had in place. Some clubs, especially when the state players were available, were as strong as first-class teams in England. Indeed, there were many aspects of grade cricket that were better than our professional game.

With my game in good order and my confidence high I was

determined to start the 2000 season strongly and make an early impression. In the opening championship match I scored my maiden first-class hundred against Northamptonshire. What made it even more special was that I scored it at Lord's. As well as being elated I also felt relieved. Surrey's Martin Bicknell had trapped me lbw when I was on 98 in the second-last game of 1999 and I was very nervous as I went through the nineties. But I got there and, like Nasser Hussain said when I was given my England cap, it was something nobody would ever be able to take away from me.

It was now the time to prove that the hundred was not a one-off performance. I certainly felt I was capable of scoring more but my season stuttered along and I failed to reach three figures again. In fact, in first-class cricket I only passed 50 on three further occasions. It was very frustrating. I kept reaching 30 or 40 and getting out, more often than not just before lunch. My Middlesex team-mates began ridiculing me for the timing of my dismissals and it started to play on my mind. By the time I got to 30 I would start thinking I was going to get out. I hit 90 against Worcestershire and 73 against Glamorgan but the season ended on something of a high when I scored 75 against Warwickshire at Lord's. It wasn't a hundred but it is an innings I am still very proud of. Allan Donald was in the Warwickshire side and he bowled extremely fast on a quick, bouncy pitch.

I have faced many of the world's leading bowlers but none of them have tested me like Donald. Fast bowlers tend to focus your mind and Donald certainly focused mine. He is a superb athlete with a classic fast bowler's action and when batting against him I did not have time to worry about my technique or getting out in the thirties. Survival was the only thought running through my head. To come through such a challenge was very satisfying and it give me great confidence. Dougie Brown eventually dismissed me but I left Lord's glowing. On my arrival in the dressing-room, and after all of my team-mates had come over to congratulate me, I sat down and thought, so that is what Test cricket is all about.

The heartening thing for me was that I had been able to cope with Donald. There are many county cricketers who skilfully avoid facing fast bowlers, and score lots of runs against the weaker sides, but my contest with him left me feeling that I could possibly play Test cricket. The frustration of not turning thirties into big scores, failing to reach a thousand runs and missing out on selection for the England 'A' team had been replaced by the belief that my career was moving in the right direction.

Middlesex, however, were in turmoil. We had finished eighth in the second division of the county championship and Gatting and Gould had been sacked as coaches. Worse was to follow. We knew Australia's 2001 tour of England would deprive the club of Langer but Ramprakash and Richard Johnson both decided to jump ship and move elsewhere. I disappeared to Sydney to play another season of grade cricket for Mosman and returned home with low expectations for the summer ahead. Angus Fraser was now club captain, John Emburey was the new coach and Stephen Fleming, the New Zealand captain, had been signed as an overseas player. But in 2001 our side was mostly made up of youngsters with career batting averages of 25 and I felt, almost overnight, that I had become one of the more experienced players at the club.

The season turned out to be a very enjoyable and successful one for me, and my pre-season fears were confounded. Middlesex should have gained promotion but we fell away badly in the final month of the season and finished fourth. The departure of Ramprakash and Langer had made the dressing-room a far more relaxed place. Fraser and Emburey were naturally more easy-going men and they attempted to change the culture. They wanted us to work hard but they also wanted us to enjoy our cricket and have some fun.

Fleming was like a breath of fresh air. He trained hard and had a great presence about him but he was very relaxed. He did not speak for the sake of it but when he said something everyone listened. Fleming combined the father-figure/mate role very well and he was very approachable. He showed the younger players in the side that you did not have to be manic about your cricket to reach the top. Fleming enjoyed a pint after a day's play and he fitted superbly into the set-up Fraser and Emburey were trying to create. It was easy to see why he was so highly regarded as a player and a captain.

I once again opened my championship account with a hundred, this time 125 in a rain-affected game against Worcestershire at Lord's. I scored two further centuries, including a career-best 176 against Durham at Lord's, a ground where I was beginning to enjoy batting. It was important for me to start scoring hundreds on a more regular basis and it was a real breakthrough to score three. Turning forties into three-figure scores is an art, and they are the performances that catch the eye of selectors.

Having achieved all my pre-season goals, I finished the summer a contented man. I had scored more than a thousand runs in a season for the first time in my career, been awarded my county cap and gained selection for the National Academy in Adelaide, Australia. I was also invited to act as 12th man for England during the Lord's Test against Australia. My fielding had always been good but it was a real thrill to get so close to the action. It also showed the selectors knew who I was.

Being in the England dressing-room helped shatter a lot of the illusions I had about Test cricket. I had an image of it being an unbelievably tough game where the players were stressed out and focused all the time. Well, that is how it looked every time a television camera panned in on the players' balcony. But once inside I realised that it was much the same as a county dressing-room. Darren Gough was joking and throwing things around, and the atmosphere appeared very relaxed. The experience helped me realise that Test cricket was basically the same game that I was playing at Middlesex, but just to a higher standard.

Watching Owais Shah, my Middlesex team-mate, play one-day cricket against Steve Waugh's side in the NatWest Series also spurred me on. Shah is a wonderful player, but if he could do it, why couldn't I? It was interesting to watch the response to Shah's selection in the Middlesex dressing-room. Most were thrilled for him but there were some players who were jealous of the extra money he was earning.

Phil Tufnell's response to Shah's selection was far from enthusiastic. England were heavily beaten by Australia and Pakistan in the NatWest series and Tufnell, after asking Shah how much he had been paid for playing, made a caustic remark about how the England and Wales Cricket Board would have to pay him far more than that if they wanted him to go out there and embarrass himself like England had done. The irony of Tufnell's comment was that he had just bared his backside on a Saturday night television show for £1,000. The moment was not lost on his team-mates.

Although I had achieved a lot during the summer I still believed there was something missing from my game, that elusive ingredient which would transform me from a good county player into a Test player. So I travelled to Australia, with 16 other ambitious young cricketers, hoping to find it at the Academy. We were fortunate enough to have everything we might possibly want right there in front of us. The facilities in Adelaide were magnificent. There were three coaches to help us in our search for improvement, and plenty of off-field activities to keep us occupied during days off. The winter, however, did not work out as I had imagined. I went to the Academy in order to change my technique and develop new shots, but the harder I tried, the worse my game became.

This was by no means the fault of Rod Marsh, or those who worked under him. He very much encouraged players to take responsibility for their own games, but I was constantly playing around with differing styles, looking for that magic cure. As a result my game did not improve as much as I wanted, but the experience was still a positive one. Away from the pitch I managed to get my fitness to new levels, and the whole set-up encouraged players to be more disciplined in their preparation for games.

It was only at the end of my time in Australia that I realised my folly. I was a player who played the pull and cut shot well, and could drive the ball down the ground. Although I wanted to do it I could not hit the ball over extra cover or whip it through the leg side like Brian Lara. I had limitations and it was up to me to make the most of what I had rather than dream of playing like one of the greatest batsmen who has ever played the game. I scored a hundred against the Australian Academy, and a couple of fifties against state 2nd XIs, but I don't think Marsh was tipping me to make it as a Test player as I packed my bags in preparation for the return home.

I can look back now and smile about the experience but the most important thing I learnt in Adelaide was that there is no magic formula. It certainly wasn't what I expected when I left for Adelaide in October yet it was still a significant discovery. My time in Australia had made me realise that what I achieved in this game was, in the end, down to me. What I had to do was back my technique and learn more about my own game. Yes, I had limitations, but so did most players. I needed to make the most of what I had and not try to be someone else. From that moment on I have stopped going up to coaches and badgering them for advice. I am still open to ideas and still looking to improve my game, but I was now responsible for my cricket, not a coach. This approach put me in a position where I could no longer make excuses when my form was poor. Many players blame a coach when they are out of form. It is a convenient excuse but I could no longer do this because how I batted and prepared was now down to me. I had to work out what was right or wrong for my game. The buck stopped with me.

Middlesex had offered me the vice-captaincy during the winter, which I had gratefully accepted, but I never envisaged the bombshell that hit me during the club's pre-season training. Angus Fraser invited Ruth and myself to his house for dinner one evening and told me that he was considering retiring from the game because he had been offered a job writing for *The Independent* newspaper, so what did I think of taking on the captaincy instead. I was shocked. The thought of being vice-captain for the season was daunting enough, but to be thrown into this ... I had not captained a team since I was at school and here I was faced with the prospect of following in the steps of Denis Compton, Mike Brearley and Mike Gatting.

I have always had the ambition to captain, and the prospect of captaining Middlesex in a couple of years' time was an attractive scenario, but to do it now – I did not know what to say or how to react. Fraser played until the end of May before making an emotional farewell and I had to learn a hell of a lot in a short period of time. Although I felt out of my depth I was quite fortunate. Most of the team was of my age and we had played a lot of cricket together. Tufnell and Paul Weekes were the only senior players and neither of them fancied the captaincy, so there was no jealousy or bickering in the background.

The prospect of becoming captain changed my attitude entirely when I was standing in the field. I was now standing at slip or backward point trying to analyse why changes to the field were being made. When you are not involved in the decision-making you tend to wander around on auto-pilot. You go where the captain tells you, and move five yards to your left when the bowler asks, but rarely do you think: why has he moved me here? The captaincy made it a very tough summer. I had to juggle the responsibility of leading a team with my ambition to go on and play for England. I am not the sort of person who often gets stressed out by issues, but by the end of the season I was shattered.

I quickly realised that picking the team, deciding whether to bat or bowl at the toss and setting the field were the easy parts of the job. I had no idea that so much went on off the field. It was all-consuming. I had suddenly gone from having a couple of days off each week to having no spare time at all. I failed to appreciate it at the time, but being thrust into the captaincy probably did me some good. I matured enormously during those four months. I had to. The job also made me realise that my batting was not the only important thing in cricket.

Despite my naivety, Middlesex gained promotion to the first division of the county championship, a sure sign that the club was going in the right direction. I failed to score a thousand championship runs, which was disappointing, but I still averaged 45 with the bat. Most importantly, though, I had coped. I had taken on the responsibility of captaining a major club and it had not had a noticeable effect on my batting. Achieving this was very satisfying. I wanted to set an example when I was batting and felt that it was very important to score runs in order to assert myself in the team. The extra responsibility helped bring out the best in me, especially when Middlesex were in a tight situation and a game needed to be won.

After an indifferent winter at the Academy I was particularly pleased to be selected to play for the MCC against Sri Lanka at Chesterfield. The MCC were, in all but name, an England A team. I scored 32 and 37 not out but I really enjoyed the experience. Not only could I play a game of cricket without the worries of making the wrong decision, I had taken another step towards playing for England. I spent the off season absorbing myself in Middlesex matters and planning for 2003. It was my first winter at home in five years and I enjoyed it enormously. Ruth and I had bought our first property, a flat in Ealing, and it was comforting to spend some time in it and to lead a 'normal' life for once.

2003 was a pivotal year for me in every way. It was the year when I really did start to think about playing for England and it was the year I got married. My name was being mentioned in the media as a possible England player but I needed to score heavily for Middlesex if I was to convince the selectors I was worthy of a place. It was the time to deliver. I knew what I needed to do. I had to score more hundreds, which I did, and I had to score runs consistently so that my name kept appearing in the papers. I managed to achieve this by scoring 40 against Essex in the first game of the season, 83 against Sussex in the second and an unbeaten hundred against Lancashire in the third. The century against Lancashire was very timely. Andrew Flintoff was recovering from injury and playing a rare game for his county. His presence raised media interest and the selectors were about. My hundred allowed Middlesex to gain a battling draw and I don't think it went unnoticed.

The opportunity I was dreaming of nearly came in the Third Test against South Africa at Trent Bridge. David Graveney, the chairman of selectors, phoned me in the build-up to the match to tell me that I was on stand-by for Marcus Trescothick who had injured his thumb. This was the moment I had been working towards since I was a spotty teenager at Radley. It was the reason why I had travelled to the other side of the world on three occasions and spent hour after hour batting against a bowling machine, but I was in shock when I put the phone down.

The feeling of elation was quickly replaced by one of dread. Was I going to be able to cope with it? Would I find out that I was not actually good enough and all the effort had been wasted? I had worked hard for seven years to get to this position but I might only get two innings to show whether I was capable of performing at this level. There were hundreds of questions flashing round in my head and I had no answers. In the end Trescothick passed a fitness test and played in a thrilling England victory. Watching on TV from Lord's, where Middlesex were playing Kent and I scored 12 and 9, the vision of moving to the other side of the television screen remained just what it was, a dream.

When I look back now at my selection for the one-day legs of the 2003/04 winter tours to Bangladesh and Sri Lanka, I probably thought I was closer to England selection than I actually was. Duncan Fletcher, the England coach, loves to show continuity and I did not feel that I would get my opportunity via one-day cricket. I had performed acceptably in limited-overs cricket, and I scored a hundred in a televised one-day game against Lancashire, but my form in first-class cricket had been more impressive. Hence my surprise when I saw my name flashing on the scoreboards at Lord's with the rest of the team announcement.

2
POVERTY TO PARADISE

I had met Darren Gough whilst acting as England's 12th man during the Lord's Test against Australia in 2001. Admittedly, we did not spend a great deal of time in each other's company but, even so, I had hoped he would recognise me two years later as I approached him at the Marriott Hotel next to Heathrow Airport. I had already introduced myself to Anthony McGrath, Ian Blackwell, Vikram Solanki, James Anderson, Andrew Flintoff and James Kirtley, who were also travelling to Bangladesh and Sri Lanka to play six one-day internationals, when Gough entered the room. Now Gough is a larger-than-life character who enjoys being recognised, and everyone noticed his arrival. He loves being the centre of attention and is usually very welcoming, but I was slightly taken aback by his reaction to my pleasantries.

'Hi Darren, good to see you again,' was the gist of my introductions. But rather than shake my hand enthusiastically and engage in small talk he simply said, 'All right, mate,' and walked off, leaving me to become slightly paranoid about our brief encounter. What had I done during my short stint at Lord's to upset him? Or was it simply a case of him not liking public schoolboys or southerners, or both? My mind began to race. Thankfully, it was neither. The next time Gough and I met he apologised for being short with me. He told me that he thought I was the new Vodafone rep, and feared that I was about to drag him away to do something.

In one way it was comforting to hear this, in another ever so disappointing.

Gough has been the life and soul of the England team for more than a decade and after a couple of days in his company it was easy to see why. He has an enormous amount of confidence in his ability and he never appears to let things get him down. England might be struggling and Gough may have been smashed around the park, yet he is still full of optimism and enthusiasm. One famous Gough story comes from the 1998/99 tour of Australia when England's bowlers were getting smashed all around the Bellerive Oval in Hobart. The game was in mid-December and Gough, who was not playing in the match, thought it would be funny to come in at the tea interval dressed as Santa Claus and hand out presents.

The dressing-room would have been a pretty glum place as Gough walked in and everyone was wondering what he would do next. 'Ho, ho, ho, Gussy and Corky. No wonder this bag feels so heavy – it's got your bowling figures in.' It was a cracking comment but it brought a mixed response. The batsmen rolled about the dressing-room in laughter. The bowlers wanted to strangle him.

Gough is also great value because of the stupid comments he comes out with. A journalist once asked him why he was nick-named 'Rhino'. 'It's because I'm as strong as a bloody ox, that's why,' came the no-nonsense reply. There have been many others, too. One morning Gough walked into the England dressing-room and informed the team that he had found a great new bar in town. It was lively and, apparently, it served excellent food. When asked what it was called, in his best Barnsley/Italian voice, he said: 'Albarone.' Albarone? The room went quiet. It was only when he explained where the bar was, and a colleague politely pointed out the bar was actually called 'All Bar One', that everyone realised his error. Gough attempted to pretend that he was having us on and we had fallen for his trick, but he wasn't and we hadn't.

Gough will talk about himself to anybody who is prepared to listen and his corner of the dressing-room was always full of the latest gadgets, each, of course, being that little bit better than anything anybody else has. But this should take nothing away from the way in which he has performed for England and the positive effect his presence had on the team. Even at the back end of his career I could see why he had been so successful. His bowling may have lost the little bit of pace that made him uncomfortable to face, but his control and accuracy were exemplary.

In a breed where giants tend to rule Gough has done unbelievably well to remain competitive. Tall fast bowlers have a huge advantage over someone like Gough, in that they get the ball to bounce to an uncomfortable height from a fuller length than a shorter man. Yet the fact that he has taken more than 460 international wickets for England is testimony to his desire and the force of his personality.

At Heathrow I had entered a different world. I was mixing with players whom I had previously only seen on television and I was involved in what appeared to be a massive logistical operation. There were people from the England and Wales Cricket Board running all over the place. My bags were taken from me as soon as I entered the hotel and I did not see them again until they were delivered to my hotel room in Dhaka. All the chores normally involved with travelling had disappeared. A representative from the airline came to the hotel to check us in and we simply walked through customs and into one of the Business Class lounges when we arrived at the airport. I had never travelled Business Class before but I became an immediate fan. The more experienced players made the most of the free bar. We were not going to see too much Sauvignon Blanc or Pinot Noir in Dhaka or Chittagong over the next few weeks and a couple settled into a bottle of wine. As a new boy I refrained. I preferred to lie back, watch a movie and enjoy the extra space.

It was a huge relief to me when I eventually met up with my new team-mates because the previous week had been one of the most stressful in my life. Ruth and I had not really considered England's winter tour schedule when we planned our wedding and, had I been selected for the Test squad too, I would have been placed in a very tricky situation. Ruth is Australian and we were to be married in Buningyong, a remote town in a beautiful rural setting 70 miles north-west of Melbourne. Most of the planning for our wedding was in place well before my England selection and fortunately the one-day part of the tour did not coincide with the happy day. Yet in order to attend my wedding and be ready to travel to Bangladesh I had to fly out to Australia for four days, where I rushed around like a lunatic, and then return home to Ealing.

The training leading up to the tour had not been much fun either. When you have just reached the end of a long hard season in county cricket, where every bone in your body is aching and mentally you are shot, the last thing you want to do is start training. But no sooner had the final ball of the 2003 season been bowled than I was off up to Loughborough for a fitness assessment. A training schedule quickly followed in the post and the only time I had off was during my stag weekend in Ireland, ably organised by my best man, Ben Hutton.

The prospect of driving to a gym in Finchley and running

around Ealing Common was far from appealing but I had no shortage of motivation. I knew that the chances of me playing were remote but I needed to make an early impression and I trained hard. England had played some very good one-day cricket during the summer of 2003. They had comprehensively beaten the touring South Africans in the final of the NatWest series, and defeated Pakistan 2–1 in the NatWest Challenge. Vikram Solanki was the only semi-vulnerable batsman in the team and he had scored a brilliant century against South Africa at The Oval. Test players filled the remaining places in the side.

My only previous visit to Asia was with Middlesex who periodically took two or three of their young batsmen to Mumbai to develop their play against spin bowling. I enjoyed my week in India and had realised their huge passion for the game, and I was looking forward to going to Bangladesh to see more of this fascinating part of the world. I was aware that Bangladesh was a poor country both on and off a cricket field, and I figured playing here would give me a gentle introduction to international cricket. I liked the idea of not yet having to deal with the intensity that surrounds playing against a side like Australia, but I was equally aware that I would be expected to score runs against a weaker opponent.

The other issue that appeared to have a flip side to it was the fact I had been selected for England in one-day cricket. At the time I was more uncertain about my one-day game-plan than the one I used in four-day cricket. I had scored runs in limited-overs cricket but the role you play in this form of the game is generally more specific than that in first-class cricket, where I had scored almost 1,500 first-class runs during the summer. In one-day cricket you can express yourself a little bit more and the analysts in the media are more forgiving when they scrutinise your technique. The down side is that you have to keep scoring quickly, and to do this you occasionally have to take undue risks. In first-class cricket you can just bat. It helps if you can score quickly but your main objective is to occupy the crease and post a decent score. As the plane flew over Europe I began to wonder whether my game would allow me to perform the tasks that would undoubtedly be asked of me.

Nobody knew quite what to expect when we touched down in Dhaka, and the first thing we all noticed was the pollution. The smog and smell, caused by millions of cars, factories pumping out toxic gases, and the general dusty nature of the land, is similar to that which you find in most major Asian cities but it still catches you by surprise.

We were accorded a police escort and it was only when we left the airport for our hotel that we appreciated how fortunate we were to have one. The traffic in Dhaka is unbelievable. It makes driving in London seem like a peaceful pastime. The roads were probably built for donkeys and carts; there are plenty of them on every main road, and it is absolute chaos. Traffic lights are situated at crossroads but they are really nothing more than a token gesture. Nobody pays any attention to them and the right of way tends to go to the biggest vehicle. Those who attempt to cross the road appear to be on some type of suicide mission and it was quite difficult to follow exactly what was taking place outside the relative safety of our bus. It was as if we had been transported into another world inside a bubble, immune to our surroundings.

Our bus driver did his best to cut through the traffic and he did not seem to be too concerned with the chaos he left in his slipstream. Cars and carts were being forced into ditches as he stormed down the middle of the road behind a police car. Visiting Dhaka would be an interesting experience for white-van drivers: it could act as their finishing school.

The poverty and smog of this vast city were not the only things that stood out as we hurtled towards our hotel. There was a huge amount of construction taking place. It gave you the sense that Dhaka is gradually developing from a rural backwater and into a major city. Office blocks were being erected on every street corner. It was with relief that we arrived at the Pan Pacific Hotel, and I was delighted to find accommodation that compared favourably to any I have since stayed in anywhere in the world.

We had gathered from the newspapers that England were embarking on a tough fitness campaign, and this was endorsed by the fact that I was given an extra pair of trainers, swimming trunks and a pair of goggles prior to my departure from Heathrow. We were expected to slip straight into the routine the Test players had been partaking in and Nigel Stockill, England's fitness trainer, had travelled up from Chittagong – where England were playing the Second Test – to ensure we were fit and ready for the one-dayers.

Stockill worked us unbelievably hard. At times we thought he was picking on us but I was amazed to see the fitness levels that had been achieved by the Test players when they returned to Dhaka. These guys had been away from home for four weeks and had played two Test matches in searing heat but they happily visited the gym each day to do an hour and a half of weight-training. Every training session was followed by a recovery session in the hotel pool. At Middlesex I thought we trained pretty hard but I had not seen anything like this.

Stockill is convinced that regular weight-training sessions help prevent injury and every player had bought into the idea. Nobody, not even the senior players like Nasser Hussain and Graham Thorpe, questioned why we were doing this, they just got on with it.

Each player was given a 'buddy' – a team-mate who they trained with – and I was paired up with Andrew Flintoff. The buddy system sounds a bit twee but it works well. Lifting weights on your own can quickly become boring, but having someone there to keep you going makes the sessions far more intense. Mind you, attempting to lift the same weights as Flintoff did little to ease my chances of picking up an injury. He picked up 70 kilograms as though it was a toothpick, whilst I struggled to move it. But it helped me forge an excellent relationship with the man who had already become England's most influential cricketer. Flintoff soon christened me Lord Brockett, after the character who had recently appeared on *I'm a Celebrity, Get Me Out of Here!* Apparently it had something to do with my posh voice and my public-school background. I accepted it but, to be honest, I had little choice. Flintoff enjoyed the nickname and is not the sort of character it is advisable to disagree with.

The bulk of our cricket training took place at a remarkable ground called the Bangabandhu Stadium. The Bangabandhu is remarkable because you are not aware that you have arrived at Bangladesh's National Stadium when the coach stops. The outside of the circular ground resembles a shopping centre, with the areas of space under the terracing at the back of the stands housing shops selling anything from fruit to refrigerators. It was only when you went through a gate and up a set of stairs that you became aware that this was a sports ground.

The facilities inside the ground were not too special. It would be incorrect to say that the outfield consisted of grass. It was more a case of weeds which were indiscriminately patched together to give an appearance of green. But at least the outfield had some colour. The practice pitches were nothing more than rolled mud. The bounce was slow and low, and it took a couple of sessions to adapt to them. The nature of the pitches, along with the humidity and the diminutive build of people living here, could explain why Bangladesh are unlikely to produce too many decent fast bowlers.

The Test squad returned to Dhaka from Chittagong with a 2–0 series win completed looking emaciated after a week in what is generally regarded to be the worst hotel in international cricket. But the arrival of Michael Vaughan, Duncan Fletcher and the Test side changed the whole atmosphere of our stay. A fairly casual training camp suddenly became a fully focused and highly specific operation aimed at winning one-day games of cricket.

As soon as Fletcher arrived meetings were arranged. In these we discussed our goals for the coming series and how we intended to play against the Bangladeshi batsmen and bowlers. Malcolm Ashton, the team analyst, supplied video footage that backed up Fletcher's reasons for suggesting we should attempt certain tactics. It was then our task to put these theories into action and we spent the next few days practising our intentions in the nets. I had expected the preparation for international cricket to be a lot more thorough than that in county cricket, simply because of the greater amount of time and financial support that is available. But to see at first hand the work that goes on behind the scenes really impressed me.

In the county game it is difficult to analyse an opponent closely because it is hard to get good video footage. Most counties record each day's play but they do very little with it because they do not have the time or resources to turn it into a package highlighting the strengths and weaknesses of the opposition. Most theories are explained verbally and hypothetically and it is often a struggle to get across exactly what you want your players to do. Having video footage makes life far simpler but it was still intriguing to sit there and see Fletcher dissect the technique of an opponent. It made me realise that I was now part of a very professional and thorough set-up.

The meetings with Fletcher were conducted in a very business-like manner. They were short and sharp, and they would start and finish at a certain time. Once Fletcher had finished his presentation he would briefly open things up to the floor so the players could express their thoughts and make observations, but long-winded debates that go nowhere were avoided.

This again was something I had been unable to prevent at Middlesex. It is good to collect the views of the team but it can often result in players leaving the room confused over what their objectives are. Fletcher is clear, simple and to the point. Vaughan has input into the planning but says very little at these meetings. Fletcher is very much the man in charge and you leave knowing what is expected of you. Vaughan has his chance on the eve of every match, when all the planning is over. Fletcher is in charge whilst all the preparation takes place, and then hands the team over to the captain who runs the show until the end of the game.

Practice sessions were conducted in a similar vein to the meetings. Bowlers would bowl off their full run-ups and be mindful of not bowling no-balls, whilst batsmen would be practising one-day shots. At Middlesex one-day practice sessions often degenerated into a bit of a slog but here players were looking to hit the ball into imaginary gaps in the field.

The fielding drills were short, sharp and very slick. They were well rehearsed and specific. A lot of time was spent throwing the ball at one stump and ideas on how we could save a fraction of a second in knocking the bails off were tested. The standard of fielding was high. At Middlesex I was one of the best fielders in the team but here I did not stand out. I knew a lack of money and time between games would make it impossible to introduce all these ideas at Middlesex but I was reassured by the fact that this was just the type of set-up I wanted at the club.

The ability of England's batsmen to play spin bowling has improved considerably under Fletcher's guidance and it was fascinating to spend an hour in his hotel room listening to his theory. Fletcher's forward press method has gained a lot of publicity, and it is something I have introduced into my game, but it is not the only tactic he advocates.

The forward press involves the batsman taking a small step forward before the bowler releases the ball. From this position he can then continue forward softly if the ball is full, or push back on to the back foot if it is short. He also believes that a batsman should remain low in his stance, as it makes it easier to see how much the ball is dipping, and that we should all be able to play the sweep shot. On England's 2005/06 tour to Pakistan the stroke received a lot of criticism when several of the team were out to it in Lahore, but Fletcher believes it has a huge amount to offer in subcontinental conditions where the ball may turn a lot. He would like each batsman to have a number of sweep shots – the slog-sweep, the square-sweep, the fine-sweep and the reverse-sweep – at their disposal.

Being able to play these shots allows you to manipulate how the field is set. The opposition captain only has nine fielders and it is easier to manipulate them if you can score runs all round the ground. To me this was all new. My play of spin was improving but I had never felt particularly confident about my technique. Now I had something to work on, and somebody to work with.

With the lack of batting berths in the side, I failed to play in any of England's three limited-over victories but I did manage to score 51 in a practice match against a Bangladesh development squad in Dhaka. I opened the batting and played pretty well before receiving a message to get out so that other members of the team could have a hit. The standard of the opposition was pretty low but it was still good to make some sort of impression.

England comfortably defeated Bangladesh in each game with Flintoff scoring three thunderous fifties, but I travelled to Sri Lanka believing I might have a chance of playing. Vikram Solanki scored 11 runs in the three games and the media were beginning to speculate about his position in the team.

The Test players were looking forward to getting to Sri Lanka, an island containing most, if not all, of the delicacies we have at home. The contrast between Sri Lanka and Bangladesh could be seen clearly on our journey from the airport to our hotel in Colombo. The plant life, the beaches and the size of the people remind you of the Caribbean, yet there is still the craziness of life that only exists in Asia. Everything in Sri Lanka was bigger and greener than in Bangladesh and we realised we were in for a far more enjoyable time when we walked into the reception area at the Taj Sumudra Hotel in Colombo to see a massive promotion for Erdinger Beer taking place. As soon as we arrived we were met by several attractive-looking girls wearing traditional German outfits who presented us each with a huge two-pint stein glass of beer. Most of the players indulged. Colombo helped us to relax. The smog had disappeared, there were shopping centres and restaurants to visit, and the view of the Indian Ocean from my hotel window was somewhat better than that in Dhaka.

Solanki's run of low scores made the solitary warm-up game in Sri Lanka an important one for me. It gave me the chance to stake a claim for selection in the first one-day game in Dambulla. Competing for a place in a team is a pretty tough and ruthless business. Every player knows that injury or the loss of form are the only two routes through which an outsider can get in a side and you learn to live with it. England rested all the big names for the warm-up game and Chris Read opened with Solanki, who scored nought. I came in at three and played well, scoring 83 off 88 balls. Sitting in my hotel room that evening I felt I had made the impression I needed to.

Dambulla is an extraordinary place, situated in the hill country 100 miles north-east of Colombo. The area is known as 'the Ancient Cities Region' and it was easy to see why. There were Buddhist cave temples and rock fortresses from civilisations dating back thousands of years everywhere you went. It was more difficult to work out why anybody would want to build a state-of-the-art cricket ground here on a World Heritage Site in the middle of a jungle. But they had, and the facilities were actually very good.

Our hotel was in the middle of a nature reserve and we slept in little huts that were separated from the reception area by 800 metres of jungle. The location gave the more mischievous members of the squad the perfect opportunity to scare the living daylights out of those who were reluctant to be at one with nature. Anthony McGrath spent a couple of uncomfortable hours in his bed one night listening to strange noises emanating from his bathroom before finally discovering that it was Flintoff scratching around and playing the fool.

At the hotel there was a palmist who was very keen to predict all our futures. I abstained but several used her. Flintoff had his palm read and was slightly taken aback when he was told that he was going to have a short life.

I knew that my innings in the warm-up game had given the selectors something to think about but it was only when Fletcher and Vaughan approached me separately during England's final practice session, and told me to prepare as though I was going to play, that I realised I had a chance. That I was going to make my England debut on the following day was confirmed to me at the team meeting that evening. It was wonderful to hear my name read out by the captain and, needless to say, I did not sleep particularly well. My mind was racing as I lay in bed considering what might happen the following day. Was I going to score a swashbuckling hundred to announce myself on the international stage, or was I about to make a fool of myself in front of millions of people? I had just scored 83 and was feeling pretty comfortable about my game, but it was impossible to keep the occasional negative thought out of my head.

What a shocker. What an absolute bloody shocker. Could there have been a worse game in which to make your international debut? The match in Dambulla was the 385th in England's limited-overs history and, it would be fair to say, never have we been so comprehensively beaten. We capitulated to 88 all out and Sri Lanka knocked them off in 13.5 overs without losing a wicket. It was possibly the most one-sided game of cricket I have ever played in.

My involvement lasted just nine balls. I played and missed at the first ball I faced from Dinusha Fernando, a young fast bowler also making his debut, left the second and missed the third. Thankfully I managed to make contact with the fourth and I survived my first over. My only scoring shot was a back-foot punch off Chaminda Vaas. Marcus Trescothick and I completed three runs and suddenly life seemed slightly less tortuous. But my joy was short-lived and I could only look up in anguish when I failed to control a straight drive at Fernando and chipped a low catch back to him. Eking positives out of a scratchy 3 is difficult but there were a couple. I may not have looked like it but I did not feel overawed by the occasion or out of my depth. I did not know how I would react to playing on this stage but it was comforting to know that I had been able to keep control of my emotions.

We left Dambulla humbled and the coach journey back to Colombo was understandably subdued. Still, I had two more games to show everyone what I was capable of and I was confident that I would register a decent score. Sri Lanka is an unbelievably hot place but it is also very wet and the next week was spent watching the rain fall. We never came close to playing either of the games in Colombo and spent day after day sitting in hotel rooms slowly losing the will to live. I found this hugely frustrating. Having worked hard to get in the side, I now wanted to establish myself and the weather was depriving me of the opportunity.

In Colombo I had my first contact with the British media. As Middlesex captain I had been put in front of the press at a couple of club open days but my experience of handling them was limited. As a group they had always been polite and welcoming with me but I became aware that there was a bit of an atmosphere between the media and those who had been in the Test side for some time. It was not nasty or hostile but the senior players became more guarded whenever journalists were around.

Who speaks to the media normally depends on what has happened in the previous game or what might be happening in the next. I was in demand because I had made my debut and very few of them knew that much about me. So I spent 30 minutes one morning in a dark corner of the hotel bar, answering questions from ten to fifteen journalists. Angus Fraser, my former Middlesex team-mate, sat at the back of the group, but he bottled out of asking me a question. Our disastrous performance in Dambulla was touched on but they seemed more interested in how I was settling in to the side, and how I had arrived in this position.

The relationship the players and the media have is a strange one. The nature of our jobs means that we spend a lot of time together – the media travel on the same flights as the players and stay in the same hotels – yet we rarely mix. However, we do both need each other. Journalists want to get as close to you as they can in order to get snippets of information about what is taking place behind the scenes. But, as a player, you are reluctant to give them these because you do not want private matters to be openly debated in the newspapers. And it is this that causes the guarded approach of the players. Yet it is in a player's interest to have a good working relationship with the media if he can. Promoting the game, and ensuring that it gets good coverage, is a part of your responsibility and as an individual you can also benefit, both in profile and financially, from receiving a positive press.

There was a brief but highly enjoyable break from the tedium of watching rain fall when the England rugby team defeated Australia to win the World Cup. Robert Croft and Dean Conway, the Welsh contingent in our party, did not seem particularly overjoyed by England's success, but the rest of us had a very pleasant afternoon in the hotel bar. It was only when I returned to England that I fully appreciated the mass hysteria that followed the victory. It made me realise what it might be like if the England cricket team were to beat Australia and regain the Ashes.

The rain had deprived me of the chance to impress the selectors and I left Sri Lanka wondering whether I had done enough to gain selection for the one-day section of the tour to the West Indies. I was satisfied to have broken into the team but I realised that I still had it all to do.

England lost a tough three-Test series to Sri Lanka 1–0 and, after Christmas at home, Ruth and I went on a belated honeymoon to South Africa. Confirmation of my selection for the West Indies came whilst we were there. It was a pleasant distraction but I felt that the coming tour was, as far as my one-day career was concerned, a make or break trip.

The one-day specialists were not due to leave for the Caribbean until early April 2004 and my preparations had centred around being fit and in form by then. So it came as something of a surprise when David Graveney, the chairman of selectors, phoned in early March to inform me that Mark Butcher had twisted his ankle in England's final warm-up game before the First Test and my presence was required in Jamaica. Time was short and I had to drop everything and get on the next plane bound for Kingston.

The tone of Graveney's conversation suggested that Butcher would probably be fit, but if he was not I sensed that I might be playing. I was some way from being where I wanted to be in terms of fitness and form but these are not the sort of offers you turn down, and less than 24 hours after the phone call I was on an Air Jamaica flight. I arrived in Kingston late at night with the squad already retired to bed. After checking in I was taken to my hotel room where I lay in bed wondering how I would cope with playing in a Test match in less than three days' time.

I met up with the team the following morning but most of them had their Test match heads on. As a Test match approaches most players begin to move into a mindset where everything they do is deliberate and geared towards achieving success in the coming match. It was only when I became a regular member of the Test team that I fully appreciated this and the differing approach to that of the one-day side surprised me. The one-day side contained younger faces desperate to impress and this, along with the nature of the game, makes the build-up to matches more exciting and dynamic.

The Test team contained bigwigs like Nasser Hussain and Graham Thorpe, legends who were playing for England when I was a teenager, and their presence created a more serious, more businesslike feel to the preparations than those I had experienced before Christmas. Test matches are unbelievably tough weeks and in the build-up to the game the aim is to conserve energy, so this was why more time was spent on the cricket and less on the training.

I immediately became aware that Butcher was likely to be fit but it was fascinating watching the way players behaved. The warm-up and fielding drills were performed diligently but as soon as they had finished most players seem to enter their own little world, a world geared towards ensuring they were fully prepared for the first morning of the Test. Batsmen like Thorpe and Hussain would have their net and then sit quietly in the shade meddling nervously with their bat handles. They would then go to a corner of the ground and give each other a few throw-downs to work on something specific. I could sense this was the cricket that made or broke careers.

Butcher passed a fitness test and played in the First Test, and I was invited to stay with the squad until the end of the game. Duncan Fletcher told me to enjoy myself and treat the remainder of my stay as a holiday, and to a large extent I did. The dressing-room at Sabina Park is small and the last thing those playing need is another set of kit clogging things up, so I played a couple of rounds of golf, had a few net practices and helped out with the 12th man duties.

Attending each day's play was beneficial, in that it gave me another chance to acclimatise to the atmosphere of a Test match. A Test match may last five days but there is greater intensity at them than one-dayers and I was nervous watching from the players' balcony. England, thanks to a frightening spell of fast bowling from Steve Harmison, won an exciting Test match by ten wickets but there were spells when a victory looked in doubt. I was amazed at the toughness of the cricket, particularly on the second day when Hussain and Butcher took a battering from Fidel Edwards and Tino Best. The atmosphere in the ground was unbelievable and the crowd went ecstatic each time Hussain or Butcher was hit. When the pair returned to the dressing-room they were in pain and had bruises all over their bodies. Harmison's 7/12 grabbed all the headlines but the batting of this pair played a major role in allowing us to spend a memorable afternoon sitting around the hotel pool revelling in our success.

England moved on to Port-of-Spain, Trinidad whilst I returned to Ealing and began pre-season training with Middlesex. Fortunately the daily trips around the North Circular to a dusty indoor cricket school in Finchley lasted only a couple of weeks before I was whisked off to Grenada with the England one-day squad. The Spice Island resort we stayed at in Grenada was spectacular. If you could pick the perfect holiday destination, this would be high on the list. Our bungalows were on the water's edge and everything about the hotel was of the highest quality. The facilities at the West Indies Cricket Academy were excellent too, but in such a location it was hard to fully concentrate on the cricket. At times it seemed a shame that we had to go and play.

Whilst we were in Grenada Brian Lara regained the world record by scoring an unbeaten 400 in the final Test of the series. It was a strange experience because watching him bat is one of the great sights in cricket but, at the same time, you gained no pleasure from watching your team-mates toiling under a hot Antiguan sun. Lara has always been the batsman I have most enjoyed watching. He has that touch of genius about him. He has the ability to score runs off any bowler in any conditions. I have had the privilege of watching several of his greatest innings. I remember being glued to the television when he scored 375 against England in 1994. And it was the same when he played brilliantly against Australia in the Caribbean in 1999. The unbeaten 153, which took the West Indies to a remarkable one-wicket victory over Steve Waugh's side in Barbados, was one of the finest innings I have ever seen.

When Lara is batting it is very difficult to turn off the television. You never know what he is going to do and he even looks good when he is blocking. To play against him during the one-dayers at the end of the tour was a great honour and it was enlightening to stand there in the field and see at first hand how he manoeuvres the ball around. His hands work together so well and they allow him to place the ball wherever he wants. Most batsmen will have certain areas that they hit the ball into and deliveries where they are better off leaving the ball alone. On certain days Lara looks as though he can hit any ball anywhere if he wants to. Like all great players he is a wonderful timer and placer of the ball. Some players spend half their career hitting the ball straight at fielders. Lara finds the gaps, and even when he doesn't seem to hit it cleanly it still races away for four.

When Justin Langer was at Middlesex he used to chirp opposing batsman who had a very high backlift. Langer used to tell them, 'There is only one player who can play with a backlift like that, and you don't look like Lara to me.' To have such a unique technique he must have an awesome eye for a ball. There are so many things that could go wrong when you pick a bat up like that, but he uses it to his advantage because it allows him to manoeuvre the ball around so well.

After a week living regally in Grenada we travelled to the rather less exotic destination of Georgetown, Guyana. Here we met up with the Test players, who were understandably buoyant following their 3–0 Test series victory. It was the first occasion England had won a Test series in the Caribbean since Colin Cowdrey's side defeated Garfield Sobers' 1–0 in the winter of 1967/68. The body language of the players and the confidence they exuded was clear to see when they arrived at the team hotel. It was that of a team that believed it was going somewhere.

The Test players were not too upset to see it rain – it gave them another day off – although those of us who had spent the last week in nets or at a gym were desperate to get out there and play. However, the prospect of this happening diminished with each passing hour as the rain became heavier and heavier. The practice match was abandoned and there seemed little chance of the one-day international taking place until the groundstaff performed a miracle mopping-up act. On the official match day there were almost 18 inches of water on certain areas of the ground but, through the recruitment of military helicopters and every sponge in Georgetown, the outfield was somehow dried and a 30-over game organised on the rain-day.

The reduction in overs and my lack of experience gave me cause for concern, and I feared I would miss a first experience of playing in front of an excitable West Indian crowd. But my worries were short-lived. We had remained at the team hotel until we knew what was happening and as soon as we arrived at the ground I was told I was playing. England narrowly won a low-scoring match, thanks largely to Chris Read, who scored 27 runs off only 15 balls at the death. I was asked to bat at three and found myself in the middle in the first over of our reply. I scored 29. I failed to go on and do what I wanted to, namely win the game, but it was a start. I had batted for over an hour and enjoyed the experience.

We then travelled to Trinidad where the rain continued to fall. England were due to play two one-day internationals at the Queens Park Oval but both were abandoned. The journey to Grenada was equally futile, with the match being abandoned without a ball being bowled, and suddenly the momentum we had had disappeared. A seven-match series had now been reduced to four and nobody had been able to have any worthwhile practice for more than a week.

The predicament tested the resourcefulness of the management because there are no indoor facilities of any note in the Caribbean. We spent one afternoon in Guyana at what would be best described as an aircraft hanger with a basketball court in the middle. Here, on the concrete, we attempted to go through our fielding drills before having some throw-downs against the corrugated iron walls.

We feared the horrendous weather would follow us to St Lucia but thankfully the sun was out and the ground was dry. Our two matches at the Beausejour Stadium followed a similar path. England batted first and scored 280 in 50 overs and the West Indies knocked them off with a couple of overs to spare. I scored 10 in the first game before being bowled by Mervyn Dillon and 67 in the second.

England lost both games but this was a true taste of cricket in the Caribbean. The sun was out, the ground was full and the crowd were, how could I say, involved. Playing cricket in the West Indies is a wonderful experience. Wherever you visit, the spectators are pleased to see you and the matches are quite often the biggest event on the island each year. West Indians do not tend to stress themselves as we do but the one thing they are passionate about is their cricket. When you field on the boundary there is the constant noise of people arguing over why a fielder is positioned where he is, or why the batsman played that shot. They all seem to have an in-depth knowledge of what is taking place and it is great fun listening to them. The noise and excitement generated at these two matches was new to me and it tantalised my taste buds. To perform on this stage and to be able to cope with the atmosphere would be hugely satisfying.

My innings in the first game was a bit disconcerting because I could not score at the rate I wanted to. At one stage I began to panic and fear that I was letting the team down. I could not get the ball away and felt I desperately needed to do something. But the harder I tried the worse it got. I was premeditating shots and trying to hit the ball too hard, and neither approach came off. It is something that happens quite regularly to batsmen in one-day cricket and it is only with experience that you learn to forget what has just happened and react to each ball as it comes your way. On this occasion I failed to do this and I quickly realised that if you let yourself down on this stage it is a very public humiliation.

I resolved to be more proactive the following day and things went much better – I scored my first half-century for England. It was an important innings for me, as was the 66 in the final one-dayer in Barbados. I had shown to myself that I could play at this level, and my second half-century had helped England win a game of cricket. The win allowed us to return home with a 2–2 draw which, when the Test series victory was added on, completed a very successful tour.

The two fifties left me feeling pretty satisfied with life as I sat back in my Business Class seat. I had by no means cracked international cricket but those innings showed me I could handle this stage. In my mind the next six months would be crucial for me but my only way of breaking into the Test side would come through one of the top four batsmen picking up an injury.

3
THE DEBUT

I strap my right pad on first as usual, making sure that the Velcro buckles are tight, but not overly so. The left pad goes on next, followed by the thigh pad, inner thigh protector and, most importantly, the box. This is a routine that I have done a thousand times during my career. The new gloves, which were 'knocked in' during the practice sessions earlier in the week, feel supple in my hands and provide perfect grip as I twirl the bat around in my hands. I start feeling a nervous energy going through my body, telling me that it is time to start moving. Now is not the time for sitting around and relaxing. I start shadow batting, pretending that a bowler has just delivered the ball at me, and rehearsing in turn all the shots in my repertoire. A straight drive, a cut, the pull shot, which normally feels so natural to me, now feels a little laborious without natural reactions taking over. I follow it up with a few fast feet drills to get the most important of batsmen's tools working.

My mind starts wondering about what type of delivery is going to be sent down to me first ball. A bouncer, surely. First ball in Test cricket is bound to be a bouncer, my mind tells me. Then again, another part of my brain takes over. It is going to be a yorker. The bowler knows that I will be expecting a short ball, so may try and double bluff me. The bell rings and interrupts my thought pattern. The players call this bell the 'worker' and it signifies to both dressing-rooms that the umpires are leaving the sanctuary of their room, and are making their way out on to the field of play. My pulse quickens a little on hearing it. Now is the time to go.

I glance to my new opening partner, Marcus Trescothick, who in turn gives me a little nod. It is time for us to make our way out. We walk through the open dressing-room door and down the steps towards the Long Room. Again, it is a journey that I have done many, many times. This time, however, we are met by hundreds of MCC members as we make our way through the most hallowed room in cricket, rather than just a few Middlesex die-hards. I can hear a few 'good lucks' and 'you can do its' in the background, but my mind is focusing on the cricket now.

We make our way on to the turf and the crowd cheers at our entry. The New Zealanders are already out there. The bowlers are marking their run-ups, and Stephen Fleming, their inspirational captain, is busy getting his fielders in position. Marcus prefers taking the first ball, and I am more than pleased to let him, both to give me a chance to see their bowling before having to face it, and to take a little pressure off by not having to face the first ball of the innings.

The umpire signals for play to start. Daryl Tuffey begins his run-up. He is a large barrel-chested bowler who wouldn't look out of place in the New Zealand rugby team. He sends the first ball down, which is safely negotiated by Trescothick. Five more deliveries pass, and the first over in our innings is a maiden. Now it is my turn.

I speak to Trescothick between the overs, and he lets me know what the bowler is trying to do with the ball. I try to listen, but my mind keeps thinking about what lies in store. I wander back to my end. I take my guard. 'That's middle,' replies the umpire. A quick survey of the field that Fleming has placed for me. A regulation field. No surprises from the New Zealand captain who knows my game so well. I look down at my bat. This is it. Watch the fucking ball, I mutter to myself. I look up. Chris Martin, a tall wiry bowler, who on his day can send them down quick, has started his run-up. He approaches the wicket, he lets the ball go. This is my first ball in Test cricket.

Just five days earlier the prospect of making a Test debut seemed as far away as ever, even though a couple of promising fifties in the West Indies had registered on the antennae of the cricketing media, despite the fact that many of the more seasoned and important of them had long since departed the shores of the Caribbean at the end of the Test series. There were calls for Nasser Hussain to be dropped after mixed performances in the West Indies, and for me or Paul Collingwood to take his place.

I had done my cause no harm whatsoever by electing to play for Middlesex on the day of my return, and getting a useful 95 against one of the strongest bowling line-ups in county cricket, Lancashire, batting at number five. With only just over two weeks between the end of the one-day series in the West Indies and the First Test starting, this was my only chance to impress the selectors before they announced the squad and, deep down, I thought that the innings may just have given me a chance, depending on whether the selectors decided to stick with the tried and tested, or take a chance on a newcomer.

I tried not to build up my hopes, but with the squad due to be announced on the Sunday morning, and the selectors' decision that all the players selected should miss their county's one-day games on that day and instead meet up in London, I expected a call one way or another before the Middlesex squad left for our away trip to Scotland on Saturday. As it was, it was left to the Middlesex coach John Emburey to break the bad news. 'I have just been on the phone to Grav [David Graveney], and you are coming with us up to Scotland. Hard lines, mate.'

The news hit me hard, but not overly so. Despite scoring those fifties in the West Indies, I knew that it was still a long shot for me to get into the team and, of the batsmen waiting in the wings, Paul Collingwood probably deserved a chance after playing a couple of difficult Tests in Sri Lanka. I consoled myself with the thought that I was now close, that people would now be taking a real interest in how I was doing on the county circuit, and that a few big scores in the early part of the season might just get me into the team if there was an injury.

It was with this thought in mind that I approached the Middlesex totesport division 2 game against Scotland. This was about as far as the county game gets from Test cricket as possible, but a score is a score, and to get a hundred there confirmed to me that I was in great form, and also added ammunition to the journalists who felt that I was unlucky to miss out on selection. I travelled back with the team from Scotland on Monday morning feeling weary, but also excited about playing Surrey later in the week, a team against whom any Middlesex player wants to do well.

While I was on the plane home, contemplating our next championship match, Michael Vaughan was in the process of twisting his knee attempting a sweep shot in the nets. This was potentially a massive blow for the England team. Vaughan, who had led the team so impressively in the West Indies, was writhing around in pain, and just about the only position that Paul Collingwood, the replacement batsman, couldn't be expected to fill in was as an opener. As I was making my way to the golf course for a relaxing afternoon stroll, frantic calls were being made by the coach to the selectors about getting a replacement on standby.

A wave of excitement rushed through me as I checked my messages after golf. 'Straussy, this is Grav here. Vaughany has been injured in the nets, and we need you down at Lord's tomorrow morning in case he doesn't recover in time.'

I rushed home, and tried to get all my kit in order as quickly as possible. Most of the England gear that I had used in the Caribbean was still in a pile waiting to be washed, but Ruth and I just about managed to get everything packed. I wasn't sure how the situation with Vaughan was developing, so didn't know whether to prepare myself to play or not get my hopes up too high again. In addition, thoughts started creeping into my head like, this could be it, are you ready for it? I wasn't sure of the answer, but I drew comfort from the fact that I was in great form, and the Test was being played at Lord's, my home ground.

I arrived at the team hotel about an hour early, to be confronted by Andrew Walpole, the England media liaison. 'Well done on your selection. There is a team media session going on this morning and, as you may be playing, there will be quite a lot of interest in you. I have arranged a table for you to sit at, and I will direct the journalists to you.' Excellent, I thought, I have turned up here, don't have the faintest idea about the situation with Vaughan, and now I have to front up to the media!

As it was, the session wasn't too bad, with most of them wanting to know about how I felt being part of the set-up. I do remember, though, being astounded about how many journalists were present. This was nothing like the West Indies tour, and it gave me an early indication that playing Test cricket in England was a different kettle of fish to playing ODIs abroad.

I just about had time for a cup of coffee and to greet the other England players before we had to be down at the ground for practice. Once I had got my kit in its rightful place in the dressing-room, and had made my way to the nets, I began to get curious as to whether I was actually going to play or not. Every indication that I had been given up to this point was that I was only there in case Vaughan didn't recover. Vaughan himself was hobbling around, working with the physio, Kirk Russell, on some light stretches, and it didn't seem as though he was taking part in the practice at all.

One of the tell-tale signals of what the team is likely to be for any match is the batting order in the nets. Right from my first trials for Berkshire Under-12s, I remember waiting increasingly impatiently for the coach to tell me to pad up. The other batsmen came and went and once the bowlers started padding up, I had a fair idea that I was unlikely to feature too much for Berkshire Under-12s that season and I was right. The same is entirely true with both county and international cricket. Coaches, because their minds are frequently on other things, such as fielding drills, or helping bowlers with their actions, usually draw up a list for nets in roughly the order in which the team will bat during the game, with the odd exception of when they want to break up two left-handers. As I surveyed the board on which Duncan Fletcher had written the order for the nets, I found my name right at the top, alongside Marcus Trescothick, and facing Matthew Hoggard and Steve Harmison. This was a sign if ever there was one.

The net passed fairly uneventfully, although I got a fearful battering from Steve Harmison. In the West Indies he had terror-

As a kid I was told always to enjoy the game.

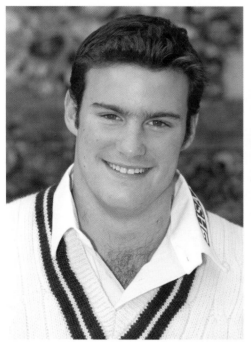

Naive, green, but eager to learn. Ian Gould, the Middlesex coach, thought I was a soft public school idiot when I started with the club – he was probably right.

John Buchanan's year with Middlesex did not work out. He went on to coach Australia, the best team in the world!

The Middlesex squad of 2003 with me as captain. The job came sooner than expected.

Right: Try to look calm and in control, even if it is all going wrong. Adjusting the field for Middlesex in July 2003.

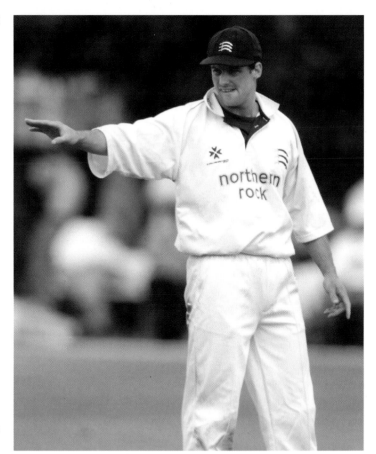

Below: You can do what you want, Adam, we will still kick your arse. Adam Hollioake and I toss in the Twenty 20 match of 2003.

Vikram Solanki and I waiting to bat in the nets at the Bangabandhu Stadium in Dhaka. 'You take Harmy, Vik, and I'll face Ashley.'

In the England bubble we can lose sight of how lucky we are. A visit to Streetpur Village, a place for abandoned children in Bangladesh, brings it home.

Duncan Fletcher is meticulous in his preparations. Here he explains a fielding drill to us.

Sweeping my way to a first international half century in the Caribbean. These runs showed I could succeed at the highest level.

Watching Brian Lara bat during the one-day series against the West Indies was a joy. It was an honour to be on the same field as him.

All the effort, all the work, all the sacrifices now seem worthwhile. Michael Vaughan presents me with my England cap on my debut against New Zealand.

Nasser Hussain and I relax on the balcony at Lord's following England's victory over New Zealand. Three hours earlier he had run me out for 83.

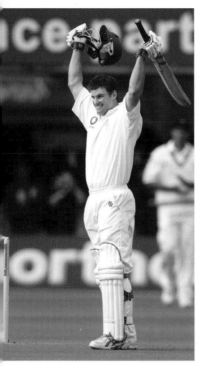

It's there, what a moment! A century on my debut at Lord's – does it get any better than this?

Marcus Trescothick and I gelled straightaway. He always wants to take the first ball of the innings and I let him.

Stephen Fleming, New Zealand captain – ct Strauss b. Flintoff. Sorry Flem, you're a great bloke but you've got to go.

Meeting the Queen was a happy and proud moment. Robert Key, to my right, and I were in the middle of a record second-wicket partnership at the time.

Isn't Lord's a great place to play cricket! After my second Test 100 at the ground, against the West Indies, I decided to plant a smacker on the pitch. It looks better than it tastes.

ised their hapless batsmen with pace, bounce and control, a deadly combination. Having played him a few times over the years, and been part of the inaugural National Academy intake with him, I knew how awkward he was to face. No batsman enjoys facing really quick bowlers, and the bounce that Steve manages to get from his high action makes him doubly unpleasant to face. Every ball feels as though it is going to rear off a length and hit you in the ribs. Just thinking about facing him can send batsmen scurrying for their chest protectors, and back in the Academy days, when his radar was liable to go on the blink from time to time, he was the ultimate no-go area during a net session. Thankfully, at the Lord's nets that day, he seemed to be getting the ball in the right areas, and it was just the sort of work-out I needed. The New Zealand team did not possess any bowlers with express pace, apart from the injured Shane Bond, but facing Harmison in the nets that day served to remind me that Test cricket was going to be a very different challenge to what I was accustomed to.

After the net came the news that I was waiting for. As I wandered over to the wicket to have a look at how the groundsman's preparations were coming on, Vaughan came up to me. 'Straussy, I think it is very likely that you are going to play. I am really struggling with my knee, and I can't honestly see any way that it is going to get better by Thursday. Just treat it like any other innings for Middlesex. You've scored a few hundreds here before, right?'

It was Michael Vaughan down to a tee. He has the most relaxed demeanour that I have ever seen in a cricketer, and is able to make the most stressful situations seem like a walk in the park. If confronted by an entire Panzer division with nothing more than a toy gun, you would half-expect him to turn to you, give you a quick wink and say, 'I reckon we can take these guys down. We'll just skip down the side somewhere, jump over that river, dive in a hole, and then launch our attack. It should be a laugh.' His manner cannot fail to inspire confidence in his team-mates, and it is the skill that was most needed during the knife-edge Ashes campaign the following summer.

His little chat churned up a range of emotions within me. Now I knew that I was very likely to play, and with that came an immense feeling of excitement, tinged with more than a little dread. He was right, I had scored centuries at Lord's before, and that was against county teams, with none of the media spotlight that accompanies Test cricket. No matter how positive you are as a person, you can't help but have nagging doubts about what lies in store. Everything that happens in Test cricket is so public. If you score a hundred, you are sure to have everyone you have ever met contact you and offer congratulations, but if you score nought on debut, and make a complete fool out of yourself in the process, it will be in every paper the next morning, well-meaning friends will look at you apologetically without knowing quite what to say, and armchair critics up and down the country will be swearing to anyone willing to listen that they have just seen the worst player ever to represent England. If you think about the negatives too much they may just consume you.

The final day prior to the Test was a constant battle with my emotions. Whenever I was busy, whether at the final practice or out for lunch, I didn't feel particularly nervous at all. This was just the normal preparation that I would go through for any game of cricket. It was when my mind drifted back into thinking about what was going to happen the next day that the butterflies came, and the inevitable doubts and questions that accompanied them. During an attempt to try to divert my attention away from the cricket, I picked up the *Evening Standard*, only to see a massive headline: 'Strauss will score a hundred on debut'. The author of this sensationalist piece was none other than my Middlesex coach, John Emburey, who went on to say that I was in the best form that he could remember, and he had no doubt that I would handle the occasion. It was pleasant reading from someone who genuinely wanted to see me do well, and it did make me chuckle. At least if I had a complete nightmare there would be two of us that looked stupid, rather than just myself!

The evening came and went, the final team meeting was completed, and the inevitable words of encouragement from team-mates were dispensed afterwards. The last few hours, sitting in your hotel room with nothing to distract you are always the hardest to contend with. Nasser Hussain apparently could not sleep at all during Test matches, and I can understand why. The mixture of anticipation, nerves, planning and, lurking somewhere in the background, dread, does not make a great recipe for sleep. I suppose I was lucky because I had been thinking about little else for the last 24 hours, I didn't have much more that could go through my head, and I eventually drifted off at about 12 in between mental images of balls flying to the boundary and stumps being flattened.

While everything prior to a Test match seems to go very slowly in the same way as watching a clock seems to slow it down, the morning of a Test is always a rush. A quick breakfast, followed by a dash to the ground to get the best parking space, and then out on to the field for a warm-up. Most of the team are not overly talkative at this stage. This is where everyone is getting themselves mentally ready for what is to come. The batsmen are preparing themselves to deal with tricky first-morning conditions if the toss is won, and the bowlers are trying to preserve as much energy as possible in case the coin comes down the wrong way.

The first morning of my first Test, 20 May 2004, was an absolute belter. The sun was shining brightly, and it was surprisingly warm for early May. Lord's looked an absolute picture as the increased light drew attention to the lovingly manicured outfield, and the incredible new Media Centre. It was obvious that whoever won the toss would bat first, and I was already setting myself to have to deal with the new ball that morning. Marcus Trescothick, who was deputising for Vaughan, failed to win the toss, and as soon as we saw Stephen Fleming being ushered towards the waiting television presenter, we knew that we were in for a long day in the field. A wave of relief washed over me. Although part of me wanted to bat first and get it out of the way, another side of me was quite happy with the delay, the opportunity to get a feel for Test cricket before having to ply my trade, and also size up the conditions.

That first day is a bit of a blur in my mind. I remember being handed my cap by David Graveney before going out, and feeling immense pride. Nasser whispered in my ear, 'Well done, mate, no one can ever take that away from you.' It was an obvious comment to make, but it really struck a chord with me. This was it, no matter how things went over the next five days, I would always be able to tell my grandchildren that I had played at the highest level.

The first hour comes and goes. The wicket is as flat as we anticipated, and the New Zealand batsmen seem to have little difficulty in fending off the new ball. Suddenly Fleming flashes outside off stump. The ball comes quick to me at backward point, and the catch nestles safely into my hands. A real nerve-settler for me, and a valuable wicket for the team. There are to be no other breakthroughs before lunch, and we all know that there is going to be some seriously hard work to do in the afternoon. We fare a little better during the latter part of the day, but with only five wickets down at the close, and with the dangerous Chris Cairns still to come, we have to contend with the possibility that they are going to get past the all-important 400 mark in their first innings.

Day two. D-Day for me. I know that I am going to be batting at some stage during the day. When will depend on how quickly we get rid of the last five New Zealand wickets. I am nervous, but in some ways the exertions of yesterday, and the tiredness that followed all the hype have dissipated it somewhat. Tuffey, the nightwatchman, goes, quickly followed by McCullum and Vettori. A last-wicket stand develops between Cairns, who uses the innings to create a new record for sixes in Test cricket, and Martin. By now I just want to get off the field and start preparing myself to bat. Finally Cairns hoists another massive blow, except this time he gets a little underneath it, and he is well taken on the boundary. Now it's my turn ...

Chris Martin lets the ball go. I pick it up quickly, despite the tricky background of the Lord's Pavilion. It's not a bouncer. There was none of the last-second energy in his action which usually accompanies the short-of-a-length 'effort' ball. It is, however, dead straight on middle and off stump. I decide to play the line of the ball, and now allow too much for the slope, which can sometimes alter its direction. The ball pitches and continues its line. My bat comes down to meet it, and immediately I feel the reassuring vibrations of the ball hitting the middle. It was only a defensive shot, but the way the ball comes off the bat at pace, bounces and hits the hands of the mid-on fielder suggests that this wicket should be easy to score on. A surge of adrenalin and relief sweeps through my body. I have safely negotiated my first ball, and now the real work begins; I have to build an innings.

Second ball. Martin, probably more comfortable bowling at right-handers at the start of the innings, lets a similar delivery go, only this time it pitches slightly outside leg stump. It is the sort of ball that left-handers pray for early in their innings. There is very little chance of getting out to it, and a little flick of the wrists should propel it away to the vacant square-leg position to get the innings off and running. Again I feel the vibration in the bat handle that tells me I have made solid contact with the ball. This time I know it is going for runs. I look up and shout, 'Two' to Trescothick. I have just scored my first Test runs.

Early in an innings I always try to set myself mini goals. Getting through the first over is always the primary objective. Getting to double figures is the next welcome barrier to overcome. Somehow it seems much better to be on 10 runs than 9, but also it means that you are starting to get to grips with the conditions, and some of the hardness of the new ball might have dissipated. With only 35 minutes for Trescothick and me to bat before lunch, it is a huge relief to have got to 15 by the time the umpires lead us off the pitch. I have got through probably the most difficult period that I am likely to face in my Test career.

The conditions aren't difficult, and the New Zealand bowling is not very different to what I have faced in county cricket, but it is in this period that you, as a debutant, feel the heat of the spotlight like nothing else. The journalists are all taking notes about how you are dealing with the situation. The television commentators are no doubt playing super slow motion footage of your technique and pointing out any flaws. The opposition are trying to get into your head with a few well chosen comments about cracking under the pressure, and finally you are having to deal with a situation that is far out of your comfort zone. You have never done this before.

The relief as I take my pads off is palpable. I have passed the first test. I haven't cracked under the pressure. If anything, I have been a little more positive than normal, and that reassures me. Going into your shell in situations like this is never a recipe for success. Most importantly, however, I feel as though I am just playing another game now. I know that I can handle the bowling. I feel comfortable with the conditions, and my focus is turning towards getting a decent score.

I give the magnificent three-course meal at Lord's a miss, and instead opt for a couple of ham and cheese rolls. I never feel hungry during an innings, but recognise that it is important to get some fuel on board. Trescothick and I make our way out of the sanctuary of the dressing-room just as the weary bowlers are stumbling out of the dining room with bellies full of rack of lamb and treacle sponge. Players love playing at Lord's more for the lunches than anything else!

I get off the mark after lunch with a clip down to fine-leg off Jacob Oram, a tall, hit-the-deck type of bowler who extracts some awkward bounce. A few more nudges and hurdles, then bang, I middle an over-pitched ball from Oram to the mid-wicket boundary. I have reached 30. Daniel Vettori, regarded by most as the best left-arm orthodox spinner in world cricket, comes into the attack. Surprisingly, he bowls from the Pavilion end, where his natural spin is negated to a certain extent by the Lord's slope. Be careful not to play at balls wide of off stump, I tell myself as he comes in to bowl. New Zealand are forced to have a reasonably defensive field after our positive start, so there are plenty of gaps to work the ball into. A few sweeps and back-foot pushes, and I have got myself to 44. Martin returns to bowl. Wide of off stump, I middle it through extra cover off the front foot. Two balls later, short and wide, I throw the bat at it, and it whistles away to the boundary for four. I have scored my first Test fifty.

I raise my bat to the Pavilion, and acknowledge the applause from the crowd. This is where playing in front of a full house is brilliant, I think to myself. Gone is the thought about making a fool of myself in front of thousands, now my mind is focused on getting a big score, and having a large number of people supporting you, as well as the honour of playing for your country, helps focus the mind. Oram sends a couple of full balls down the leg side, which I get down to the fine-leg boundary. Easy runs.

Vettori is proving more difficult, bowling from the other end. He seems to have settled on a line which makes it difficult to score singles, and the presence of two fielders around the bat unnerves me. I have a decision to make. Either I suck up the pressure and am prepared to play out a couple of maidens, or I take the game to him, hit one over the top, and hopefully open up more options if Fleming changes his field. A well-known cricketing cliché is 'If your heart and your head say to go for a big shot, then do it. If your heart says yes, but your head no, then refrain.' I size up the situation. We are 160/0, and I am hitting them well at 75 not out. We don't want to lose a wicket now, but it is important to keep the momentum going. I know that I only have to get half a bat on the ball, and it should go over mid-wicket for four. I decide to take him on. The ball is well flighted, I skip down the wicket, get to the pitch and middle it over mid-wicket for a one-bounce four. Adrenalin surges through my body. I have taken the risk, and it has come off. Fleming hastily positions a man at deep mid-wicket and takes out one of the men around the bat.

Scoring is starting to prove more difficult now. The fields are defensive and the ball is getting softer. It takes me ten overs to get from 80 to 90, and I am starting to get edgy, especially after the loss of my opening partner, Trescothick, who edged a ball from Oram to the wicket-keeper. I am frustrated about scoring slowly, and the thought of getting a hundred on debut is starting to consume me. I am thinking too much about the final result, getting a hundred, and not enough about the process, getting 10 runs. I resolve myself to play every ball on its merits, but the adrenalin is flowing. Martin bowls a length ball wide of off stump. I should leave it, but it seems like the first wide ball I have received in days. I flash at it, only to hear the snick as it catches the inside edge of the bat. There is another sound also; I look back to see the ball travelling down to the fine-leg boundary and my stumps are intact. What was that noise, I think to myself, but decide to forget about it and concentrate on the next ball. Television replays later show that the ball clipped off stump but did not dislodge the bails.

Three balls later, I think that I see a bit of width on a short ball from Martin. I prepare to cut it. There is no width though, and I end up having to steer it through gully, where Oram dives low but cannot hold on to the catch. I run through for a single, but berate myself for trying to invent scoring shots. I am now on 96, it has taken an age to get the last 6 runs, and I can feel the anticipation in the crowd. Everyone seems to know that I am going through a difficult patch and they are willing me to get through it. I, on the other hand, am hating the pressure. The emphasis has changed from he 'could' get a hundred to he 'should' get a hundred, and that makes things much more difficult. It is now much more of a battle with yourself and your emotions. The bowlers have been trying in vain to get you out for hours and are now resigned to waiting for you to do something to get yourself out. All I have to do is wait patiently and score off the bad deliveries but I am finding it difficult to keep concentrating. I have an almost uncontrollable urge to hit a boundary. Scoring a four is going to relieve all the pressure, and take me to a hundred, but I have to wait for the right ball.

Tuffey bowls me one short of a length. I see it early and play my favourite pull shot. I feel the ball come off the middle of the bat and look up, expecting to see the ball whistling to the square-leg boundary. I have got it a little fine though, and the fine-leg fielder moves swiftly to his right to cut it off. I am now on 98. Martin starts another over. Surely, I think to myself, it has got to happen this over. I let a couple of length balls go through to the keeper. I am so close. Another length ball, this time I try to take a risk by hitting through the line, but the ball bounces more than I antici-pate, and I am fortunate that it finds the splice of the bat, rather than the edge.

Butcher walks down the wicket casually. He has seen this all before. 'Keep watching the ball, Straussy. In a minute he is going to bowl you a wide one, and you are going to smack it through the covers for four. Be patient.' I nod my head in reply. Martin runs in again and lets go. The ball is full and wide, just as Butcher said. I slash at the ball and feel solid contact. The ball has gone between the two cover fielders and, as I look up, I know that I have just brought up my hundred.

I sprint down the other end, knowing that the ball is going for four, but I don't know how to react. I punch the air and wave my bat with so much force that I nearly fall over. In one moment, all the tension, adrenalin, fear and nerves leave my body, to be replaced by pure unadulterated joy. I raise my bat to my team-mates, all of whom are on the balcony cheering me on. I look around the ground. Everyone is on their feet cheering. The giant scoreboard displays a message: 'Congratulations Andrew Strauss on scoring 100 on debut.' I cannot believe this is happening to me.

I got out to Vettori shortly afterwards, playing a tired defensive shot on 112, but for just about the only time in my career I felt no disappointment. There were handshakes and congratulations from all my team-mates, and it took me an age to calm down. I walked around the dressing-room in a daze as the last half an hour of play went by, and I had to keep pinching myself to be sure that it had actually happened. For years I had looked at the honours board in the home dressing-room at Lord's, which commemor-ates hundreds and five-wicket hauls at the ground, hoping that A. J. Strauss would one day appear there. It would be a few days before my name would be painted up there properly, but my England team-mates had taken the liberty of putting a strip of white sticky tape with my name on it under the last centurion. I had fulfilled any schoolboy's dream, scoring a hundred at Lord's on debut. It doesn't get any better than that.

That night, however, as Ruth and I were having a quiet cele-bratory glass of champagne in a St John's Wood restaurant, the enormity of what had just happened hit me. It was the stuff of legends, but it was only the beginning. I had opened a very heavy door by scoring my first Test hundred, but I wasn't sure what lay beyond it. Are there going to be more successes? What are the press going to make of all this? Is my life going to change? Am I going to cope with it? These questions all filled my mind as I sipped on the Veuve Clicquot, but I let them all pass me by. There would be plenty of time in the future to worry about those things. For the time being both Ruth and I were determined to enjoy the ride.

As I awoke the next morning, feeling tired but still elated, I thought that most of the work that I would be expected to do in the game was already done. We were cruising at 240/2 in reply to their 386, and I was looking forward to a day of relaxation while my team-mates put the game completely beyond them. I have come to realise over the couple of years that I have played for England, however, that things rarely go according to plan. Some good bowling with the new ball reduced us to 311/6, and we ended up doing well to reach 441. New Zealand were still very much in the game, especially when they reached 180/2 in their second innings, a lead of 125.

As has often been the case with this England side over the last few years, someone has stuck their hand up when needed and, with the game delicately poised, this time it was the turn of Ashley Giles, who was getting attacked from all sides of the press after a quiet tour of the West Indies, to bring us back into the game. His 3/87 in 39 overs was a fantastic effort on a wicket not helping the spinners, and he did much to take the pressure off our seam bowlers. For New Zealand it was Mark Richardson, following up his first-innings 90 with a century, who got them in a position possibly to win the game. With just over a day to go, we were set 282 to win on a wicket that was showing signs of wear and tear. It was a tough ask.

For me the drama of the game had not finished. Despite seeing us reduced to 35/2, Nasser Hussain and I were able to put on a hundred to put us in a position to win the game. After my first-innings hundred, I was used to their bowlers and the wicket, and was finding batting a much more enjoyable occupation than in the more testing first innings. Despite the relative ease with which Nasser and I were putting on runs, the equation for us to win the match was becoming slightly more difficult as New Zealand were bowling defensively and generally trying to slow down the scoring rate. It was with this in mind that Nasser approached me between overs about an hour after lunch. 'We just have to be a bit careful that we don't score too slowly. Let's try to get our running between the wickets a bit sharper,' he said. I nodded in agreement, and immediately started looking for more quick singles to rotate the strike.

Our momentum was just building when Nasser's words came back to haunt us as he smashed a ball straight at point and set off running. My first reaction was to shout, 'No', but the way he was sprinting down the wicket to me made me realise that it was too late, he was not turning back. I set off, quickly at first, but then slowing down as I realised the futility of my task. McCullum gathered the throw safely and whipped off the bails. I was run out for 83, just 17 short of achieving a century in each innings.

I trudged off the ground feeling disconsolate, but not overly upset with my team-mate. His idea to get us scoring more quickly was correct and, although even he might admit that there probably wasn't a run on offer, it was a mistake of judgment that we all make from time to time. As Nasser came up into the dressing-room at tea-time, the first thing he did was to come up to me, place a hand on my shoulder and say sorry. I could see that he really meant it and was quite devastated about what had happened. My reaction was to tell him not to worry and go on and win the game.

Fortunately, he did exactly that, showing the full range of his repertoire as he smashed the New Zealand bowlers everywhere on the way to a century in what turned out to be his last Test match. It was a fairytale ending to his career and, after all the blood and guts that he put into English cricket while captain, he deserved nothing less. I really could not be unhappy at how my first Test match turned out. Okay, I didn't get the century in each innings that I was so close to achieving, but a century and an 80, and Man of the Match were beyond my wildest dreams. More importantly, England won a vital and extremely tight Test match, by chasing a record fourth-innings score in a Lord's Test. We had shown immense character to chase a score like that on the fifth day and, looking back, that game was probably a watershed, both in terms of result and belief, that set us off on an incredible summer.

4
THE MAGNIFICENT SEVEN

As I rested my tired and hungover body at home I began to reflect on what I had achieved at Lord's on my Test debut. I knew I had accomplished something very special. I had fulfilled a childhood ambition in my very first game for England, a feat nobody could take away from me, but I also realised that I could not afford to dwell on it for too long. People's expectations of me were going to be much higher from now on and I had to make sure that I did not let my standards slip. One match, after all, does not make a career, or a summer for that matter.

Sitting in our flat on Ealing Common, Ruth and I were confident that I would retain my place in the side for the next Test, but it was by no means guaranteed. My performance had created a problem for the selectors. Michael Vaughan was expected to be fit for the Second Test at Headingley. Naturally he was sure to play, but mathematicians are yet to work out a way of getting three into two. So who would they drop? The England team had taken shape on the tour of the Caribbean. There was a good, confident feel about it, we were all enjoying each other's company and success, and you sensed something special was taking place. England had now won four of its last five Test matches, but who were the selectors going to drop?

Nasser Hussain solved the problem two days after our memorable victory by announcing his retirement from international cricket, and it was only when the news reached me that I realised I would definitely be travelling to Leeds.

Nasser kept his intentions pretty quiet at the end of the New Zealand match but there was something in the way he behaved as he walked off Lord's that suggested he was thinking of calling it a day. There were also a couple of throwaway lines whilst we sat enjoying a beer on the balcony. 'There cannot be a better way to go,' was the gist of what he was saying. But he had not made any announcements and we as a team were not aware of a decision. It was only a few days later I learnt he had spent the night before his match-winning hundred informing Duncan Fletcher and members of his family of his intention.

In one way there seemed a certain symmetry about what was taking place. I had had a fairytale start to my career and he had finished his in the best possible way imaginable. At times Nasser could be stroppy but he had given his heart and soul into becoming the best possible England player he could. As a captain he was totally committed to England's cause, too. Not all of his actions were popular but he had a vision of the England side he wanted to lead and he worked tirelessly towards that goal. Heaven knows how many sleepless nights he had thinking about how he could turn the team into a force to be reckoned with. For these reasons alone he deserved to go out on this note.

I expected there to be a certain amount of media interest in me at the conclusion of my First Test debut but I was not really prepared for the furore that followed. There were times when I felt a little bit out of control. Everybody seemed to want a piece of me and my mobile phone did not stop ringing. In the following week several interesting articles appeared in the newspapers. Journalists had contacted old coaches, colleagues and friends for their views on me and I was finding things out about myself that I wasn't really aware of. In the past any interviews had been cricket-related but now I was reading what people thought of me at school or university. It was a strange experience but, thankfully, they were all pretty positive in what they said.

Playing for Middlesex on the Saturday became a welcome change, in that it allowed me to get away from the media frenzy. Once again I could concentrate on cricket. I knew I could play cricket; I wasn't sure how I came across on television, radio and in the newspapers. As I drove to Lord's for Middlesex's Cheltenham & Gloucester Trophy match against Glamorgan it dawned on me that it had only been five days since the last time I had played at this famous old ground, yet it seemed so much longer than that. So much had happened. So much had been said. The memory of hitting the ball through the covers to bring up my hundred was still vivid but it is now, strangely, somewhat distant.

The contrast between the last time I set foot on the Lord's outfield and this game was stark. On the Monday 30,000 people had cheered England and me to victory. On Saturday most stands in the ground were empty. The C&G fourth-round tie against Glamorgan was an important game for Middlesex but I struggled to get myself up for it. As the Middlesex captain, I was determined not to give the impression that my England success had lessened my commitment. I tried harder than ever, but the body would not respond to what my brain was telling it. It appeared to be some-where else. I scored a bright and breezy 19 but it wasn't exactly what the team or I was looking for. However, it was great to see the Middlesex boys again and win our way through to the quarter-finals. It was also nice to see that my team-mates were genuinely happy for me. This is not always the case in team games and quite often an international player's return to his county is greeted by snide and jealous remarks.

Naturally there was the odd comment from the opposition. David Harrison, the Glamorgan opening bowler, gave me a couple of reminders of where I was. Harrison bowls off the wrong foot and, after beating my bat on one occasion, told me that I wasn't playing for England now. I felt like saying, 'I'm aware of that, facing a bowler with an action like yours,' but I bottled out and got on with my batting.

Whilst playing for Middlesex my selection for the Second Test at Headingley was confirmed and on the Monday morning I packed my bags for a week in Leeds. For Lord's all my kit had been given to me at the ground and it was only when I started filling my bags at home that I began to realise how much I had. I was only going up there to play in a game of cricket but it felt as though I was setting off on some sort of pilgrimage.

The contrast between Lord's and Headingley could not have been greater for me. Lord's is a ground that I had played at every other week for four years yet my sole experience of playing at Headingley was a Middlesex 2nd XI game six years earlier. When we left the team hotel in the centre of Leeds I had to follow a team-mate because I did not have a clue how to get there. And when I arrived I felt as though I had never been there before. It had completely changed with new stands dominating most of the ground. Throughout the West Indies tour in the winter I had told myself that I had to become accustomed to playing at grounds that I did not know. I firmly believe that it is better to have no memories of a ground than bad ones but it always takes time to feel comfortable at a new venue.

Headingley is a unique Test ground. The blue seats on the

terracing, the Leeds Rhinos Rugby League ground at one end, the terraced houses at the other and the slope give it a completely different feel to any other in England. The pitch is also a one-off and there are a lot of batsmen, whether they be Test or county players, who are mentally scarred from playing here. The ball can behave unpredictably and there are times when batsmen fear more for their fingers than their wicket. But I had none of that baggage. I had no bad memories of the place so I entered the Second Test with a Test hundred to my name as well as a fresh, open mind.

The big debate leading into the Test concerned who out of Marcus Trescothick, Michael Vaughan and myself would open the batting. We all wanted to do it but only two of us could. I was prepared to bat anywhere England wanted me to but it would have been hard for me to slip down the order. I had batted at three in the one-dayers in the West Indies but I had opened in all but a couple of my first-class games for Middlesex.

Vaughan informed us that he would drop down to four on the Monday evening. It was reassuring to hear this but I also felt a little bit guilty. Michael had performed brilliantly for England in this position for a couple of years and now he was moving down the order to accommodate me. In a way it added to the pressure I felt going into the game. I wanted to prove that my performance at Lord's was not a one-off, and I also wanted to show that I was a worthy replacement for Vaughan.

Nasser's retirement had secured me a place in the Second Test but his departure did cause me some distress. At practice on Tuesday I was told that I would be taking up his position at short-leg. I was surprised I was not put there at Lord's – the shin-pads and helmet are usually reserved for the new kid on the block. It was the case at Middlesex where, as an expendable young player, I had been thrown in there at the start of my career. This ceased when I became Middlesex captain and I returned to the rather less dangerous fielding position of slip or mid-off. Nasser had a playful little dig at me before the Lord's Test about fielding at short-leg, and I reminded him that Mike Gatting and Graham Gooch finished their careers fielding here. Nasser actually seemed happy to continue fielding there, so I decided to leave it to him. But once he had gone I had no excuse and Duncan Fletcher, realising I was a bit out of touch in the position, drafted me off for extra practice.

The previous week also taught me that what you say in interview always filters through to your team-mates. After Nasser retired I was interviewed by the BBC and stated that England would be a weaker side without him. I thought nothing of it and was trying to be complimentary about a great servant for England. But before the Second Test Michael Vaughan came up to me and told me that what I had said was wrong. He told me that England was not a weaker side without Nasser, we were a stronger side with me in it. From the England captain this was lovely to hear.

At the eve of Test team meeting we were informed that there would be a second change to the side that won at Lord's. Simon Jones had been feeling discomfort in his left foot and Kent's Martin Saggers was being rushed up the M1 to play.

It was Saggers who took England's only wicket on a wet and miserable first day. The only other positive that came of the day for me was the fact that the short-leg helmet works. Mark Richardson clipped one at me off Steve Harmison and it struck me on the bonce. The blow caused much merriment amongst my team-mates, who suggested that, technically, it was a dropped catch and that I would have to do a little more work on my reactions.

New Zealand dominated the second day and worked themselves into a strong position on a pitch that offered the fast bowlers help. In the mid-afternoon the news that we had all been wondering about finally reached the dressing-room and Michael Vaughan dashed off the pitch, changed quickly and set off down the M1 to Sheffield to attend the birth of his first child. That the England captain had been allowed to do this brought mixed reactions from the media and spectators, as it did when I returned home from Pakistan in November 2005 to be present at the birth of my son, Samuel. In the past such an action has been frowned on. Chief sports writers love pontificating on matters like this, and I know I received a fair amount of stick for missing the Third Test in Lahore. I take great pride in representing England but there are some things in life that are more important than playing cricket for your country, and being at my wife's side when she was giving birth to our first child is one of them. There is still the odd remark made now, normally by people who have been divorced on at least one occasion, but I have absolutely no regrets about doing what I did.

At Headingley the feeling amongst some journalists was that Vaughan should either withdraw from the match or miss the birth of his first child. They felt the imminent arrival would be an unwelcome distraction that would affect his captaincy and batting in an important match. This, however, was not the case. Vaughan never let the stress he was under show and England were a better team with their captain there to captain them.

The way in which Duncan Fletcher handled Vaughan's predicament highlighted a change in the approach of the management to players. In the past England players have been expected to forget their private lives once they walk through a dressing-room door and concentrate solely on the cricket. This, of course, is impossible and under Fletcher England now attempt to ensure that the whole cricketer, rather than just the batsman or bowler in the player, is happy.

England finally bowled New Zealand out on the Saturday morning and the Test then followed a similar trend to that at Lord's. I scored 62 but it was the batting of Marcus Trescothick, Andrew Flintoff and Geraint Jones, who scored his first Test hundred, that enabled us to put New Zealand under pressure when they batted for a second time. Trescothick scored a quite brilliant 132 on a difficult pitch. It was a score he needed. During the pre-Test debate on who should open there were suggestions that Trescothick should be the player who made way. He had not had the best of winters, and had scored only three fifties in his previous 17 innings. He was not under any pressure for his place but he needed this innings just to get people off his back. It is thrilling to stand up the other end when he is in this sort of form. Trescothick has a simple technique and he hits the ball very hard. At times he makes you feel inadequate at the other end as you mistime another one to mid-on, and it was his innings that took the initiative away from New Zealand.

Vaughan, with daughter Tallulah safely born, scored only 13, and it was left to Flintoff and Geraint Jones to ram home our advantage. For the second match in a row we had grabbed hold of a game on the fourth day when the pressure was on. It was a good sign. As was the batting of Jones, who underlined the importance of having a wicket-keeper who can bat. England added almost 200 runs to their score whilst Jones was at the crease and his 118-run partnership with Flintoff played a major role in us winning the game. It is always hard to evaluate how many runs a great keeper will save you, in terms of the catches he takes and the presence he has on the field, and every international team is looking for an Adam Gilchrist figure. Fletcher and Vaughan have been given a fair amount of stick over the selection of Jones but it would be safe to say they both felt vindicated at the end of this Test match.

I woke up on the final morning feeling slightly nervous. Sunday's exploits had taken England to the brink of a series victory but I could not help feeling that this game had another twist in it. There was a real sense of anticipation among the rest of the side. Being in a team that is becoming used to winning means that when an opportunity to win presents itself the players have the confidence to play the smart cricket and do whatever is required. And that is exactly what happened.

A clinical bowling performance from Matthew Hoggard and Stephen Harmison meant that New Zealand's last five wickets added only 59 runs and that we were left chasing 45 for victory. Trescothick saw us home, but unfortunately his opening partner became a consolation casualty for the New Zealand bowlers. I had a quick glass of bubbly in the dressing-room, then hit the motorway for Nottingham, where we celebrated properly. The Third Test may have been only three days away but we all enjoyed a good night out in Nottingham. And why shouldn't we? We had just won a series against a highly rated New Zealand side and we were playing excellent cricket.

This was my first experience of back-to-back Test matches and I found them incredibly hard to prepare for. A skinful on a Monday night was not the ideal way to start these preparations but it is the mental fatigue that is harder to overcome than the physical. It is very difficult to refresh yourself mentally and I was absolutely exhausted after Headingley. A two-day break gives you no chance of recharging the batteries, and I really struggled in the Third Test against New Zealand because of this. I did not know how to cope with it. I did not know how to switch off between the matches.

It brought home the reality of how tough Test cricket is. In between Lord's and Headingley the excitement of playing on this stage for a second time had allowed me to cope with any fatigue but in Nottingham it hit me hard. I suppose it was inevitable. Whenever there is a huge up there is a down as well, and this comes after the game when you are absolutely shattered.

Vaughan and Duncan Fletcher are fully aware of this and we only had a light gym session on the Tuesday and a light practice on the eve of the game. After practice I attempted to remedy my reputation for having terrible dress sense by going into Nottingham and splonking out on some new clothing. James 'David Beckham' Anderson and Matthew Hoggard were my fashion gurus and I am not totally convinced with the result but they may grow on me.

Although the series was won, we had the opportunity to complete a clean sweep over a very good side and this was something that Vaughan and Fletcher stressed to us at the pre-Test meeting. Winning is definitely a habit and it was not a habit we wanted to get out of. We were desperate for Vaughan to win the toss and bat first so that we could put our feet up and rest, and we were all using reverse psychology – 'It's a bowling day, boys, feels like a bowling day' – before the coin was flipped. Bugger, Stephen Fleming, the New Zealand captain, called correctly and out we went on what looked like a good batting pitch.

The effort of the previous week took its toll on the first day. Mark Richardson continued his excellent form and Fleming scored a chanceless century. New Zealand, on 272/2, appeared set to post a huge total but then Harmison struck twice in two balls. Ultimately it changed the course of the game. New Zealand's final eight wickets only added a further 112 runs and we were once again in the match.

Trent Bridge is a place of which I have fond memories. It is a cricket ground where it is easy to feel comfortable and I had scored a hundred there for Middlesex in 2002. My fondness for playing there did not transfer into runs this time, however, and I nicked the third ball I faced through to the wicket-keeper for nought. I had dealt with getting through the 'nervous nineties' on my debut and scored a hundred, but now I had to deal with the emotional turmoil of avoiding the dreaded pair. For some reason I had got it into my head that, after starting my England career so well, the game was going to bite me back. I was convincing myself it was inevitable that I would bag a pair in my third Test and when these thoughts start nagging away at you it is difficult to remain positive.

Fortunately the ordeal did not last long. Chris Cairns' generosity allowed me to avoid the ignominy of bagging them when he bowled me a slower ball that I tucked away for four runs. Cairns' charity failed to continue but he had a little help from the umpire who gave me out lbw for 6 to a ball that pitched about six inches outside leg stump.

Graham Thorpe scored a brilliant hundred to help England win another remarkable game of cricket. Each of the three Test matches against New Zealand had followed a similar pattern. New Zealand had batted first and worked themselves into a strong position. England had then fought back, grabbing hold of each game on what became known as 'Super Sunday'. We then went on to win each match. In doing this we had proved that we were a very resilient and competitive team. We had shown the ability to win matches, even though we had not bossed the whole game, and this was a big development for the England team. At Lord's and Trent Bridge we had successfully chased record fourth-innings totals and at Headingley we had won after conceding more than 400 in the first innings.

I had only played in one Test series but I could already sense that there was not a huge difference in class between the eight leading Test sides in the world. There are no weak teams and matches are decided on such small margins. I had noticed England's attention to detail in the West Indies and it was these little things, along with making the right decisions at the important moments, that end up winning you Test matches.

At the end of the series I sat down and had a beer with Fleming. He had spent the 2001 season playing for Middlesex and we had got on very well. He is a lovely man and was very popular. But at the end of the series and after being beaten 3–0 he was understandably very disappointed. New Zealand had arrived in England with genuine aspirations of becoming the second-best side in the world. They had competed well with Australia in Australia, they had beaten India and drawn with South Africa – they were a decent side. Fleming told me that this had been the hardest series he had ever had to captain. New Zealand had had their injury problems – Shane Bond did not play in any of the Test matches and Daniel Vettori had a bad back throughout – and their bowling had been poor but he was also very complimentary about the England side. New Zealand had been unable to handle the pace and hostility of Harmison and had buckled when under pressure. We, however, had raised our game at the pivotal moments, and this boded well for the Test series against the West Indies.

*   *   *

But before we took on Brian Lara's side in five-day cricket we had the midsummer one-day extravaganza of the NatWest series. And it was during this period that I had my first experience of the tug of war that takes place between club and country. I was not a centrally contracted player and this meant Duncan Fletcher could not dictate when and where I played cricket. I was contracted to Middlesex who, naturally, wanted their captain to play in every game he could.

There was no problem with me playing for Middlesex in the quarter-finals of the Cheltenham & Gloucester Trophy two days after the scheduled finish of the Third Test against New Zealand, a game Middlesex lost. Problems surfaced at the end of the NatWest series when Middlesex wanted me to play in a couple of National League games and two Twenty 20 matches. Whatever people say about Twenty 20, and it has its critics, they surely could not argue with the concept if they were part of the 27,000 spectators who turned up at Lord's for the game against Surrey. There was a fantastic atmosphere at a fantastic event. The only disappointment was Middlesex's performance.

After three limited-overs matches I asked Middlesex whether I could be rested from the National League game at Durham so that I could focus my mind on Test cricket. I had had four weeks of trying to slog the ball out of the park and I wanted to prepare properly for the Test series against the West Indies. The intricacies of one-day cricket had left me feeling out of form and I had scored very few runs in any of the matches I had played. During the same period the West Indies were playing three-day games and getting decent Test practice. It left me thinking that this was surely not the right way for me to prepare for a Test match.

Yet, despite my reservations, I ended up playing for Middlesex and my last game of cricket before the Test involved me making a 600-mile return journey up to Durham. I arrived home at 2 a.m. on the Monday morning, having scored a duck and suffered the ignominy of losing with two balls to go. To make matters worse, when England met up next day, Steve Harmison, who was playing for Durham, gave me a barrage of abuse as soon as I walked into the dressing-room at Lord's, where we were about to take on the West Indies. Harmison had been the last man in and I, as captain, had set a field that had allowed him to play a couple of trademark sweep shots to get off strike in the last over of our match. He was amazed that I had not paid more attention to his batting whilst on England duty. My mistake had probably cost us the game.

Once again England's preparations for the Lord's Test were affected by injury. Against New Zealand Vaughan's knee problem gave me the chance to make my debut, and here, before taking on the West Indies, Mark Butcher's whiplash, sustained whilst driving to The Oval for treatment on a thigh strain, gave Rob Key the chance to prove his undoubted class. Having seen Rob play at the Academy in Adelaide and for Kent, I knew what a good player he is but he needed to translate that into Test runs.

England had had a disappointing tri-nation one-day series. We had failed to make the Lord's final, in which New Zealand had defeated West Indies by 107 runs. If we had performed well in the NatWest series I am sure Vaughan and Fletcher would have drawn on that success but, from the moment we arrived at Lord's to take on the West Indies in the First Test there was not a mention of one-day cricket. It was as though it had never happened. The attitude was that we were now playing a form of the game that we knew we were good at.

At Lord's, even on practice days, England change in the Pavilion and walk over to the nets at the Nursery End to train. It is a journey I have made on countless occasions but when I arrived on the Nursery ground I was horrified to see a huge image of myself on a wall of the Nursery Pavilion, an area used for corporate hospitality on match days. The picture was in black and white and alongside it was a quote from me saying what it meant to score a hundred at Lord's.

Before my hundred on debut the only picture of me at Lord's was a passport-sized photo in the Middlesex diary. I was flattered to see this new version but I wasn't quite sure what my team-mates would make of it. There are other similar banners and pictures scattered around Lord's containing quotes and highlighting out-standing performances here by the likes of Sachin Tendulkar, Glenn McGrath, David Gower and Graham Gooch. These are the greats of the game, so it was slightly embarrassing to be set amongst them. It did not take long for the media to notice the picture and, before I knew it, I was being asked to have my photo-graph taken in front of it.

The Test proved to be a memorable one for Key and myself. Despite not feeling in great form I managed to score my third consecutive century for England at Lord's. The second hundred came in a NatWest series match against the West Indies. It was an important innings, in that I had proved that the first hundred was not a fluke, and it also helped me relax when I came to Lord's again. To this day I do not know how I achieved this feat. The pace and bounce of the Lord's pitch suits my style of batting but there must be an element of fate behind it. The emotion of reaching three figures for the second time in a Test was never going to be the same as the first but it was still hugely satisfying.

I was thrilled to see Key post his first Test hundred, a brilliant innings of 221. Indeed everyone in the side was chuffed for him. He had been in good form in county cricket and this, in some ways, placed him under more pressure. Rob was, in essence, representing county cricket and he needed to show that he could make the step up. Butcher's misfortune had given him a one-off chance to show he was good enough to be an England player and this innings proved he could.

Rob has an endearing character and is a lot fitter than he looks. He has a physique that no amount of miles on a treadmill can change. He could do a thousand sit-ups a day for the rest of his life but he would never develop a six-pack. All the same, he is looked on as a tough opponent on the county circuit and he has an approach to cricket that is similar to that of many Australians. He has a never-say-die attitude and difficult situations tend to bring the best out of him. The harder the game the more likely he is to score runs.

Robert is great company and his views on a situation are rarely bog-standard. He often comes from left-field. I don't know whether it is deliberate, and he just does it to stir people up, or whether he actually believes what he says. In a funny way he is also one of the most miserable men in world cricket. He just loves a moan but, unlike some, he is one of those people whose whinging is very amusing. We were due to meet the Queen during the tea interval at Lord's. Rob was unbeaten on 90 at tea and as we walked out to bat after meeting Her Majesty he kept going on about how an earth he was expected to keep his concentration after meeting her. No matter the situation, there will always be something for him to moan about.

We had got to know each other well during our winter at the

Academy and when he reached his hundred we hugged in the middle. The memory of scoring my first hundred here was fresh in my mind and I said something like: 'It feels good, doesn't it.' To which he replied: 'You're fucking right it does.'

We put on 291 together for the second wicket and we had a ball. The pitch was good, the sun was out, there was a full house at the home of cricket and we were both striking the ball well. There were times when we felt we could take the piss out of the opposition by hitting the ball and playing the strokes we wanted no matter what they did. It is the only time in my international career when I have felt like this.

Batting on the first day gave me the experience of facing two of the more enigmatic fast bowlers in West Indian cricket. Fidel Edwards and Tino Best can both bowl quickly but if you were to pass them in the street you would not think they were West Indian fast bowlers. Joel Garner and Curtly Ambrose they are not – both are about five feet eight inches tall. Edwards has a low slingy action, in the Jeff Thomson mould, and the ball comes from in front of the umpire. I had never seen a bowler like him before and it took a bit of getting used to. Best, meanwhile, enjoyed a chat, spouting out absolute rubbish after each delivery. It was probably just as well we could not understand his thick, deep Bajan accent. But what did become clear was that he rated bowling at above 90 mph as much as taking a wicket. We did not know what to expect from him. Beamers, bouncers, Best could bowl anything at you and this was rather disconcerting.

On my debut I had clammed up when I reached 90 and nervously stuttered my way through to three figures. Here it was somewhat different. Omari Banks, the West Indian offspinner, was bowling at the time and he had no fielders out on the leg-side boundary. I did not feel any nerves as I approached my second Test hundred and the field set gave me a free hit on the leg side. It was an invitation I could not ignore and I hoicked him over there, moving from 90 to 100 in about four balls.

Rob and I were not the only England players to put in potential match-winning performances. Vaughan became the eleventh player to score a hundred in each innings of a Lord's Test and Ashley Giles took 9/210, the best match figures of his England career. Ashley improved on these in the Second Test against the West Indies at Edgbaston but the events that took place at Lord's must have given him greater pleasure. On the final day of the Test he dismissed Brian Lara with a beautiful delivery to give him his hundredth Test wicket. Lara, Lord's, good ball, Test win – perfection.

Naturally, we were all delighted for Ashley, who had been receiving a lot of criticism in the early part of the summer. Ashley is no Shane Warne or Muttiah Muralitharan, he is the first to admit that. He is an honest, much-loved and valuable member of the team who works bloody hard at his game. Those who are not privy to dressing-room instructions do not appreciate the full extent of his contribution to the side.

Vaughan's two hundreds were equally important. When Michael Vaughan is in full flow there are few, if any, better batsmen to watch. At the crease he possesses the elegance and grace of a right-handed David Gower. His cover-drive is a sight to behold and, without appearing to put any effort into his shots, the ball rockets off to the boundary. Vaughan walked off the field to a standing ovation after scoring his second hundred and, once in the dressing-room, he came up to me with a big smile on his face and said: 'That's how you do it, Straussy.' I laughed before reminding him that he did not have to run between the wickets with Nasser Hussain.

Although the victory seemed fairly straightforward we were all absolutely knackered at the end of the game. It had taken five days of hard graft to beat the West Indies, and we definitely felt as though we had earned the right to hold the initiative in the series. England had now won seven of their last eight Test matches – Brian Lara's unbeaten 400 led to the only draw – and comparisons were being made between our side and the great England teams of the past. The best run by a post-War England side took place between July 1978 and July 1979 when a team containing Ian Botham, David Gower, Graham Gooch and Bob Willis won nine of the ten Tests it played against New Zealand, Australia and India.

As a team we were now beginning to feel we could complete our second whitewash of the summer. Before the First Test against the West Indies we had talked about winning the series 4–0, and the 210-run victory had strengthened the belief that we could win seven consecutive Test matches.

Back-to-back Test matches once again gave us little time to celebrate then rest our weary limbs. We were given the Tuesday off and I spent the day relaxing on our sofa at home, before sorting my kit and driving up to Birmingham for the Second Test. Our solitary practice session before the Test was very light and I passed the afternoon shopping in the city centre with Vaughan and Anderson. It was whilst with them in a packed café that I suffered the embarrassment of somehow managing to fall off my chair, grasping at nothing but thin air in an attempt to keep myself upright, tumbling down three steps next to the table and ending up in a sorry heap on the floor. Anderson and Vaughan predictably found the whole episode extremely amusing and, needless to say,

I will not be going back there in a hurry. I managed to regain my composure by the time we had our team meeting in the evening. A massage from Vicky, our masseuse, had eased the pain in my sore muscles, and it was only my ego that needed further recovery.

What a captain Michael Vaughan is. We were desperate for him to win the toss and, had he not, it is unlikely that the bowlers would have spoken to him all day. There was plenty of analysis by Vaughan and the team on how he managed to pull off this monumental feat. It was generally agreed that wearing Jimmy Anderson's cap and the presence of a mascot made the difference. But he did win it and it was difficult to wipe the smiles off the bowlers' faces. Feet up, give lunch a crack – what an easy life a bowler has. No matter how the coin came down I was walking out with the umpires. The pitch was dry and it looked pretty flat. My experiences of playing here have taught me that the bounce can become unpredictable towards the end of a game, so it was an important toss to win for cricketing reasons too.

Edgbaston is a fast-scoring ground and we probably should have done better on the first day, where we scored 313/5. A few of us, myself included, had got ourselves in before contributing to our own downfall. Fortunately, Trescothick was not one of them, and he was at his pugnacious best, scoring his second hundred of the summer. We knew we needed at least another hundred runs on the second day if we wanted to control the game but no one in the team expected us to go on to post a total of 566/9. A swashbuckling partnership of 170 between Flintoff and Geraint Jones allowed us to dominate proceedings. These two seem to enjoy batting together and the desire to play attacking cricket allows them to bring out the best in each other.

Flintoff was once again awesome, hitting 17 fours and seven sixes in a career-best 167. The most amusing moment of his innings was when he hit Jermaine Lawson over long-on for a huge six. The ball dropped in the area where the players' guests sit and Colin Flintoff, Andrew's dad, dropped the catch.

Brian Lara, no doubt angered by poor West Indian bowling, completed a stunning day's cricket by racing to 74 before the close. What a player he is. Four hundred and thirty-seven runs had been scored in the day – perhaps it is a batsman's game after all.

Flintoff got Lara early on the fourth day, which surprised us all. Lara is famed for going on and posting huge scores once he gets in. Ramnaresh Sarwan scored a century but once Lara went the result became something of a formality. Ashley Giles took four first-innings wickets, and five in the second, including Lara again. Giles was not the only player to star, as Trescothick became the ninth England player to score a century in each innings of a Test match.

With the Wisden Trophy retained we were all looking forward to a much-needed rest. It was lovely to get away from the pressures of Test cricket and spend some time at home, but is amazing how quickly these special days pass. Most people will think that when a player has a week off he just takes the phone off the hook and puts his feet up on the sofa for seven days. In reality it is quite different. Every player is on some sort of fitness programme, either through the ECB or their county, and a week off is an excellent time to catch up on the gym-work you miss when playing and to recover from niggles. Inevitably some time is spent attempting to keep the technique sharp in the nets and before you know it you are checking that all your kit is clean, and packing your bags.

Because the final two weeks of the season, with back-to-back Test matches, were going to be very demanding, I tried to do as little training as I could get away with during the week off and as a result I felt slightly unprepared when I arrived at Old Trafford for the Third Test. Getting the balance right between rest and practice is a constant battle, one that players rarely perfect, but there was still plenty to play for and I felt the next two matches were very important for me. Another big score in either of the games would complete a great summer, while a couple of failures would result in it finishing on a bit of a flat note. There was also a great deal for the team to play for. Seven consecutive Test wins would be a fantastic achievement, and there was also the small matter of central contracts and winter tour places up for grabs.

It is only natural that the handing out of central contracts and selection for the winter tour of South Africa occupy a part of every player's mind. They can be used as a source of motivation but you cannot afford to let them become all-consuming. Money was not my motivation for playing cricket in the first place, as I hope it never will be. But I knew that if I scored runs, everything would look after itself, and to do this I had to knuckle down and do what I did on my debut.

Inclement weather meant that I had to wait until Wednesday to have a grass net but practice went well. One of the qualities of this side was its ability to switch on when it needed to. It is great for teams to laugh and joke when there is no cricket taking place but in other sides I have played in there has been a tendency for this to infiltrate into the cricket once it starts. Yet in this unit each player knew his role and what to do to get himself into the right frame of mind to play in a Test match.

The seven-wicket margin of victory at Old Trafford suggests that this was another easy win for England but the West Indies pushed us very hard in the Third Test. They batted first for the first time in the series and dominated the opening three and a half days of the match. Dwayne Bravo highlighted what an exciting cricketer he is by top-scoring in the West Indies first innings and then taking 6/55 with the ball.

I scored 90 and put on 177 with Graham Thorpe. England were struggling on 40/3 when we came together and I really enjoyed the challenge of building an innings in a backs-to-the-wall situation. On each of the previous occasions I had scored runs for England I had felt in control of events. I had opened the batting and we had got off to a good start. This was the first time I had been placed under pressure by the match situation, and it was very satisfying to come through it with a decent score.

Thorpe scored a wonderful hundred, batting for a considerable part of his 114 with a broken finger. The innings was an example of him at his best. When he bats Graham gets in his own little bubble. Off the field he has been a great help to me. As fellow left-handers we share the same problems and I have spent more time talking with him about batting than any other England bats-man. He would advise me how to play bowlers who bowled at more than 90 mph or how best to deal with left-arm spinners who aim for the footholes. From time to time I also pick Trescothick's brain but Graham's style of batting was more similar to mine.

He loves to chat about cricket but in the middle he said very little to me between overs. The contrast took me slightly by sur-prise because this was the first time I had batted with him. It was not that he was not interested in me. He was. It was just that batting was serious stuff and he wanted to focus on what he was doing. I learnt a great deal from batting with Thorpe that day. He adapted his game superbly to the match situation, choosing his

shots accordingly, highlighting why he was the best England batsman of his generation. Michael Atherton, Alec Stewart and Nasser
Hussain were all fine players but Thorpe was the one who could
be most relied upon to score valuable runs in difficult situations.
And by consistently doing this he showed that he had a great
understanding of what was needed during demanding periods
of play.

Graham is a quiet, softly spoken man who undemonstratively
went about his business. Rarely was his voice heard above that of
others in the dressing-room, but he was great to have around.
It was reassuring to see him fiddling with his bats in the corner
and, whilst he was at the crease, you always felt there was a way
out of a tricky situation. The breakdown of his marriage and
the inability to see his children affected him badly. I was aware
that he had been through a great deal of heartache, but during my
brief association with him he appeared to be coping with his
predicament.

Once again we grabbed hold of the match on the fourth day.
At 88/1, and with a lead of 153, the West Indies were well placed
to push on for a much-needed victory. Andrew Flintoff, Steve
Harmison and Ashley Giles had other ideas, however, claiming
nine wickets in 31 frantic overs. Flintoff, predictably, was the catalyst and his ruthless dismissal of Brian Lara, who gloved a short
ball to me at third slip in the same over he had become the fourth
batsman in Test cricket to pass 10,000 runs, sent shudders through
the West Indian batting line-up.

Our target of 231 looked some way off following the early loss
of Trescothick and myself, but Key and Flintoff guided us home
with an unbeaten fourth-wicket partnership of 120.

The victory took England to a sixth consecutive Test victory and left us within one match of a clean sweep. When things are going well for a side cricket seems like a very easy game. You turn up at pre-match meetings, reaffirm your aims and attempt to continue doing what you have in the past. Winning, and the ability of team members to produce a match-winning performance when it is needed, gives players confidence in themselves and those around them. You feel that if you have an off day someone else will make up for it and it is a wonderful situation to be in. The victory at Old Trafford confirmed these beliefs. The West Indies had given us their best shot but we had got up off the floor and beaten them. It is impossible to instil into a team the confidence that comes from winning and, understandably, we turned up at The Oval, for the final Test of the summer, feeling that we had won the game before it had even started.

Thorpe's broken finger ruled him out of the final Test and Ian Bell came in to make his debut. There was a festive spirit during the game at The Oval. Every England batsman reached double figures but not one of us went on to post a hundred. Bell looked every inch a Test player during his 70 but the highlight of our innings was the batting of Harmison and Matthew Hoggard, who both carved their way to career-best scores. Harmison then ripped through a dispirited West Indian side, taking eight wickets on the second day, and James Anderson took four in the second innings as we romped to a ten-wicket victory inside three days.

So ended a fairytale summer for both the England cricket team, who had won seven consecutive Test matches, and myself. Winning every Test in a summer is a wonderful achievement and we had a great deal to feel proud of. But the most satisfying aspect of our cricket was our ability to win games from difficult situations.

In four of the seven matches the result could have gone either way after three days, yet we reacted positively and decisively on each occasion, and walked away as worthy victors.

All in all the West Indies series proved to be another good one for me. I scored a second Test hundred at Lord's and hit an important 90 at Old Trafford. Yet there were moments within the series where I did feel very undisciplined. It probably had a lot to do with the fact that I had runs under my belt and I was less keen to sit back and wait for the bad balls. I attempted to get on with it and, as a result, against bowlers who generally came across me, I got out chasing a couple of wide ones. I also found I was trying to pull balls that were probably too wide of off stump. I had proved that my hundred on debut was not a fluke and that I was not a flash in the pan, but I still felt that there was plenty of work for me to do.

I believe I had a relatively gentle introduction to Test cricket in some respects, especially when one considers the challenges that lay ahead. Against better bowlers, like Glenn McGrath and Shaun Pollock, I was not going to get many balls to hit and I would need to decide how to counteract them. Should I just try to see them off and look to score at the other end, or was I going to develop methods of getting off strike? Shuffling across and working to leg, or attempting to pull each of them off a good length were options but there was an element of risk attached to these. I also had to remember that Test matches offered me the chance of batting for a very long time and it is not all about crash, bang, wallop like it had been for us all that summer.

Overall, though, I had to be happy with what I achieved that summer of 2004. I scored 590 runs at an average of 45. It was a pretty good way to start a Test career, and I took a lot of pleasure from it. There were sterner tests to come but it was good to know that I would be part of a tough winter series against South Africa with runs under my belt and confidence high.

5
PLAYING POLITICAL CRICKET

The undesirable prospect of travelling to Zimbabwe had been hovering over our dressing-room like a black cloud throughout the summer. The topic, and the stance we should take as players, had occasionally been raised in conversation but nobody really wanted to turn their attention to the subject until the Test series against New Zealand and West Indies and the Champions Trophy had finished. The media drifted in and out of the subject with views being expressed on television and radio as well as in the news, sport and opinion pages of newspapers. The consensus was that we should not be touring Zimbabwe. It was the view held by the players too.

According to many observers there were cricketing as well as moral reasons for the tour being cancelled. Cricket within Zimbabwe was in turmoil. Accusations of racism and corruption had been aimed at the Zimbabwe Cricket Union by 15 of the country's leading players who had refused to sign contracts until matters had been sorted out. The rebel players wanted Ozias Bvute, the chief executive, and Peter Chingoka, the chairman, to resign. In response to these demands the ZCU had sacked all 15 players. The dismissal of men like Heath Streak, Stuart Carlisle, Grant Flower and Sean Ervine meant that the team we were due to play against would be the weakest in international cricket. Understandably there were calls for the International Cricket Council to kick

Zimbabwe out, but it was a pressure the game's governing body was resisting.

The Zimbabwe Cricket Union, sensing that the swell of opinion was moving against them, took the matter out of the ICC's hands by temporarily withdrawing from Test cricket. The move resulted in England's two-Test, three one-day international tour becoming a 12-day trip containing five one-day games. It is fair to say that each player was happy with the outcome of Zimbabwe's decision. After all, it meant that we spent less time in the country.

The cricketing reasons for not touring, and the view that the weakness of the Zimbabwe team was threatening the integrity of international cricket, was understandable, but to us, as players, they were largely irrelevant. It is not our job to judge whether a team is good enough to play cricket at the highest level. All we can do is go out and score runs, take wickets and win games. Yet it was correct for the England players who expected to tour to reflect on whether it was morally right for them to travel to and play sport in a country that was being governed in such a despicable way.

Inevitably, the issue gathered momentum as the tour neared. Stories were appearing in newspapers stating that two or three of the team would be declining to tour. It was Steve Harmison who was the first to announce that he had made himself unavailable for the tour in his Sunday newspaper column. Harmison's decision became the catalyst for us to discuss the matter, and for the media to rev things up. Before Harmison's declaration we had presented a united front, stating that we would take advice from the England and Wales Cricket Board before dealing with the matter at a later date.

We all felt very uneasy about the tour, especially after what had happened in South Africa in the 2003 World Cup, when Nasser Hussain's squad spent a traumatic week deliberating on whether they should travel to Zimbabwe for a qualifying match. In the end England refused to travel on the grounds of safety and security, even though they knew the decision was likely to cost them a place in the next round of the tournament. It did, and it was the enormously stressful week spent pacing around the Cullinan Hotel in Cape Town that played a big part in Harmison's decision.

BBC's Radio Five Live immediately began holding phone-ins and it quickly became apparent that the public did not want us to visit Zimbabwe. We were all aware of this but we also understood what a difficult position the ECB were in. David Morgan, the chairman of the ECB, gave each player the option to withdraw from the tour if he wished but his offer did little to ease the position we found ourselves in. Our emotions were being thrown around as though in a cement mixer. The ECB were telling us that they would lose millions of pounds if England failed to fulfil its obligation to tour, and this was stressed to us throughout our deliberations.

I had major moral objections to touring Zimbabwe but there were several factors that ultimately resulted in me signing my contract and getting on the plane. The principal reason was my loyalty to the game of cricket in England. The game was paying my wages and I felt I had a responsibility to ensure that cricket continued to flourish at home.

Had the ECB been fined £3 million, which was the figure bandied around, domestic cricket would have been placed in a very difficult position. The financial repercussions of Zimbabwe refusing to tour England the following summer, and a possible fine from the ICC were spelt out very strongly to us by the ECB, who suggested that the anticipated loss could result in some counties going bust. The fact that my actions could lead to colleagues and mates being made redundant was not something I particularly wanted on my conscience either. What did become clear was the fact that the ECB would be sending a side to Zimbabwe no matter what. If we, as a group, chose not to go the next 15 or so players would be asked and I, along with others, did not want to give the impression that we were passing the buck on to somebody else.

I read as much as I could on the internet and in the papers, and received information on what it was like in Zimbabwe from the ECB, yet I still found it very difficult to work out exactly what was taking place. I also listened to the views of Andy Flower, the former Zimbabwe cricketer who had left the country at the end of the 2003 World Cup. Flower had worn a black armband in one of the qualifying games to represent the 'death of democracy' in Zimbabwe and his views were worth listening to. He wanted England to tour because, for a short period of time, they would focus the world's eyes on what was taking place there. His view proved accurate because some members of the media who got into Zimbabwe did go around searching for non-cricket stories. They filed reports on the state of Zimbabwe as a country and this was probably the reason why Robert Mugabe, the President of Zimbabwe, did not want certain individuals in the country in the first place.

The ECB opted to rest Andrew Flintoff, Marcus Trescothick and Ashley Giles from the touring squad, although Flintoff subsequently stated that he would not have toured anyway. Giles, however, turned the opportunity of rest down, preferring instead to offer support to his close friend, Vaughan, who was tour captain.

Nobody was happy with what was going on in Zimbabwe, and

it was difficult to forget descriptions of the atrocities that were allegedly taking place there, even though it is dangerous to trust everything you read in the papers or see on television. Zimbabwe only appeared to grab the headlines on quiet news days. It would then dominate briefly before disappearing off the agenda again. The problems facing the people of Zimbabwe were, how-ever, there all the time. As for myself, I felt as though I was a pawn in a huge and contentious game of politics.

After a six-week break I felt rested and ready to go when we gathered at Heathrow Airport on 15 November. I arrived in the morning to do the usual round of bat-signing and it was great to catch up with the boys again. The prospect of leaving the comforts of home, knowing that, barring injury, you were not going to be back for three months was, however, fairly daunting. Zimbabwe was not the only country we were due to visit. After the one-day series there, we were to go straight to South Africa for a five-Test, seven one-day tour. This was the first time I had to deal with such a full schedule.

After wasting money in duty-free shopping – why does every-body buy stuff they don't really need just because it is a little cheaper? – we eventually departed for Namibia. I was one of the few members of the party to have visited Namibia before, on an MCC tour four years earlier. I knew that the practice facilities in Windhoek were excellent and they would provide us with all that we required. What might possibly take place off the pitch would be another matter.

Rain limited the amount of cricket we played during our trip but we managed to get the practice we needed in two warm-up games against Namibia. What Mick Hunt, the head groundsman at Lord's, would have made of the methods used to get the ground fit for play does not bear thinking about. Initially a helicopter was brought in to dry a damp area, but when this failed the groundstaff began digging out huge sods of turf and replacing them with drier sods dug up from outside the boundary. It was a remarkable sight but it allowed us to get a 42-over match in.

Ever since boarding our flight at Heathrow, we knew that there was a chance that at some stage during this politically sensitive tour we could get embroiled in something other than cricket. And as we prepared for our second practice game in Namibia we were blissfully unaware of the dramatic events that were to unfold within the next 24 hours.

We were well into the second innings of the match when news began to filter through to us that 13 cricket journalists, who had applied for accreditation with the Zimbabwean government, had been refused entry into the country. Suddenly the optimism generated by the hospitality of our Namibian hosts began to diminish. It took us some time to digest what this meant for the tour itself. The prospect of waving goodbye to a dozen journalists in Johannesburg next day seemed slightly amusing initially, and some of the boys began joking about this being the best thing Robert Mugabe had ever done. But we quickly realised that the government of Zimbabwe had made a political statement on the back of the England cricket team touring its country and this changed everything.

At the barbecue that followed the game we were all jittery. All sorts of questions were forming in our minds. What does this mean for us? Will the ECB/ICC still let the tour continue? What do we do?

My summary of the situation was that this new development had put us in a much tighter corner than we had previously been in. At the start of the tour, the players felt that although we had moral objections to making the trip, it was a necessary evil if we did not want to put the game of cricket in England in a perilous position. Now it had become abundantly clear that the cricket and the politics could not and would not be separated. Suddenly the cricket journalists, and indirectly the players themselves, were being used as pawns to serve Zimbabwean political ends. It was not right that Mugabe could stop cricket reporters entering his country to cover cricket matches, and if he was going to do it there was, in our minds, a very good reason for the tour not to go ahead.

Not one of us knew what would happen next. We were very unhappy about what was taking place and we were less than 24 hours away from flying to Harare. Matters were moving along at a frightening pace and decisions had to be made.

I woke up feeling particularly uneasy about the situation the following morning. The topic dominated conversation around the breakfast table and during our flight from Windhoek to Johannesburg. Waiting for us in Johannesburg was Richard Bevan, our representative from the Professional Cricketers' Association, who immediately shepherded us into a meeting. The predicament we found ourselves in must have brought back horrendous memories for Michael Vaughan, Paul Collingwood, Ashley Giles and James Anderson, veterans of England's World Cup squad of 2003. The ECB and the PCA had given us assurances that there would be no repeat of that fiasco. Prior to the tour we had stated that we would be on the next plane out of Zimbabwe should anything like that happen whilst we were in the country. There was no question of us sitting around in Harare whilst they held meetings to decide the future of the tour with the ZCU. These views settled us a little, as did the feeling that lessons had been learnt from Cape Town 21 months earlier. But we were in no mood to set foot in Zimbabwe until all the journalists had received their accreditation. It was definitely a case of we all go, or we all stay away.

A stressful and emotional meeting with Bevan ensued where we were given the opportunity to express these views. The ECB were initially keen for us to fly to Harare and sort the matter out once we were there but it was agreed instead that we would remain in Johannesburg until the issue was resolved. The decision meant that all the team's luggage had to be removed from the plane bound for Harare and Phil Neale, the operations manager, attempted to get us into a hotel close to the airport for the night. It was crystal clear that we had become involved in something much bigger than cricket when we were met by a huge media scrum as we exited the airport. This only served to heighten the atmosphere. In some ways we were relieved that we did not have to board the plane, yet we were all still concerned about what was going to happen next.

After another restless night the morning was spent trying to find ways of occupying ourselves. A weights session in the gym was followed by a game of head tennis on a tennis court. A couple of players partook of a bit of sunbathing as lunch approached, but we were still very much in the dark as to what was happening in the negotiations between the ECB, the ZCU and the Zimbabwean government. The press were loitering around the hotel foyer sniffing for snippets of information, and there were dozens of television news crews with the satellite dishes on their vans stationed in the driveway. It had become a massive news story and they were all waiting for smoke to drift out of our hotel chimney. We were being told that the Zimbabwean government was unlikely to back down on the issue, so gradually, as the day wore on, we began to prepare ourselves mentally for the fact that the tour was about to be cancelled.

Shortly after lunch, however, we received news from David Morgan, the chairman of the ECB, who informed us that the Zimbabwean government had, in fact, climbed down. The news was followed by an announcement on television that the tour was back on. Even so, we were not entirely sure that this was the case and it was only when John Carr, the ECB's director of cricket, arrived from Harare that we truly believed we were on our way to Zimbabwe.

Once the Zimbabwean government had backed down from refusing the journalists entry, the ECB felt it had no choice but to continue with the tour. To not go then would have meant that the ECB was likely to suffer the same financial consequences that had, in effect, forced us to make the tour in the first place. In the eyes of many observers the ECB had missed a golden opportunity to get out of a tour that they did not want to make, but at the time they were looking to build bridges with other countries in the ICC. England's image is not very positive amongst many of the other full Test-playing members. We are viewed as arrogant and demanding when we tour. So through fulfilling their obligation, even though they were swimming against public opinion at home, the ECB were showing willing.

But who was to blame for the whole sorry saga? Was it the ECB, who could have jeopardised the future of cricket in England? Was it the ICC, who acted in accordance with the views of its members? They were in a horrendous position too. If anyone was to blame it was the British government because they clearly did not want us to go and they had the means to prevent the tour going ahead.

But they were not prepared to do this in case it set a precedent. The government kept using the line that it was not in their mandate to prevent its citizens from travelling anywhere when the ECB just wanted them to say enough to cancel the tour.

The government's inability to make a decision did not prevent politicians from getting political mileage out of saying that they did not want us to go. Politicians enjoyed the fact that the rest of the country echoed their views, yet they were not prepared to do anything to stop England touring, or make up the shortfall had the ECB been fined for refusing to travel. I thought they handled the situation very poorly. It was the same when Sky Sports secured the rights to exclusively televise England's home matches between 2006 and 2009. Once again, when there was political mileage to be gained from the fact that cricket could no longer be seen on terrestrial TV they started getting involved. But once again they were not prepared to act in a decisive way. One does wonder whether the politicians would have been so concerned about cricket's future had England failed to regain the Ashes in 2005.

The government's handling of the Zimbabwe affair led to several cynical comments being made at Downing Street after we had won the Ashes in 2005. 'You're happy to be involved with the England team now, but where were you when we needed you ten months earlier?' was the gist of our slightly drunken conversations.

The following morning we set off for Harare, not knowing what sort of reception would greet us. But there was a feeling of relief when we arrived in the Zimbabwean capital. Relief that maybe now all the politics would end and we could just concentrate on playing cricket. Harare Airport was modern, spotless and far smarter than we expected. There were pictures of Robert Mugabe hanging from every wall as we made our way through customs, which was quite spooky. It left us feeling that he would be watching every move we made whilst we were in his country.

Our arrival, along with that of the travelling media, went smoothly and we made our way to the coach that took us to our hotel. The journey into Harare was surreal. We knew the police would prevent masses of people hanging around the airport but we did expect to see the odd protester as we made our way to the Zimbabwean capital. But there seemed to be a total lack of interest in our arrival, and there were no signs of trouble either.

There was a part of me that expected to see burnt-out cars on the side of roads and houses in a state of ruin but as we made our way through the suburbs everything seemed relatively normal. People were getting on with their everyday life. There were fruit and wooden-carving sellers sitting at their kerbside stalls attempting to earn a living, and we passed a reasonable-looking golf course. There were no queues at petrol stations and the only sign of reaction to our arrival was on a white wall within 200 yards of our hotel. Here 'England go back' and 'Shame on England' had been daubed in bright red paint.

After 48 hours of concerning ourselves with matters off the pitch it was a relief to get to the Harare Sports Club and focus on cricket. We knew that the only way for us to react was to try as hard as possible to register a 4–0 whitewash. The series was intended to be a five-match affair but the delay in Johannesburg had reduced it by a game. It did not really matter to us, we just wanted to get it over with before turning our attention to the South African leg of the tour.

The apathy of the local population to our arrival made the whole experience rather eerie. But it was understandable. This is a country that is in the process of dying on its feet and the arrival of the England cricket team was going to change very little. They, quite rightly, had far more important things to worry about. Having been to Zimbabwe six years previously with Durham University, there were several differences that I noticed. On my last visit it had looked a pretty impressive place with the major centres resembling those in South Africa. But it was now a lot more run down. It appeared like a third world African country.

The other noticeable difference to me was the nature of the people. Whether it was in our hotel, at the cricket ground, or just walking around the streets, very few people were to be found smiling. Everyone looked dejected. If you looked into people's eyes there was no sign of life or fun in them. It had all been knocked out by Mugabe's oppressive regime. The sight of men and women trudging around in a hopeless situation reminded me of images of Eastern Europeans living under communist rule. Colour was no barrier because the white faces had the same ghostly appearance as the black ones. It was so sad to see a race of people that had been so active and alive looking so dispirited and dead. During the trip I chatted with both black and white people and you could tell they had lost hope. They were resigned to their fate in what was basically now a shambles of a country. It was very hard to take.

During the entire trip we all felt extremely paranoid. There was talk in the dressing-room that all our hotel phones had been tapped and we were being followed by the Zimbabwe secret police but you did not know how much of it to believe. Miekle's Hotel was as smart as any I have stayed in, and a couple of the local restaurants served excellent food too. It created a strange sensation. We had been led to believe there were shortages of this, that and everything but the menus were wide and varied and everything was available. The contradiction continued at the Harare Sports Club, which is a beautiful cricket ground with a lush green outfield and superb practice facilities. It is a gorgeous place to play cricket but, sadly, not with the backdrop of this series.

Amongst the many fears we had was that of anti-Mugabe protestors being pulled out of the crowd by police and beaten before getting dragged away, never to be seen again, and during the first one-dayer I spent more time looking in the stands than I had ever done before. Our entrance on to the ground was also unforgettable. Normally cheering and applause greet the appearance of the teams but there were hardly any spectators in the ground. All I remember hearing as I walked out to field were reporters at the side of the pitch finishing their pieces to camera by saying, for example: 'This is Jeremy Boden reporting here for Sky News live at the Harare Sports Club.'

Another reason for angst was the proximity of Mugabe's house. To enter the Harare Sports Club you have to travel down a road that runs parallel to the President's house. Armed guards stand on every corner and there were rumours that Mugabe or members of his government would come and meet us. This was a hypothetical situation that the media had talked about but we had agreed how we would react if it happened. Had Mugabe or any of his officials attended and asked to meet us we would have refused. Not only that, but we would have immediately packed our bags and got on the next plane out of the country.

There was, however, a small incident away from the cricket when the innocent views of Ian Bell were misinterpreted, highlighting how careful we all had to be when making public statements. Bell had scored runs in the first one-day match and was made available to the media on the following day. And his comments grabbed the headlines in the *Herald* newspaper, which is believed to be under the control of Mugabe's regime. Under the headline 'England players appreciate Zimbabwe' it said: 'One by one the England cricket players are beginning to queue to give their approval of their tour to this country.' Bell, in an effort to be courteous and pleasant, was quoted as saying that he had been 'pleasantly surprised' by what he had seen in Zimbabwe and that he 'would like to come back and play some more here'. The ECB immediately expressed its disappointment over what had been written, stating that 'nothing Ian Bell said was intended as a political comment'.

England won the series 4–0 but the cricket was irrelevant. We had been asked to come here and perform a job, and we had performed it. The one-sided nature of the cricket had made it unenjoyable. In reality it was just a side-show to the main event, which was England fulfilling an obligation to play cricket in Zimbabwe.

The result only fuelled the views of those who feel that mis-matches like these do nothing for the image of the game, and that Zimbabwe and Bangladesh should be booted out of international cricket. My feelings on the two countries are completely different. Bangladesh may be poor, and getting walloped every time they play is not doing them an awful lot of good, but you can see the potential there. There is a huge interest in cricket in Bangladesh and they do have some talented players. It may all be embryonic but cricket there should only move in one direction, and that is up. Zimbabwe is a completely different situation. There are such a small number of people playing the game there, and a lot of those who do play are leaving or do not want to be associated with the national team. It is a shame because four or five years ago they were quite a competitive side, especially in one-day cricket. The shortage of players and their lack of ability will make it very hard for them to get back their Test status.

There were a lot of relieved and happy faces on the plane that left Bulawayo heading for Johannesburg on 6 December. The players and every travelling member of the ECB breathed a massive sigh of relief. England had fulfilled their obligation and there had been no incidents. We all knew that we would not have to go through this for at least another six years.

Even now, a couple of years after the tour, I am still not sure whether we did the right or wrong thing. But I suppose if I looked at what took place, and what has taken place since, I would agree with Andy Flower's assessment of the situation. Since we left Zimbabwe the media have shown very little interest in the place. We did not go to Zimbabwe to make people aware of the problems that existed there, and the fact that it was high on the news agenda for a few weeks does not justify our decision. But as a by-product of the tour the world gained some idea of what was happening there and that had to be good.

There were a few positives that came out of the tour. There is no doubt to me that the experience of visiting Zimbabwe brought the squad who travelled closer together. It was a tough time for us all, and there were occasions when players became quite emotional about the position they found themselves in. In numerous meetings we had opened up to each other and expressed views that we held very closely to ourselves. That had never happened before, and as a result we got to know each other far better.

6
REACHING NEW HEIGHTS

With the Zimbabwe ordeal thankfully over and the exciting prospect of a five-Test series against South Africa to look forward to, emotions were high as we came in to land at Johannesburg International Airport. It was only a short alcohol-free flight but each of us felt as though a huge weight had been taken off our shoulders. Now was the time to relax, concentrate on the cricket and not feel guilty about going to a decent restaurant in the evening.

It was now that we said goodbye to Darren Gough, Kevin Pietersen, Matthew Prior, Vikram Solanki and Alex Wharf, England's one-day specialists, and reacquainted ourselves with Andrew Flintoff, Steve Harmison, Matthew Hoggard, Rob Key, Chris Read, Graham Thorpe and Marcus Trescothick. It was great to catch up with the Test guys again. Tales of what had taken place in Zimbabwe were regaled to those who were interested and a couple of knowing glances were sent our way by veterans of the World Cup fiasco when we described the emergency meetings. But there was something missing, something not quite right as the two groups attempted to become one happy family.

Initially we found it hard to integrate. It was difficult to put a finger on why things felt different because we were coming off a successful summer, where we had become a very close-knit group who had supported each other and enjoyed each other's triumphs.

But I suppose it was down to the fact that those of us who had been to Zimbabwe were still preoccupied with what had taken place there. The 12 days we spent in Harare and Bulawayo, and the traumatic 24 hours spent deciding whether or not we should travel to Zimbabwe had taken their toll. The baggage of the trip was still with us, whilst the newcomers were fresh and enthusiastic after a two-month break.

In my mind the differing attitudes and the lack of togetherness was one of the principal reasons why our tour of South Africa got off to a worrying start. Naturally, there were cricket reasons too. Those of us who had been to Namibia and Zimbabwe were reasonably well prepared for what was to come. The cricket had not been particularly testing but our preparations were well ahead of the new arrivals' who had not played a competitive game since the Champions Trophy final on 25 September.

One thing that we all knew, however, was that the facilities in South Africa would be fantastic. It is, without doubt, one of the best places in the world to play cricket. Having been born in Johannesburg, it was fascinating to see how much the place had changed. There were still huge concerns about crime, which appear to have been ever-present for much of the last decade, but judging by the amount of new building, and the atmosphere of the place, South Africa definitely seemed like a country moving forward. Anyone who has been there will know that sport is like a religion, and this goes a long way to explaining why South Africa have been so hard to beat at home since their re-admission to international cricket. It is also the reason why we had to make sure that we were as well prepared as possible heading into the First Test.

The task of re-integrating the squad was made harder by the fact that our itinerary did not allow us to spend much time socialising together before the competitive matches began. Within two days of our landing in Johannesburg we were playing the opening game of the tour against a Nicky Oppenheimer XI at his beautiful Randjesfontein ground. England won a rain-affected one-day game but it did not provide those who needed it with the practice they wanted. It was a waste of time.

We then travelled to Potchefstroom, a small agricultural town 75 miles to the south-west of Johannesburg, for a three-day game against South Africa A. It was our only competitive fixture before the First Test and we understandably played our strongest team. But the match proved to be a nightmare for us. We did not play very good cricket at all and lost comprehensively by seven wickets.

Each of the batsmen who went to Zimbabwe managed to spend some useful time in the middle, but Trescothick, Butcher, Thorpe and Flintoff – the newcomers – scored a total of 48 runs and batted for just 165 minutes during eight visits to the crease. There was, however, one moment of amusement, although nobody laughed when a bolt of lightning hit the ground within 800 yards of the stadium. A deafening clap of thunder followed and several players – including Ashley Giles who was fielding closest to the bolt – hit the ground. Once we had become aware of what had taken place we dashed back to the dressing-room, fearing for our lives. As we began joking about the incident one member of our squad suggested that our top-order would be safe to go outside as long as they carried their bats. This was because they had looked incapable of hitting anything with them.

Michael Vaughan summed up our situation after the match when he said: 'If we continue to play like this over the next couple of weeks we are going to be in for one hell of a surprise. We

117

may have been a little bit complacent and underestimated the opposition, but we should certainly not be losing games in two and a half days to South Africa A. This may yet give us the kick up the arse we need and remind us that we have not yet reached the standards that everyone thinks we have. In the first innings our shot selection was poor. Six of us got out playing flamboyant drives in conditions where it was a difficult shot to play. They dangled the carrot outside off stump and six of us had a go at it.'

With the captain's words ringing in our ears we set off to Port Elizabeth, the venue of the First Test, desperately searching for two or three days of high-quality practice. Vaughan was right to say what he said. After seven consecutive Test wins there was an air of complacency about the side. The result against South Africa A showed us that we had no right to win a game of cricket. It proved to be a timely reminder.

On each of the England tours I have been on there have been questions asked about the volume of cricket in the lead up to the First Test. Most journalists feel that England do not play enough competitive matches, but it is Duncan Fletcher's job to assess what we need at the start of a tour and weigh that up against the stamina needed to get through to the end of a tour. Warm-up games are necessary but they can be overrated and they can often do you as much harm as good. This is definitely the case if you enter them with a relaxed attitude. For practice to be beneficial it needs to be done with real purpose and intensity. You need to go into the matches with specific things you want to work on, and our current group of players manages to do just this in net as well as middle practice. The key to being ready for a Test match is not the volume of runs you have scored in the build-up. Obviously it is nice to enter a Test with a hundred behind you but the real key to success is being switched on mentally and feeling prepared when you take guard or mark your run out.

The fact that we regularly play back-to-back Test matches makes life extremely difficult for those who are not selected in the Test side too, as the scheduling gives them no chance of showing what they are capable of. The days have gone when England spent a month or so acclimatising and playing games in three or four states before the First Test. It may be unpopular but the ICC's Future Tours Programme, and the increase of international cricket being played, dictates that teams nip in and nip out of countries for two-, three- or five-Test series. It is a very difficult situation to manage. Having only one serious warm-up game before a Test match in a foreign country is not ideal but, given the way tours are scheduled these days, you just have to get on with it. Our record over the last few years, along with the way we have performed in the opening Test match of tours, suggests Fletcher has got it just about right.

The belief gained from winning seven consecutive Test matches in the summer had not disappeared but the South Africa A game had rattled us slightly, and in an effort to overcome these problems we had a couple of long and thoughtful meetings when we re-affirmed what we had achieved during the summer. We looked at what we had done right against New Zealand and West Indies, and talked about how we could apply these positives to the conditions in South Africa.

Because I was born in South Africa, my arrival had created quite a bit of attention. The media love stories about a player returning to the country of his birth, and as I had spent the first six years of my life in South Africa the local journalists wanted to talk about the time I had spent there and the role it had played in my development. It was gratifying to return to South Africa as an England player because it gave members of my family the first chance to watch me play Test cricket live. I did not feel as though I had to justify my inclusion in the England side. I feel 100 per cent English and South Africa had played no part in my cricket development.

But I was looking forward to the tour because South Africa is a fantastic country and it would allow me to see parts of it that I had never seen before. The reception I received from the public was nothing like that meted out to Pietersen when he arrived for the one-dayers, although his presence did drag me into the whole South-Africans-turning-their-backs-on-their-country-of-birth debate. But the flak I copped was very mild compared to Kevin's.

Our preparations at St George's Park in Port Elizabeth, the venue for the First Test, were extensive and we spent almost four hours at the ground attempting to get things right. The First Test of a series is always an important one because it allows players to make an early impression on the opposition. If the impression is good it can set you up for a good series, but if someone gets the better of you it can be hard to wrest the initiative back. In the build-up there were several things I kept reminding myself to do. The first was to be patient. Against the West Indies I got myself out on a couple of occasions by looking to be too aggressive too early in my innings. I kept telling myself that I did not have to score a hundred before lunch on the first day. I had five days to bat. I also needed to make sure that I stayed focused and that I enjoyed the experience. My aim was to go out, grab the game by the scruff of the neck, and make the most of the wonderful opportunity I have been given.

Above: Tino Best is not yet in the league of previous generations of West Indian fast bowlers, but he is quick.

Right: 'Phew, it's missed me.' Facing fast bowling is the ultimate buzz, and that red ball hurts when it hits you. Tino Best gives me a taste of chin music.

You can't bowl there at Freddie. Andrew Flintoff was awesome in the Second Test at Edgbaston, where he scored 167.

I picked Graham Thorpe's brain at the start of my Test career. He was a great help. At Old Trafford he scored a century with a broken finger.

The whitewash is complete and captain Michael Vaughan has an early shower as we celebrate our series win over the West Indies at The Oval in 2004.

Enjoying a relaxing afternoon off at Windhoek in
Namibia. Later, in Zimbabwe, the mood changed
when the government refused to let some English
journalists into the country.

Keep your eye on the ball. This one may
have got away, but practice makes perfect.

Some countries have developed innovative ways of drying out a damp outfield. At Windhoek, a
helicopter provides an unusual backdrop to my shadow batting.

Above: Richard Bevan (*right*) of the Professional Cricketers' Association helped guide the England players through the Zimbabwe affair.

Left: The Zimbabwe team were no match for England in the one-day series, but the cricket was largely irrelevant.

Below: Darren Gough has a word for most occasions. Here he celebrates a wicket on England's tour of Zimbabwe.

Above: I always appreciate Duncan Fletcher's sound advice, here delivered at Newlands before the Third Test versus South Africa in January 2005.

Right: Fitness became an integral part of our preparations under Michael Vaughan – training at a gym in Durban in December 2004.

Below: Minutes after this photo was taken a bolt of lightning hit a field next to the Potchefstroom Ground, forcing us to run for cover.

Life just gets better and better. Here I celebrate my third Test century, this one against South Africa in the First Test at Port Elizabeth.

Stumps in hand as souvenirs, Graham Thorpe and I walk off at Port Elizabeth after seeing England to a record-breaking eighth consecutive Test victory.

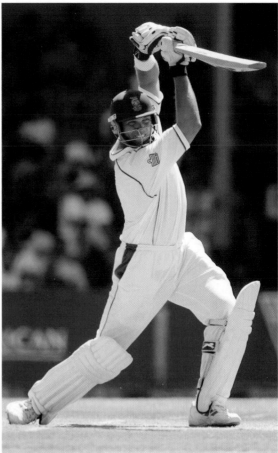

Above: Jacques Kallis batted superbly throughout the England/South Africa series of 2004–05.

Right: Technically, few batsmen in the game are better than Kallis. Here he executes the perfect cover drive.

Below: Shaun Pollock is always probing at your defences with his nagging accuracy. He and Makhaya Ntini make a challenging opening pair.

Speaking to the media is part of an international cricketer's brief. Here I am trying to make sense in South Africa.

Marcus Trescothick and I were involved in a record opening partnership at Durban. We batted together for almost six hours and put on 273 runs.

I had scored a fifty in Potchefstroom but I was not feeling in great touch. My form may have been better than most of my team-mates' but there were parts of my game that did not feel quite right. Yet despite this I had one of the strangest sensations of my career in the build-up and during the first couple of days of the Test. Only a fool would tempt fate by openly stating before a match they would score a hundred but in the quiet moments before the game I developed a strong feeling that it was going to happen to me. I don't know where it came from, and it has not happened since, but it was there. I kept it to myself as we bowled South Africa out for 337, which was a pretty good effort when one considers they were 178/3 at one stage. Boeta Dippenaar scored a painstaking hundred and the wickets were shared amongst our five bowlers.

When I walked out to bat the sensation was still with me. In fact once I had got in, it kept popping up in my mind. And it was there when I drove Makhaya Ntini straight down the ground for four to reach my third Test century. Naturally I was delighted to get there but, bizarrely, the belief that I was always going to reach three figures made this special moment a little less satisfying. I cut Shaun Pollock to A.B. de Villiers at backward point on the third morning after adding just 6 runs to my overnight score of 120. This disappointed me, but by then we were within a hundred runs of South Africa's first-innings total.

Simon Jones gave us the first glimpse of his destructive powers in South Africa's second innings when he trapped Jacques Kallis plum in front before ripping through the tail. Jones instigated a second-innings collapse by holding on to a brilliant catch in the deep to dismiss Graeme Smith, the South African captain. Cricket is never dull when Simon is involved and he has the happy knack of making things happen.

I scored an unbeaten 94 in England's second innings, enabling us to romp home to a seven-wicket victory. The innings completed a wonderful week for me. The match had entered a crucial phase when I went out to bat in our second innings, and that 94 turned out to be my most satisfying innings of the tour. The pressure on me rose when both Trescothick and Butcher fell for nought in the opening four overs, and it was a real thrill to see England through to victory. I had the honour of scoring the winning runs, when I cut Ntini for four, and walking off the pitch that morning was one of the highlights of my career.

It was also hugely satisfying because the win had allowed us to complete an eighth consecutive Test victory. To break the previous England record of seven, set by Arthur Shrewsbury's side of the 1880s and Percy Chapman's side of the 1920s was an outstanding achievement. It was also a remarkable turnaround, when one considers the fragile state in which we entered the match.

I had never batted so well in my life and for much of the game I felt in complete control of what was taking place in the middle. But over the course of the next week I had to keep my emotions in check and not get carried away and take my form for granted. One thing I have been guilty of doing in my career is taking things a little easy in the match after the one I have done well in. I was determined not to let this falling out of form happen on this tour. When you are hot you have to make sure you stay hot, and I was intent on scoring further hundreds!

The hundred in Port Elizabeth was a reward for the extra practice I had put in at the end of the 2004 season. At the end of the summer I was concerned with my pull shot. It was something that had not been lost on Geoffrey Boycott, who came up to me when I was inspecting the pitch before the First Test and said: 'I suppose you are going to get out twice pulling in this game like you usually do.'

I knew the pull would be an important stroke on South African pitches, and that on these surfaces the ball was unlikely to stand up to be hit if it was banged in short. I had got out playing this shot during the summer, so I had spent several net sessions facing a bowling machine attempting to hit the ball down. To do this I had to get my weight forward in the stroke rather leaning backwards on the back foot.

It was also very satisfying to successfully negotiate facing Makhaya Ntini and Shaun Pollock, who are an excellent opening partnership. Fidel Edwards and Tino Best, the West Indian opening bowlers, were quick but they did not have the skill of this pair. Once again the attention to detail we showed in our preparation came off. We had spent a lot of time getting a bowling machine to bowl from really wide of the crease to imitate Ntini, and then really close to the stumps to imitate Pollock. As bowlers they are completely different and they offer completely different challenges to you as a batsman. It is not just where they bowl from that varies. Ntini is a wonderful athlete. He runs in and bowls his socks off every day. He gives you a little bit more to hit than Pollock but he is also more likely to produce an unplayable ball. Pollock's nagging accuracy means that he is always probing away at your defence and the crucial thing about facing these two was having a very specific game-plan in your mind about how to play each bowler.

As a left-hander I had to be very disciplined outside my off stump against Ntini. He is always angling the ball across you and you have to be prepared to leave a lot of balls. If you go after him and drive loosely there is a good chance you will edge him to the slips. Pollock, however, gets very tight to the stumps and therefore you have to play at far more deliveries. When facing Ntini I tried to shuffle across my crease, whereas against Pollock I stayed very still.

The theorising happens off the field but when you are out there you have to get it right straight away. You have to be sure of what you are trying to achieve and adapt in the first 20 to 30 deliveries you face because this is when bowlers are at their most potent. If you are waiting to react to what they are going to do there is a really good chance of you getting out. Scoring runs in the opening Test of a series does wonders for your confidence but, even more importantly, the extended period of time you have spent at the crease allows you to learn how their bowlers operate. During your time in the middle you have the ideal chance of working out how to counteract them. If you do not get runs early you can be searching for ways of doing this for three or four Test matches.

Celebrating Christmas in a place like Durban is a strange experi-ence. The heat, the proximity of beaches and a Test match starting on Boxing Day makes it hard to get into the festive spirit. By now all our wives, girlfriends and families had arrived and it was lovely to share Ruth's company again. Our hotel, 30 minutes up the coast in Umhlanga Rocks, was idyllic. We had trained on Christmas morning and in the afternoon I, like most players, felt like a killjoy. Ruth had come over to spend Christmas Day with me yet I could not relax with her and enjoy a couple of bottles of wine. I was too wrapped up in what was going to happen at Kingsmead the following day.

We arrived at the ground on Boxing Day believing that we could beat anyone. The victory in Port Elizabeth had led us to believe we had the measure of South Africa but by the end of the first day this confidence had taken a huge dent. South Africa bowled us out for 139. This was new territory for me and it was the worst day's cricket I had experienced since coming into the side. Ntini and Pollock, whom we had managed to counteract so well in the First Test, shared seven wickets. We came back strongly on the second day, reducing South Africa to 118/6, before watching Jacques Kallis play one of his finest innings. We had struggled to come to terms with a difficult pitch but it was incredible to see how easy he made it look when batting.

I was just starting out as a professional cricketer in 1997 when Kallis spent a season with Middlesex. I was learning my trade in the Second XI at the time and I did not get to know him very well. Even then we all knew he had huge potential. Kallis had played half a dozen Test matches and achieved very little but Don Bennett, the former Middlesex coach, who is a man not known for making big statements, felt that he had the potential to go on and become the best all-rounder in the world.

Kallis is without doubt one of the world's best batsmen. To average 56 in Test cricket is a phenomenal effort. One of the reasons for his success is that he has a game-plan that he sticks to rigidly. On occasions this game-plan has received criticism for being one-dimensional, but you cannot argue with the number of runs he scores, and only those in the South African dressing-room know the role he plays in the side.

His technique is as good as any in the world and he is one of the few players – Rahul Dravid and Inzamam-ul-Haq are the other two – who has looked at ease against our bowling attack. At the end of his 162 he showed he has the ability to take an attack apart but more often than not he chooses not to use it. Anyway, his presence seemed to breed confidence in the South African tail.

They made us work very hard for the last four wickets and added 214 runs.

Walking out to bat facing a deficit of 193 is pretty daunting but the way in which the South African tail had batted suggested the pitch was flattening out. Marcus and I had a bit of luck against the new ball but once we had overcome it we felt quite comfortable at the crease. In some ways having such a large deficit to overcome acted as an aid to concentration, as we both knew that we could not afford to play a rash shot and give our wicket away. It was exceptionally hot in Durban that day, highlighted by the fact that Marcus lost four kilograms of weight during the morning session. Nigel Stockill, the team physiologist, was concocting all sorts of weird drinks in the dressing-room, but they did seem to work as we ticked off one milestone after another. A 50 partnership became 100, which became 150 and then 200. When we congratulated each other on putting on 200 together it seemed ludicrous that, after so much hard work, we were now only seven runs ahead.

Our fun ended just before the close when Marcus edged a catch through to the keeper. It was a shame because we wanted to bat for an entire day together and this goal was one of the things that kept us going as we tired. When Marcus was out we had taken our partnership to 273, the fifth-highest by a pair of England openers and the best for 44 years, and we were right back in the game. I returned to my hotel room that night absolutely knackered and was in bed by 9 o'clock. I'm not sure my wife was too happy with my uncommunicative state, but she understood the situation and was delighted that I had scored my fourth Test hundred. After spending an evening doing all the right things – rehydrating, eating carbohydrates and getting to bed early – I then got out in the fourth over of the day. It is at times like this that you wonder what would have happened if you had gone out and celebrated with a few drinks.

Thorpe, Flintoff and Geraint Jones helped move us into a position from which we could declare, with the potential for one of the most dramatic wins ever. But stubborn South African resistance and bad light meant we had to settle for a draw. It was a bitter pill to swallow, as victory would have completed the greatest comeback that I had ever played in. Our run of victories had come to an end and, as we flew to Cape Town that night, we had to satisfy ourselves with the positive thoughts of how well we had played for the final three days of the game.

New Year's Eve is very much like Christmas Day, in the way that it is hard to really let your hair down when you have a Test match to play in two days' time. But after an exhausting week in Durban I did not have the energy for a huge night out. As cricketers we get to travel to some of the most exotic locations in the world but, unfortunately, we seldom get much time to see the sights. Days off are rare but we were given one on New Year's Eve, and Ruth and I used it to go to the top of Table Mountain. If Ruth had not been in Cape Town I would probably not have made the trip. I would have stayed in bed all day. But I am glad I did: it was stunning. The more adventurous of us spent the evening at a bar near to our hotel in the Waterfront area of the city, and had a few beers seeing in the New Year. Practice had been organised for 11.15 a.m. on New Year's Day so we had to take things a little easy!

Everything was beginning to feel a little crazy to me at this time. The cricket could not have been going any better, and following up what I achieved at Port Elizabeth with a 25 and 136 in Durban was something I could feel very proud of. The cricket was taking its toll though and I felt exhausted. After batting for so long in

Durban, spending a stressful final day in the field and then arriving in Cape Town and meeting up with so many people for New Year's Eve, I did not feel as though I had much left in the tank. But as Justin Langer used to say – don't fuck with form. I was in the nick of my life and I could not let it slip. I had the opportunity of achieving something very special. The pitch at Newlands, the venue of the Third Test, was supposed to be a belter, and I could not think of a better way to starting the new year than with a hundred. It would make it three hundreds in three Tests on the tour, and that became my goal.

Unfortunately, the whole team seemed to be in a similar state of fatigue to myself in the Third Test and we were duly trounced by 196 runs. Our form with the bat had been something of a concern throughout the entire tour, and in our two innings here not one player scored a fifty. Steve Harmison, with 42, top-scored in our second innings and that was not good enough.

I felt in good form in each innings in Cape Town, scoring 45 and 39. When I reached 33 in the first innings I scored my thousandth Test run on my nineteenth visit to the crease. In terms of innings I was the fourth-fastest Englishman to reach the landmark, after Herbert Sutcliffe, 12, Len Hutton, 16, and Wally Hammond, 18. Naturally it is a huge thrill to be up there with the greats of English cricket but I actually found the experience of chasing records counterproductive. Golf has highlighted this to me on many occasions. How often does a golfer who is leading the Open Championship fall away once he starts looking at the leader board? I felt a bit like that as I approached 1,000 runs. It did not help my batting at all. The journalists seemed to think that I had some sort of magic formula, which I found very interesting.

In my brief international career I have realised that the best players are the ones who are able to treat a Test or one-day match just like any other game of cricket. The crowd and the television cameras need to be treated as incidental. If you are able to do this, then you are only concerned with what the opposition team are doing, and therefore able to concentrate completely on the job in hand. This sounds very simple in theory, but in reality it is far more difficult, especially when you are not in form or under pressure for your place. So far I have avoided a run of low scores, and I am certain it will be a far greater challenge to stick with a simple game-plan and a clear mind when things are not going so well. The one thing I have tried to do is keep my emotions on an even keel. I have deliberately stopped myself from getting too carried away when things have gone well, and tried to stop thinking negatively when they have not.

I had also developed a pre-match, pre-innings routine that I try to stick to rigidly. It sounds a bit sad and anal but it worked throughout the South African series. It would start at the end of the team meeting on the eve of a match. After the meeting I would return to my room and sit down for an hour or so and write my thoughts down in my diary. I found it important because it helped me clear my mind and focus on what lay ahead. I would write down how I was feeling and what I had to try to do in order to score runs the following day.

I started making these entries after my winter at the National Academy in 2001/02 and to begin with I concentrated on batting. But when I began playing for England I decided to expand on what I put in the diary because there was a lot more going on. On tour there are many different thoughts going through your head. You can get a bit bored in your hotel room and become tired of spending so much time with the same people. Inevitably you do have the odd low day. But by putting it down on paper I was almost putting it out of my mind. It was my way of dealing with it. I would then compare and contrast my feelings with previous entries in order to get my mind into a positive state. When you are in form this is not too difficult to do because you don't have any technical concerns and your mind is pretty clear. The challenge for me is to continue doing this when I am out of form because then there will inevitably be countless thoughts pinging around in my head.

The first morning of a match. I eat cereal and toast for breakfast and listen to Joss Stone on my iPod as we drive to the ground. On the team bus there is always a lot of nervous chattering, or people taking the piss out of each other, but on the first morning of the Test I always prefer to have some time to myself. Listening to music helps me focus my mind and helps me get into my own little cocoon. All my preparation batting-wise would have been done on the practice days so, after the warm-up and fielding practice, all I want is a few throw-downs. Very occasionally, when I want to feel bat on ball, will I have a net. But during these sessions I am not really thinking about my batting, I am simply going through the motions.

I always watch the toss, and generally assume we are going to lose it, so I am often trying to work out what the opposition will do. If we are batting I wait until 20 minutes before the start before I begin preparing myself. I check my kit, look for a bit of peace and quiet and try to keep as relaxed as possible. Then five minutes later I put my pads on and do some shadow batting to get my feet moving. Then, with the bell looming, I go and sit on my own outside so that I can get my eyes adjusted to the light and relax. If I am tense and nervous and the adrenalin is flowing too much there is a danger that I will do something I may regret at the start of my innings, like going for a big drive or playing at a ball I should have left alone. So I am trying to get my mindset when I face the first ball to be as close as possible to how it is when I have scored 20 or 30. Marcus Trescothick had been my only opening partner up to this point but there is no special chemistry between the two of us. Conversation is kept to a minimum as we walk out to bat and Trescothick always wants to face the first ball.

Maybe it was weariness, or maybe it was just luck evening itself out that prevented me going on to post a big score at Newlands. I played a dreadful shot in the first innings, edging a big drive on to my stumps, but got a poor decision in the second. Jacques Kallis batted superbly for South Africa again, scoring 215 runs in the match, and Charl Langeveldt claimed a five-wicket haul on his Test debut. The other disappointing aspect of the defeat was that so many England supporters had travelled to South Africa to watch us. Walking out on to a cricket ground and seeing the stands covered in England flags is very uplifting but, sadly, we saved our worst performance in a long time for the week they were there.

Rather than rush to the nets for extra practice, we were given a couple of days off in Cape Town before flying to Johannesburg for the final two Tests. It was much needed. Our hotel in Sandton, a suburb of Johannesburg, stood next to a huge shopping centre that had several high-quality restaurants in it. Ruth did not waste the opportunity and dragged me out for a serious shopping session. We spent a couple of the evenings in Johannesburg catching up with friends and family, and it was nice to get out of the complex and see a little of the real Johannesburg. With so much development going on, it really seems as though things are looking up in this part of the world.

On one afternoon after practice we had an honest team talk about what went wrong in Cape Town. The talk, the days off and some good practice had the desired effect and we were all really looking forward to the coming match. The Johannesburg Test was the most important in my career so far. With the series being level at 1–1, and with two Tests to go, anything could happen. The ground in Johannesburg is affectionately known as the Bull Ring. It is an intimidating stadium with incredibly high stands that tower over the pitch, and it is not difficult to imagine what it is like when it is full of patriotic South Africans baying for English blood.

Vaughan won his first toss of the series on a pitch where he would have been happy to lose it. He chose to bat and the moisture in the pitch made life difficult for myself and Trescothick. It was the first time in the series we had encountered any lateral movement and Shaun Pollock was a real handful. The ball flew past the edge of my bat on numerous occasions but as it softened and the pitch dried out batting became easier. I spent most of the first day batting with Rob Key, which was great fun. We really do seem to enjoy each other's company when we bat together.

It was an incredible feeling to get my third hundred of the series. Not even in my wildest dreams would I have expected to reach such heights. I had had patches of good form in county cricket before, but I had never experienced form like this. What is slightly more strange is that I did not once walk out to the middle feeling completely comfortable. There had always been a deficit to overcome, a tricky run chase ahead, or a slightly damp wicket to contend with, and I am sure these situations helped focus my mind. One of the great benefits of being in form is that generally you have no demons in your head telling you that your technique is wrong, or that a bowler is going to get you out. Naturally, the aim is to keep this going for as long as possible.

The timing of my dismissal spoilt a brilliant day. On 147, my highest Test score, I drove tiredly at Pollock and edged a catch to second slip. When I returned to my room after the second day's play, and sat and thought about scoring another hundred for England, I did feel a little confused. I was confused because I was struggling to come to terms with what was happening to me. A rain-affected second day meant I had time to read the newspapers and surf on the web, and maybe my state of mind was due to the attention that kept coming my way. In the papers and on-line people were comparing me with the greats – Bradman and Headley – because of the rate at which I was scoring runs and hundreds. It was very spooky to see your name next to players like this, and it did not seem quite right.

I kept telling myself that the important thing was not to get caught up in the publicity. The media overstate things when you play well, and likewise when you play badly. I knew deep down that things would not keep going like this forever, but I had to ride the wave for as long as I could. This was an incredibly exciting but strange time for me. I knew that millions of people around the world would love to be in my shoes and I would be a fool to waste it, so the challenge was to live the dream, whilst at the same time live in reality. In an effort to keep in touch with reality I even considered stopping reading the papers. Me, Andrew Strauss, in the same sentence as Don Bradman – what a joke.

Vaughan made a bold declaration on the third morning in order for us to make the most of perfect bowling conditions. Four hundred and eleven is not a huge total but by declaring we showed our desire to win the game and move 2–1 up in the series.

Herschelle Gibbs made us spend a lot of the next four sessions wondering whether we had made the right decision. Gibbs had missed the First Test with injury, and not looked in particularly good form in the Second and Third, but here he showed what a destructive and classy player he is. He batted beautifully for his 161, getting good support from Mark Boucher and Nicky Boje at the bottom of the order.

Jimmy Anderson had a bit of a torrid time but he did pick up the crucial wickets of Boucher and Gibbs. Neither wicket was taken with a particularly good ball, but there will be plenty of occasions when he bowls well and gets little reward. Matthew Hoggard was the star for us, taking five wickets in South Africa's first-innings total of 419. Hoggard bowled even better in South Africa's second innings but before he got his hands on the ball Marcus Trescothick played one of the finest innings I have seen. Hoggard quite rightly claimed most of the plaudits for his 12 wickets in the Test but it was Trescothick's 180 that set up our thrilling victory.

You know you have taken part in something pretty special when, sitting on the balcony after the game with a beer in hand and singing along to the tunes being played on the music system, Graham Thorpe declares the win as his best ever for England. This was a man who had played 97 Test matches at the time. He had played in winning sides in the Caribbean, Asia and Australasia, but nothing, he said, compared to this.

I had only played in 11 Tests and it was the most satisfying win of my career. Hitting a career-best score is always going to make the match memorable but this was a game that had everything. There had been scintillating strokeplay from both sides, some inspirational bowling, excellent catching and, going into the last session of the fifth day, all four results still just about possible. What more could you ask for?

Hoggard had been a menace to the South Africans all tour, and I am sure his inswingers had already given Graeme Smith and Gibbs – prior to his hundred here – nightmares. His five-wicket haul in South Africa's first innings was down to heart and determination but his 7/61 in the second innings was heart, determination and class. It must be one of the finest-ever displays of swing bowling from an England bowler.

We thought that our chances of winning were slim when Vaughan declared bravely for the second time in the match, but victory became a distinct possibility after Hoggard took three wickets, including Kallis first ball, in his opening five overs. He took three more in his second spell and by now we had all realised that we were witnessing something special. Graeme Smith, who had been forced to bat down the order after being hit on the head during practice, nearly kept us out but it was fitting that Hoggard took the wicket that sealed a remarkable victory.

To the media Hoggard remains the unfashionable member of England's fast bowling quartet but his value is definitely not underestimated by those of us in the dressing-room. He can be a stroppy, cussed, stubborn bugger but he has a heart the size of a basketball and is as honest as the day is long. He is one of those players who never quite seems to get the recognition he deserves, no matter how well he performs, but I feel there is a part of him that quite enjoys this. Matthew doesn't particularly enjoy the limelight. He would rather be out walking his dogs on the Yorkshire moors than posing on the red carpet at a movie premiere. But behind the slightly dopey 'Farmer Giles' exterior is a surprisingly sharp mind. He does not like people knowing it but he has three high-grade A levels to his name. I am not sure if it would ruin his credibility up on the Yorkshire Moors if he admitted to being clever, but in his intellect, rather like his bowling, he prefers to be underestimated.

Communicating with him before 10 a.m. is a nightmare, and even the most good-natured of comments are likely to be greeted with a Neanderthal grunt. He is blunt and to the point with any-one who cares to listen. An example of this came on England's 2005/06 winter tour of India. In Delhi the England team were invited to the British High Commission for a huge party to cele-brate the Queen's eightieth birthday. Prince Charles and Camilla were at the do and, as Camilla came through a room on her own, Hoggard caught her eye. He said, in the same way he would engage a team-mate: 'Don't tell me that you're sneaking out of here before the party is over. If you are, though, I'm coming with you.' It was classic Hoggard.

The victory celebrations in Johannesburg went on long into the night and we looked a pretty bedraggled lot when we met up the following morning. But behind the hangovers was the realisation that we still had a job to finish. South Africa are a proud and competitive sporting nation. Many people had written them off after the Second Test, yet they levelled the series in Cape Town. We were now 2–1 up but we did not want history to repeat itself.

England rarely feature in a dull Test, even if a considerable chunk of the game was lost to rain, and this match was no excep-tion. For four days we controlled the match, taking a 112-run first-innings lead, and killing any chance of a South African win. A.B. de Villiers and Kallis scored hundreds that put us under a bit of pressure on the final afternoon. We had a little wobble when we lost three wickets in the opening 12 overs of our second innings but, realistically, we were never going to be bowled out in 44 overs. If anything the rain had had a detrimental effect on our cricket because we wanted to be off the pitch for as long as possible and we spent more time looking for thunderstorms than a win.

But we got there eventually. After seven weeks of hard, exhausting cricket, it was fantastic to come through and become only the second overseas side to win here – Australia were the other – since South Africa's readmission in the early 1990s. What made it all the more memorable was that we achieved it without ever getting out of third gear. This said a lot about the team but it also served as a warning against complacency. We knew that we could not afford to make the same mistakes against Australia if we were to regain the Ashes.

I scored 44 and nought in the final Test. I did not score the fourth hundred I was looking for but things could not have gone better for me on the tour. Scoring 656 runs at an average of 72 is something I am still really proud of. It was satisfying to return to the country of my birth and do well, and family members who are still out there were very proud of the way I had played. Even now I cannot remember ever striking the ball so well for such a long period of time. There is no doubt that people's expectations of me would continue to rise on the back of this series but I had no doubt that I would carry on scoring runs if I did not allow off-field distractions to get in the way of my cricket.

The only concern for me on the tour was that I got out chasing wide balls on five occasions in the series. It was not something I was likely to lose sleep over but it showed that there is always work to be done on at least one aspect of your game.

It was with slight envy that I watched the Test specialists return home for a much-deserved rest. By now I had been away from home for ten weeks. However, those of us who play both forms of the game faced another two and a half weeks travelling around South Africa playing seven one-day matches. England's away record in limited-overs cricket has been poor for quite some time and our 4–1 defeat – one game was tied and one rained off – highlighted that we still had some way to go before our one-day performances matched those in Test cricket.

7
ONE DAY AT A TIME

There are countless theories as to why England has been unable to produce a decent one-day side. The current team is not the only one to struggle to come to terms with this intense and highly skilled form of the game. Mike Gatting's side reached the World Cup final in 1987, as did Graham Gooch's in 1992, where they lost to Australia and Pakistan respectively. Adam Hollioake picked a team of supposed specialists during his brief time in charge and they won a mini tournament in Sharjah in 1997, but other than that England has had very little success in limited-overs cricket.

English domestic cricket should, in theory, produce good one-day cricketers and a strong England team because we play more limited-overs cricket than any other nation in the world. English counties were the first first-class sides to play in a competitive limited-overs tournament when, in 1963, the Gillette Cup was initiated. And since then the England and Wales Cricket Board – formerly the Test and County Cricket Board – have introduced 65-, 60-, 55-, 50-, 45-, 40- and 20-over competitions. For more than 30 years English counties have had three limited-overs competitions to play in each summer yet they, and successive England coaches, are still to produce a World Cup-winning side.

It is hard for me to comment on what went wrong during the 1980s and 1990s but the one-day cricket I have played with Middlesex since 1997, and England since 2003, has given me an insight into why we have struggled. In an attempt to explain why England have failed to make the same progress in one-day cricket as Test cricket we have to appreciate the differences between the two games, and the different challenges they bring to those who play them.

Fellow batsmen may not thank me for saying this but in Test cricket the onus of winning games is with the bowlers. They are the stars because in Test cricket you are not likely to win many matches if your bowlers are not capable of taking 20 wickets. This, therefore, is the challenge and thus bowlers are the most influential figures at every match. Teams that have a very good bowling attack will win a high percentage of their matches. Australia's success has been based around the ability of Shane Warne, Glenn McGrath and Jason Gillespie, and England, in the guise of Steve Harmison, Andrew Flintoff, Matthew Hoggard, Simon Jones and Ashley Giles, possesses an attack to envy. England's batsmen have played their part in England's success since I broke into Test cricket in 2004, but it is the bowlers who have made the biggest contribution.

All this changes in one-day cricket, a game where runs equal entertainment and the regulations restrict the possible impact a bowler can have. The attributes that make a bowler effective in Test cricket can also make him a liability here. The ability to swing the ball and the possession of searing pace make for a dangerous Test bowler, but these assets can often lead to the concession of runs. The most effective bowlers in one-day cricket tend to nip the ball back into a batsman and aim for your thigh guard. This style of bowling is less likely to get you out in Test cricket but in one-dayers it reduces the number of scoring opportunities a batsman has. In one-day cricket a batsman loves width because it gives him the opportunity to throw the bat at the ball. To a large extent he could not care less where the ball goes, but if he gets a good strike there is a strong chance it will go for four.

Bowlers who bowl short of a length and straight give away fewer run-scoring opportunities and this can frustrate a batsman, a situation that can lead to his demise. Teams obviously want to take wickets, but not at any cost. In a Test match a team can tolerate a bowler taking 3/70 in ten overs because bowling a side out for less than 300 would be deemed a success. But in a one-day game these figures would cause alarm because the main job of a bowler is to keep the number of runs conceded down to a minimum. A team can win a one-day game without taking a wicket: all you have to do is score more runs than the opposition.

The best bowlers adapt their game to circumstance. Glenn McGrath and Shaun Pollock create pressure and bowl wicket-taking deliveries, but most tend to be more defensively minded in this form of the game. In Test cricket the slips are there waiting for an edge and you can give him protection by placing a fielder on the cover boundary if you want to. In one-day cricket, however, you are only allowed two players outside the 30-yard circle for 15 overs, and this means you have to do without a third man or a sweeper on the cover boundary. Fewer slips are positioned and possible slip catches slide down to third man for runs. The fact that the ball is leaving the batsman also gives him the room he requires to throw the bat at the ball and Hoggard would concede a lot of one-day runs in the 90-degree section between the wicket-keeper and cover-point.

The factor that most limits the possible impact of a bowler, though, is the maximum allocation of overs they are allowed. In a Test match there is no limit to the number of overs Shane Warne,

Muttiah Muralitharan or Andrew Flintoff can bowl, but in a limited-overs game they can only bowl one-fifth of the total numbers of overs.

So the onus is on batsmen to win one-day games of cricket. It is we who can bat for 50 overs and it is we who the fielding restrictions and powerplays are intended to help. In one-day cricket, where the bowling resources of a team are levelled out, England competes against teams containing several match-winning batsmen. And with England's bowling being slightly stronger than our batting this makes life harder.

For batsmen there are technical and psychological differences between the two forms of the game. If you bat like Chris Gayle or Shahid Afridi you can just go out and play the same way but most players have to adapt their games. In Test cricket there is no pressure on a batsman to score runs. Five days is a long time and you can just sit there and play, and runs will eventually come. In one-day cricket, however, a batsman cannot afford to sit in his crease and wait for the bad ball to come along. He needs to be proactive, creative and possess the ability to hit the ball in to unconventional areas.

Overseas players appear to be better at doing this than English batsmen. I believe this has a lot to do with how they are coached and the fact their games have developed in a more natural way. In England we are coached the fundamentals of the game at an early age. As a batsman you are told to play straight and meet the ball with the full face of the bat. This approach gives you the best chance of scoring runs in Test cricket. But in one-day cricket, in order to score singles and rotate the strike, you have to be able to deflect the ball in to gaps and down to places like third man. You have to be able to improvise and use your wrists, which is quite hard when you have spent ten years practising hitting a cricket ball straight back down the ground.

These problems can be overcome if you have a game-plan of how you intend to score your runs off each individual bowler. The state of the game generally dictates how aggressively you bat against a certain bowler, and you have to work out when is the best time to sit on him and when is the best time to take a few calculated risks. Knowing when to make these decisions is crucial and it takes a great deal of experience to get them consistently right.

The media believe that Duncan Fletcher was simply making excuses when he stated that lack of experience was responsible for England's failure to win games. But he was right. One only has to compare the number of one-day caps in an England side to that of the opposition to realise that they have handled tense situations far more often than we have. These matches have also enabled them to develop their game-plans and skills. I am sure Sachin Tendulkar made the wrong decision on a number of occasions at the start of his career.

The final reason why I believe England struggle with one-day cricket is the attitude towards the game. When there are two forms of the same game it is inevitable that one is deemed to be slightly more important than the other and in England one-day cricket is considered the poor relation. Test cricket is the game people talk about most in England. Newspapers give Test matches greater space and journalists cover them with greater enthusiasm. During England's 2005/06 one-day series in India, only one of the cricket correspondents from a broadsheet newspaper stayed on to cover the tour. Again, if a player is tired and in need of a break, where are you likely to rest him? The answer is probably during the one-day series and this does give a slight indication of where our priorities lie as well.

Test cricket is the form of the game that carries the greatest kudos. These views are traditional, and they are understandable. I, like most international cricketers, will look back on my Test career with the greatest pride, because it is those figures that will tell the world how good a player I was. This does not mean that I do not take pride in the way I perform in one-day cricket but to be a great of the game you have to excel in the Test arena.

I do not believe my views are any different from those of other international players, but I do feel that the administrators and the public in other parts of the world value one-day cricket more than Test cricket. This becomes apparent when you visit places like India, Pakistan and South Africa where attendances at Test matches are often small, yet every one-day match is an absolute sell-out. The hype before a one-day series in these countries is huge, and you often feel that the Test series is acting as an appetiser for the big event that is to come.

There is a belief that the current England side does not take one-day cricket as seriously as Test cricket. It is absolute rubbish. We work as hard at one-day cricket as we do at Test cricket, and the attention to detail behind the scenes is just the same. Given the time we have, it is hard to believe we could do any more on the practice front, and the playing schedule does little to help us. In English domestic cricket you only have to look at the fixture list each summer to see where our priorities lie. The Benson & Hedges Cup, whose zonal rounds were played during a two-week period at the start of the season, used to give counties the chance to pay specific attention to one-day cricket. The Twenty 20 Cup is now given the same luxury. But, even so, the majority of one-day games are played the day after a four-day game has finished, and this gives players little or no time to practise and prepare properly, creating a 'we'll worry about Sunday's game when we get round to it' sort of attitude.

When I was captain of Middlesex I used to look at my bowlers with sympathy on a Sunday morning as they drifted into the dressing-room. More often than not they were knackered from four days of hard toil, and the first place they visited on arriving at the ground was the physiotherapist's room. What chance had they got of developing new tricks? Most of them wanted the day off and I was just happy to get them out on the field.

The fact that most one-day games are played on the same ground as the four-day matches that preceded them gives grounds-men little chance of preparing a decent pitch. Good pitches are a fundamental part of one-day cricket and sub-standard ones, of which there were too many when I was captain at Middlesex, lead to low-scoring matches which do little to prepare players for the next step up, where they must become accustomed to chasing or setting scores in excess of 270. In county cricket a score of 270 normally wins the match because players are not sure how they should play when chasing down a big total. But at international level, and especially when playing abroad, teams regularly set and overcome scores of this size.

The problem is psychological as much as physical. A team are unlikely to know how to pass a huge opposition total if they rarely score one themselves, yet when England are on tour opponents give the impression that they are capable of chasing any total we set them. The introduction of Twenty 20 is helping English cricketers to overcome this problem because batsmen are becoming accustomed to scoring at 7 or 8 runs per over for a sustained period of time. These skills will inevitably feed through to the England team – who play very few Twenty 20 matches – and that can only be good news.

In county cricket it is very difficult to compete in all competitions at a high level and something has to give. There have been counties that have prioritised one-day cricket, and the advantage it gave them brought huge success. Gloucestershire are a great example of this. Under the guidance of their coach, John Bracewell, and captain, Mark Alleyne, Gloucestershire dominated domestic one-day cricket in England between 1999–2004, winning seven trophies in six seasons. Good luck to them for capitalising on an area of the game where other teams failed to pay attention. Gloucestershire's success made their supporters happy and gave the players several nice pay-days, but it did not do a great deal for English cricket. One of the principal roles of the counties is to produce England cricketers and during this period Gloucestershire failed to supply the Test side with one decent player.

Despite everything, I firmly believe England have the potential to produce a highly competitive one-day side. In Marcus Trescothick, Kevin Pietersen and Andrew Flintoff we have three of the most destructive one-day batsmen, capable of winning any game of cricket against any side in the world. The prospect of Trescothick, Pietersen and Flintoff batting in England's top five should offer our supporters great encouragement.

Pietersen is an astonishing player. I first saw him at Lord's in 2001 when he scored his debut first-class century for Nottinghamshire against Middlesex. Even then his audacity took me by surprise. During that innings he showed complete disdain for Phil Tufnell who was still the best slow bowler in England. Having shared the same dressing-room with him, I have come to realise how much he loves the big stage. Indeed, the bigger the occasion the better he plays. He benefits from being a tall man with long levers and this gives him the ability to get over the ball and hit good length deliveries for four. He also has a great eye and wonderful reflexes that enable him to see the short ball early, and these attributes, along with immense power, make him a daunting opponent.

But Kevin's biggest asset is the confidence he possesses. He has absolute faith in his technique and his game-plan. While some players spend hours talking about shot options and looking through video footage with their coaches, he will sit in the corner reading magazines and checking out his text messages. No matter what shot he plays he backs himself to complete it successfully. It is an incredible attribute to have and it allows him to go fearlessly after any bowler in the world.

Pietersen made his one-day debut for England in Zimbabwe where he played a couple of sparkling innings, but it was difficult to truly judge his class there because the opposition was so weak. But those scores gained him selection for the one-dayers in South Africa where he was unbelievable. England lost the series 4–1 but Pietersen scored three hundreds and a 75. The stick he received from the crowd – Pietersen was born in South Africa but chose to qualify for and play for England – acted as a huge motivation but I do not think it is possible to play one-day cricket any better than he did on that tour.

In recent one-day matches he has looked to be positive from the moment he sets foot on the field, yet in South Africa he took time to get himself in before treating us to an amazing array of stroke-play. When he is in that sort of form bowlers cannot bowl at him. He has the range of stroke to hit the ball anywhere in the ground and the power to hit any bowler over the boundary for six.

Pietersen's particular brand of confidence is very un-English. Born-and-bred Englishmen tend to be a little reserved when they talk about their exploits. Cricketers, in particular, are very super-stitious about saying or doing things that might come back to haunt them. But these issues do not concern Pietersen because he does not feel he needs to conform to any cricketing stereotypes. He is more than happy to juggle fame, fortune and outrageous batting. In his Test career he has already scored hundreds against Muttiah Muralitharan and Shane Warne, the two best spinners in the world, and Brett Lee and Shoaib Akhtar, the two fastest bowlers in the game. If he can keep his huge appetite for runs he has the potential to become a truly great player.

But even with Pietersen in our one-day side our win ratio has failed to increase dramatically, and that is largely down to the inconsistency of our cricket. I am as responsible as anyone for the lack of harmony that has prevented England from getting on a roll. Good one-day teams need confidence and once this has been generated it is amazing what can be achieved. Once a team starts winning they seem to keep on winning. Test sides rarely win five or six Tests in a row, yet in one-day cricket teams regularly put together runs of ten, 12 or 15 victories.

I am the first to admit that our form when abroad has been disappointing. But our record at home has been reasonably good whilst I have been associated with the side. I made my one-day debut for England at Dambulla in Sri Lanka in November 2003, a match we lost heavily, and our next series of games were in the West Indies, where we drew 2–2. The summer of 2004, when

England played New Zealand and the West Indies in a triangular competition, was a bit of a nightmare. We failed to get to the final but we were largely playing an experimental side and Flintoff was injured. Pietersen was yet to grace us with his presence and we were very reliant on Andrew in those days.

At the end of the summer, however, we proved that we were capable of playing high-quality one-day cricket when we reached the final of the Champions Trophy, only to lose narrowly to the West Indies in the September gloom. It was a game we should have won and, coming on the back of seven consecutive Test victories, it would have sealed a remarkable summer for us. Trescothick highlighted what a great one-day player he is by scoring 104 in our total of 217. And victory seemed a formality when we had reduced Brian Lara's side to 147/8. But Courtney Browne and Ian Bradshaw batted superbly to take the match away from us in very difficult conditions. How they were able to see the ball in the gloom at The Oval is beyond me. Steve Harmison was roaring in and bowling at 90 mph plus and the streetlights outside the ground were on. But Browne and Bradshaw remained calm and guided the West Indies home with seven balls to spare. Hurricanes had recently devastated parts of the Caribbean and the West Indies team had said they would donate their match fees to a fund set up to help rebuild what had been demolished. Perhaps they were meant to win.

On the way to the Champions Trophy final we comfortably beat Australia at Edgbaston, the first time we had defeated them in one-day cricket for more than five years. It also brought an end to a run that had seen us lose 14 consecutive matches to them. At the end of the game Fletcher was delighted in the way that we had ruthlessly gone after Australia and chased down a total of 259 in

47 overs. We had showed no fear and it supplied the team with the embryo of how we were going to conduct ourselves during the Ashes the following year.

In the summer of 2005 our one-day cricket was pretty good too. We defeated Australia once in the group stage of the NatWest series and tied with them in the final at Lord's. And in the NatWest Challenge that followed we lost 2–1 in the three-match series. These games were the first to be played using the new ICC initiatives of supersubs and powerplays. The powerplays – five-over segments where the fielding side had to position nine players within the 30-yard circle – were tolerable, but the supersub ruling – where a player could be replaced at any time – was a waste of time. It gave too much of an advantage to the team that won the toss, and we lost it twice in the NatWest Challenge.

Ideally, Duncan Fletcher would like to see the same personnel representing England in both forms of the game but achieving this is virtually impossible. There are bound to be at least a couple of changes and these are far easier to manage in England than when abroad. At home it is easier to get the facilities you want for practice and the one-day specialists you draft in are usually in reasonable form because they have been playing county cricket prior to their selection. When you are away on tour it is far more difficult. The one-day players turn up fit but their preparation has often been limited to an indoor school and it naturally takes them time to find their best form.

The timing of the matches should not have any influence on the quality of cricket we play, but it does. This will infuriate many people, and I accept that we are professional people who are being well paid to do a job millions would love to do, but at times it is hard to manage the challenges that come with being away from home for a long time. I am not looking for sympathy, far from it. I know how fortunate I am to be playing cricket for England, but it is inevitable that your thoughts start turning to home at the end of a Test series, especially when several members of the side are about to leave.

I feel it would help England if our one-day games were played at the start of a tour because there would be no shortage of motivation for the Tests that followed and we would play the limited-overs games when everyone is fresh. The games would also give us greater time to acclimatise before the start of a Test series. In the end, though, we are largely in the hands of the country that is hosting us and they want to finish England's visit off on a high, and that generally means one-day cricket.

It would also be beneficial if England occasionally went on a mini tour where we played just one-day cricket. Other countries do it. They spend a month playing Test cricket here, three weeks playing one-day cricket there, and it allows them to concentrate on one particular form of the game. The England tours I have been on, with the exception of Zimbabwe – which was meant to encompass both forms of the game – have involved us playing a combination of Test and one-day cricket.

These issues are relevant but the biggest reason for our lack of success when abroad is our inability to adapt to the conditions we face whilst on tour. The responsibility for this lies principally with England's top four or five batsmen. It is our job to score the bulk of the team's runs and on too many occasions we have lost two or three wickets in the first 15 overs. We know it is an area that we have to work on and if we can get it right we will give Pietersen and Flintoff the perfect platform on which to show their class. I have to accept a fair portion of the blame for our problems at the top of the order because I haven't provided the platform required as often as I would have liked.

The team's shortcomings can be seen when you look at the list of century-makers in one-day cricket. Sachin Tendulkar, Sourav Ganguly, Ricky Ponting, Saeed Anwar, Brian Lara and Sanath Jayasuriya have each scored 19 or more one-day hundreds, whereas Trescothick, England's most successful current player, has posted just ten. These figures are obviously influenced by the number of games we play compared to our opponents, but the fact that the current England side has scored only 20 one-day hundreds highlights our problems. Hundreds win one-day games of cricket and the sooner English batsmen begin scoring them regularly, the sooner we will become a top side.

8

BACK DOWN TO EARTH

After three hectic months sampling the sights and sounds of Africa, it was an absolute pleasure to return to the freezing shores of home in late January 2005. It is at this time of year that most in the UK start praying for the longer days and higher temperatures that the onset of spring brings, but after spending so long exposed to high factor sun-cream and the unsympathetic African sun, a few weeks rugged up in front of a log fire sounded like absolute bliss. Also, if things started to get a little frigid, I could always use the warm afterglow of a hugely satisfying and successful personal performance in the southern hemisphere to keep me going.

Everything in my life could not have been going better. Ruth had completed the unenviable task of moving into our new house while I was away, and I had the distinctly more enviable task of coming straight from the airport and walking through the door to find everything unpacked and the transformation from house to home completed. They say in sport that timing is everything, and in this instance they are entirely correct. In addition, I was able to pack all my cricket kit away and forget about the game completely. I had no real technical work to fit into my schedule, as the runs were flowing, and I intended as much as possible to heed the advice of the England management to rest and recuperate as much as possible prior to the most eagerly anticipated Ashes summer in recent history. The offshoot of all this was that I had a period of two months where my only real responsibilities were to reaccustom myself to living at home, and wander off to the gym every so often to keep the fitness ticking over.

The going to the gym bit was not difficult to do, but getting used to being at home again took a little longer. After three months of being waited on hand and foot, I was a complete nightmare to live with. While on tour it is extremely easy to get into what I call hotel mode. Got dirty plates in your room? Just chuck them outside the door. Got laundry to do? Call Housekeeping. Need a bed making? Put a sign outside your door. Does the bathroom need to be cleaned? No way, Jose! Need bags to be taken to the airport for you? Simple – call Phil Neale and he will sort it out. It is the sort of lifestyle that people dream about because all those annoying little tasks that we all have to do in our everyday lives are taken care of. The actual touring aspect of always living out of a suitcase gets tedious after a while, but having a chore-less existence never does. So having worked so hard to get into those habits, it is a little difficult to revert back to being a good, industrious New Age man. The bags, when I return home, are plonked in the living room to be dealt with in a few weeks' time, coffee mugs are left strewn throughout the house, and the wife can easily be employed as my personal butler, housekeeper, receptionist and Phil Neale clone. Needless to say it lasts about 48 hours before I am told in no uncertain terms to buck up my ideas.

After about two weeks Ruth and I decided that being at home in the English winter was not all it is cracked up to be and, buoyed up by the possibility of being waited on hand and foot again, disappeared off to Cuba for ten days of sunny rest and recuperation. As we jetted out I was vaguely aware that my colleagues at Middlesex were dusting off their training gear, last worn in September, and getting back to business.

March for a county cricketer is a fantastic time of year. New sponsored cars start appearing alongside the daffodils, pristine new items of kit are handed out like Christmas presents, and the players feel fresh, motivated and excited about the prospect of a new season. They launch themselves into the indoor net sessions, and even the gruelling training days, administered by David and Aaron Heard, the Middlesex fitness trainers, don't dim the enthu-siasm. I, on the other hand, was not feeling so enthusiastic. The first Test match against Bangladesh was still over two months away and, although I was available to play the first four championship matches for Middlesex before that, I was extremely keen not to peak too early, get worn out, and feel drained by the time the Aussies graced us with their presence.

I decided, wrongly, that I would only start my preparation two weeks prior to the start of the season. Although I was in the gym and keeping physically fit, it may have been a combination of a false sense of security and wrong priorities that kept me from working on my batting until very close to the onset of the cricket season. Also, I was beginning to find it a little difficult to fit everything into my schedule. The ECB had me lined up to do a few personal appearances throughout the month of March, my sponsors, Gray-Nicolls, wanted to use me to launch their new range of equipment for the summer, and there were various requests from radio and newspaper journalists to attend to. I figured that as the season had not started yet, it was the perfect opportunity to get these off-field distractions out of the way before the serious stuff started, but found that time was becoming increasingly more precious.

When I finally joined up full time with my team-mates at the beginning of April, just over two weeks before our first fixture, everything seemed to be progressing well. I was a little behind in my fitness, and I had to endure countless taunts from the likes of David Nash and Ben Hutton, my mate and newly appointed captain of the club, along the lines of 'Gracing lowly Middlesex with our presence, are we?' and 'I'm surprised your head can fit through the door' etc etc, but the batting seemed to come back without too much difficulty. The net sessions went well, and a pre-season game against Surrey gave me valuable time in the middle as I made 40 and 75 before retiring. I was enjoying being back with my mates again, and not having to prepare in quite such a pressurised environment. Looking back it was a little bit of a recipe for disaster, but I did not spot it at the time.

On 17 April the 2005 cricket season kicked off for Middlesex with an away one-day match against Nottinghamshire. Despite catching Jason Gallian at second slip first ball of the season, my involvement in a comprehensive Middlesex victory was limited by both a spirited first-wicket partnership between Paul Weekes and our new signing Ed Smith, and the inclement April weather, which brought an early halt to proceedings and had everyone scurrying around for the slightly incomprehensible Duckworth-Lewis sheets. These sheets give teams the scores that they have to have achieved in a given over, depending on how many wickets they have lost, in order to *tie* the game. Try explaining that one to an American. They are filled with so many figures that you could be forgiven for thinking that they are part of some sort of World War Two code book, but with a little patience, and a few mistakes along the way, most teams seem to have got to grips with them. Also Messers Duckworth and Lewis do seem to have come up with a decent system to decide rain-affected matches. Fortunately on this occasion they ruled in Middlesex's favour, and we went on our merry way back to Lord's to play our first championship match in a buoyant mood. I had missed the opportunity for more time in the middle, but wasn't overly concerned.

I should have been. On an absolute belter of a wicket, I left a straight one early in the first innings and was bowled by Ryan Sidebottom for 4, and then had the much greater humiliation of being bowled by the very occasional offspin of David Hussey, the Notts overseas player, on the final afternoon of the game for 2. He was bowling because Stephen Fleming had long since given up hope of forcing a result in another rain-affected game, and was trying to improve their over-rate. It was as close as any batsman can get to free runs, and I was the mug who had to watch my team-mates feasting on the assortment of half-volleys and long hops. My day was further ruined by one of the clowns from Notts writing 'Husey's bunny' all over my sponsored Vauxhall some time after the game. I consoled myself with the fact that at least whoever did it, and I suspect it was Graeme Swann, a buddy of mine from the Academy days, couldn't spell his team-mate's name correctly, and also that the only player to get fewer runs than me in the match was Stephen Fleming himself who registered a nought and 1. It was good to give him some stick in the Tavern after the match, but secretly I was seething at allowing myself to get off to such a poor start to the season.

Fleming had become an absolute legend at Middlesex during the year he spent with us in 2001. He came into the side with the reputation as being the world's greatest cricket captain and a bloody good player to boot. As a primarily young side we were all slightly nervous but incredibly excited about meeting and playing with this tactical guru, although he was not due to captain our side. Despite coming unstuck in the Russian roulette that is the early-season University game against Oxford, he immediately proved to us all what a fine player he was by getting a hundred against a Durham side including Steve Harmison and went on to have a very successful season.

It was off the pitch, however, where his impact was felt most of all. For a man with such a weighty reputation he was remarkably down to earth and willing to join in with the youngsters, and his unflappable nature and genuine warmth as a person made him immensely popular as a result. He also had the unique ability to have a dressing-room hanging on his every word when talking about cricket. It wasn't that he was saying anything particularly revolutionary, but the way he articulated his thoughts was incred- ible. It was a real education for all of us, and left none of us in any doubt as to why he was so highly rated as a captain.

Fleming captained Middlesex when Angus Fraser, our old war horse, picked up an injury, but this period in charge could hardly be described as successful. In fairness to him, he did not yet know any of the players, but we had to endure the shock and despair of losing a one-day game to Durham off the last ball, largely down to his blunder. A crucial run-out was disallowed in the second-last over, and the ball proceeded to deflect off the stumps for four because he had failed to notice that only three fielders were within the circle. It is the sort of mistake that all captains make from time to time, but we made sure that he never forgot that incident for the rest of the summer. You really do expect better from the world's best captain!

Fleming also had the dubious pleasure of captaining a certain Phil Tufnell, a man who had tested the resolve of many a skipper.

Tufnell's rebellious nature pushed Fleming to the limit and he was more than happy to see Fraser return to the side, admitting that he had never captained a player like Tufnell before and that Fraser was welcome to have him back.

There is nothing more frustrating than seeing opposition players rack up runs without the slightest indication that they are in any trouble, and then to follow their momentous scores with a failure of your own. Our second championship match provided another kick in the teeth for me as Ian Bell smashed our bowlers to all parts in registering a double century, while I grafted away for 13 and 37. I was beginning to feel a little out of sorts in the middle, and the banks of confidence that were overflowing in South Africa were reaching worryingly low levels. I was not helped by a ridiculous fascination most reporters following Middlesex matches had with basing 80 per cent of their articles on my struggles at the wicket, and only 10 per cent on the actual game. I didn't usually get to read the final 10 per cent as I had thrown down the paper in despair by that stage. I was finding it increasingly difficult to cope with the ongoing battles with my lack of form, as well as the attention it was creating. It's only two games, I kept telling myself. Everyone has a couple of bad games. But with everyone else focusing on how this lack of form was likely to affect England's Ashes chances three months hence, retaining perspective became difficult.

More difficult was having to keep fielding questions from well-meaning friends and unimpressed Middlesex members as to why the runs weren't flowing. Everyone seemed to have a theory, and I was having to play the cricketer's head-in-the-sand trick far too often. This trick, which is played by just about any cricketer who has faced a period of poor form, requires you to respond to all questions about your form as though your head has been buried since your last big score, and you are unaware of any problem. 'Why haven't you got any runs lately then?' an inquirer may ask. 'Absolutely no reason. I am hitting the ball well in the nets, I feel very confident out in the middle, and I am sure a hundred is just around the corner,' you reply, as though the thought that you might be going through a horror run had never entered your head. Inside, of course, you are thinking, I haven't got any runs lately because my head keeps falling over, my bat feels like a toothpick in my hands, I keep getting 'jaffas' from even the most moderate of bowlers, and I have literally forgotten what it feels like to hit a boundary. It is all a big act, and I defy any batsman to disagree with me. The problem with the head-in-the-sand trick is, however, that the longer you go without breaking the sequence, the less you believe what you are saying, and the less credible the reply becomes. You start fidgeting nervously when answering the question, and failing to look the person in the eye The ordeal will only finish when you break the sequence of low scores.

The prospect of my own sequence of low scores being broken was made somewhat harder by the fact that our third championship game of the season was away at Hampshire. Not only did I have to contend with probably the most challenging wicket to bat on in county cricket, but I also had to face my first duel with Shane Warne, who was captaining the south coast side.

The Rose Bowl wicket has been seen as a batsman's graveyard ever since the ground was completed in the late 1990s. It is very difficult for a groundsman to produce a wicket suitable for four-day cricket in the first few years, and following the earlier example of the Riverside ground in Durham, this wicket seemed to be taking its time to settle down. As a match wore on, the gremlins in the wicket came out to play. Balls could either roll along the ground, or rear off a length and hit unsuspecting batsmen right between the eyes. It was not a great recipe for shot-making, and few batsmen managed to trouble the scorers. Ironically in the first few years, it was the Hampshire batsmen, who should have been more adjusted to the vagaries of the pitch who struggled. Perhaps it is because they knew how many demons lay lurking in the wicket that their strokeplay became more inhibited, whereas opposition players just adapted to whatever came their way without thinking about it too much. I was fortunate enough to have scored a century there on my last outing in 2001, so the return to the ground did not daunt me as much as some others.

Also the task of facing Shane Warne did not overly daunt me. I knew that the press were likely to draw conclusions about how my Ashes series was likely to pan out on the evidence of my facing the great legspinner in this match. I, however, drew much confidence out of the fact that I had scored hundreds against both Stuart MacGill and Mushtaq Ahmed in recent years, and felt I had a pretty good game-plan against legspin. I was looking forward to the challenge of facing Warne, and eager to get some experience facing him before the added pressure of the Ashes series.

I did not have to worry too much about game-plans for legspin in the first innings. Warne, as captain, always seems keen to try out unorthodox fields, and against me he employed a square-leg fielder in no-man's-land, somewhere between saving a single and cutting off a four. Sean Ervine, the Hampshire bowler, then proceeded to bowl a series of half-trackers, which I in turn kept pulling hard, straight at the man positioned at square-leg. I found this increasingly annoying, as the shots deserved to go for four and, in my frustration, I managed to hit the next long hop even harder, and it travelled straight to the man again, but this time in the air. I was out for 6, and my season was getting worse.

Hampshire then proceeded to show us how to play on the wicket by setting us 300 to win, a very difficult proposition at the Rose Bowl. Ben Hutton and I managed to get through the new ball, and when I saw Warne warming up a shiver of excitement pulsed through my veins. It was an important moment in the context of the summer, and I was looking forward to the challenge, despite my poor form. Straight away, however, I found that Warne bowled very differently to other legspinners. He seemed to vary his pace more and, when bowling around the wicket, he bowled with a round arm, so as to get a greater angle on the ball. This, in turn, meant that left-handers find it very difficult to leave the ball, as there is always a chance that it could spin back towards the wicket and trap you lbw. Also it was much harder to get the ball towards the leg side, thus forcing you to play against the spin, and increase your chances of getting caught by the close-in fielders. With the inconsistencies in the wicket also helping him, I knew that I had to take some measure to get off strike, otherwise I was a sitting duck. I tried a sweep, I tried coming down the wicket, and I even tried using a reverse sweep, but he had me firmly planted down at his end. Eventually a ball kept impossibly low, and I was out bowled Warne for 19. It concerned me that I had found him so difficult to contend with, and with another low score under my belt, I was beginning to feel that I would struggle to get runs against Shane Richie, let alone Shane Warne!

Things were not going well. I felt frustrated about my poor form, and also more than a little embarrassed about letting my team-mates down. Here I was, having scored Test runs at will for the last 12 months, struggling to justify my selection in the Middlesex side. My mood wasn't improved particularly by the news that I had been nicknamed 'Andrew Strauss OBE' by the more unforgiving of the Middlesex supporters, the OBE standing for 'Only Bats for England'. Looking back I suppose it was just a little joke at my expense, but I didn't find it particularly funny as, if I kept playing the way I was, I wouldn't be batting for England very long either.

My final championship game for Middlesex prior to the start of the international calender saw us return to the less demanding wicket at Lord's for the visit of Gloucestershire. I saw this as the perfect opportunity to get some much-needed runs, return to form just in time for the first Test, and put all the tough times behind me. I worked much harder than usual in the build-up to the game, grooving shots, and tweaking my technique. In the nets I did feel good but I knew that playing in the middle when out of form was a different matter altogether.

Wednesday 11 May was the sort of spring day that makes everyone want to get outside. The sun was beating down on the Lord's outfield, and the smell of cut grass was perfume to my nostrils. Ben Hutton did the right thing on winning the toss and elected to bat, and he and I made our way to the wicket knowing that we had the perfect opportunity to get Middlesex off to a great start. Both of us, however, were short of runs, so despite the flattest of wickets we made batting look very difficult for the first half hour. After a couple of cover-driven fours against Steve Kirby, the nutty Gloucester opening bowler, who had once famously sledged Mike Atherton by saying he had seen better players in his fridge, I began to feel reasonably comfortable at the wicket for the first time in ages. With the wicket right on the edge of the square, and the Grandstand boundary not more than 50 yards away, I decided that if he dropped one short, I would take on the bouncer and try to hit it for six. The bouncer duly came, I went for the shot, and managed to hole out straight to fine-leg. I was absolutely livid. The one thing that you cannot afford to do when out of form is to throw your wicket away, and I had just done it. My pads were thrown down in a fury, my training kit was put straight on, and I set off on a run around Regents Park, which would last close to an hour. I returned more tired, but only a little pacified, to find the rest of the boys doing a great job without me. I resigned myself to having to score the runs in the second dig.

It didn't happen though. Same thought process, different bowler, and I was out for 10, trying to pull James Averis. I had officially hit rock bottom. The head-in-the-sand trick could no longer be played. I knew I was horribly out of form, my team-mates knew it, the press knew it, my wife knew it and even the guy working in my local post office knew it. There was no running away from the fact. The only positive about reaching the lowest of low ebbs is, however, that things cannot get any worse. Sure, I could keep on getting out cheaply, but the way I was playing, I half-expected that to happen anyway, so I made a conscious decision to not be too hard on myself, try to enjoy the games, rather than concentrating purely on my own performance, and attempt to do things a little more naturally. This attitude was not going to help me score runs for Middlesex as I had just played my last game, but I was increasingly sure that it could only help me to score runs against Bangladesh in the first Test match the next week.

After four championship games I had scored 118 runs at an average of 14, but I had learnt a number of valuable lessons. Firstly, I had to prepare myself one hundred per cent properly in order to perform, regardless of the standard of cricket, Secondly, county cricket is much harder than many people give it credit for, and thirdly, getting yourself out of a bad trot requires you to let go and use your instincts.

Out of the England players I was not alone in my struggles. Marcus Trescothick, my opening partner, was in the middle of a run of scores that made my meagre returns seem fruitful, Graham Thorpe was having a difficult time with both his back and his bat, Geraint Jones wasn't overly troubling the scorers, Kevin Pietersen was finding the Rose Bowl wicket hard to adjust to and even the captain himself, Michael Vaughan, got a run of low scores before redeeming himself with a century. Looking back, it does seem a little strange the supposed cream of English batting all failed. Was it because county cricket was much stronger than previously? Was it because we were not a hundred per cent focused? Was it because we were used to a Test-match routine? Or was it simply a case of a bit of bad form on sporting early-season wickets?

The reality, I believe, is that it was a combination of all of the above. Also, the advent of central contracts, which have done so much to improve the England side, probably as a by-product divorce players to a degree from their counties. Whereas in years past the likes of Angus Fraser would have felt like a Middlesex player playing for England, these days it is more a case of an England player playing for Middlesex. The contracts have given the England team an identity where there was none before. Perhaps the counties are disadvantaged because of this but, as the Ashes series later in the summer showed, there is no substitute for a team spirit.

9

THE PHONEY WAR

Some players can't help salivating about the prospect of easy runs against poor quality opposition. The games against the universities generally provide county players with a gilt-edged opportunity to get valuable first-class runs deposited in the bank early season, so as to protect their average in case things don't go so well later in the summer. Of course, these runs are of no value to the team whatsoever, as the result is usually a foregone conclusion, and even if a county side were to lose, it is of no consequence.

What these runs do tend to do, though, is help players when negotiating their contracts at the end of the season. 'Well, Mr Chief Executive, I scored 1,000 first-class runs at an average of 45. Surely I deserve a pay rise.' What those figures don't show, however, is that without his 150 not out against Oxford UCCE, he actually only averaged 36, and most of those runs were in games destined for a draw. There are definitely some players out there who are as, or more, interested in protecting their averages than winning games of cricket. For these players games against the universities and touring 'A' teams are manna from heaven.

I can't say that I have ever enjoyed playing in these games. My first four scores against university sides were 12, 5, 0, 3. Hardly the sort of score likely to impress tight-fisted county chief executives. I did rectify the balance somewhat by scoring a century against Cambridge the following year, but the prospect of playing against the universities has always been enough to bring me out in a cold sweat. The problem with fixtures like these is that there is no upside. If you get a hundred, there is no joy because everyone feels that you should do. If you get a low score, cricket followers throughout the country will be wondering why something has gone so badly wrong that you can't even score runs against the minnows. All this combines to ensure that these are the games that I get most nervous for. Against teams like this, I am always in a hurry to score runs, end up trying to hit good balls for four, and mistime the bad balls because I am trying to hit them too hard. Obviously once a batsman does get in against a weak bowling attack, then the easy pickings do become easier to take advantage of, but you have to still be at the crease to do this.

The international equivalent of the university games are the fixtures against Bangladesh and Zimbabwe. Bangladesh, the newest Test match nation, is really in its infancy in terms of cricket development. Their elevation to the highest level probably owes as much to the very powerful cricketing nations that surround them as it does to the quality of their cricket. They have never really shown that they are a team ready to take on the likes of Australia but the country does have an incredible passion for the game and, with some talented youngsters in the team, they can only improve as a side in the future. In the meantime, however, it is very much a case of lambs to the slaughter.

Both Bangladesh and Zimbabwe lack the quality really to trouble Test-class batsmen, and there have been so many easy victories for the established nations against them recently that the results are as close as you can get to a foregone conclusion. Players turn up for these games with one of two thoughts going through their heads. Either they are thinking about the easy runs on offer to

Not the most graceful of positions to end up in, especially if you are given out. Matthew Hoggard caused Graeme Smith endless problems on England's 2004–05 tour to South Africa.

England celebrate another series win after beating South Africa in 2004–05. Michael Vaughan holds the splendid Nelson Mandela trophy.

Shane Warne bowls me in the Hampshire versus Middlesex game, a disappointment before the Ashes series of 2005. My best man Ben Hutton is lucky to be at the non-striker's end.

Darren Gough shows his intent in the Twenty 20 match at Southampton. He wanted to show Australia we meant business from the first time we played them.

The astonishing Kevin Pietersen hits an Australian bowler down the ground. Pietersen's brilliant unbeaten 91 ensured we made a positive start against Ricky Ponting's side.

Left: Simon Jones apologises to Matthew Hayden after an errant throw hit him at Edgbaston.

Below: Hayden didn't want to accept the apology and Paul Collingwood and I became involved. Ponting comes over to calm things down.

Right: Ashley Giles runs the first of the two that tied the scores off the last ball of the final game of the 2005 one-day international series.

Michael Vaughan and Ricky Ponting share the NatWest one-day trophy in July 2005 after the series was drawn.

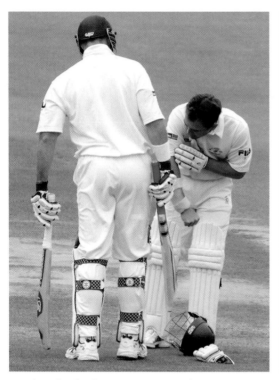

Hayden checks that Justin Langer, his opening partner, is OK after being hit by Steve Harmison with the second ball of the first Ashes Test.

The great Glenn McGrath holds the ball aloft after taking his 500th Test wicket, that of Marcus Trescothick at Lord's in July 2005.

Harmison hit Hayden, and Ponting, in a fiery spell on the opening morning of the Test, and ended with figures of 5 for 43.

Ashley Giles received a lot of criticism after our defeat at Lord's. At Edgbaston he showed his worth with a fine all-round display.

I share one of Flintoff's bear hugs after Steve Harmison dismissed Michael Kasprowicz to clinch a two-run win at Edgbaston.

Shane Warne bowled me twice at Edgbaston but here I get the better of him, hitting him back over his head for four.

Left: The hours of practice against Merlyn, the bowling machine that attempts to imitate Warne, proved worthwhile when I passed three figures at Old Trafford.

Below: I don't remember the dive, or the change of mind to go at it with one hand, but I will always remember the catch to dismiss Gilchrist off Flintoff at Trent Bridge.

boost their averages, as Jason Gillespie proved with his double hundred against them, or they are adopting the more negative outlook that they might miss the boat, and be forced to sit in the pavilion and watch the mismatch develop. Neither thought is likely to make players' hearts beat faster.

As the England team met up to prepare for Bangladesh, it was clear that everything we did during this series had to be geared towards the far greater challenge later in the summer against the Aussies. Bangladesh were to be a rehearsal for the main event, and we had to get into the right habits well before the Aussies landed at Heathrow. This task was made harder by the fact that a large proportion of the team had long since forgotten what the right habits were. Generally the batsmen had been struggling in county cricket, and even a couple of the bowlers weren't using the early-season wickets to their advantage. We knew that we had to change this quickly if we were going to be competitive against the Aussies, and right from the off it was a pleasure to be in an environment where everyone was completely focused.

If our time playing county cricket had been a case of making sure we didn't peak too soon, this was now the time where we had to get everything spot on. Nigel Stockill, our fitness trainer, informed us as soon as we walked through the door of the team hotel, that the three-week period when the Bangladesh Test series was being played would also double up as a time for conditioning work. This meant that we had to be prepared to do gym-work before, during and after the Test matches to make sure that we were in the best possible shape for the arduous one-day series that followed before the Ashes.

Perhaps, however, the most important moment in the days leading to the First Test was the outcome of meetings designed to set our goals for the summer. Here we set out what we wanted to achieve on the cricket field, but also dealt with the off-field challenges we would run into prior to the Ashes. The Aussies were already using the press as a propaganda tool, much like they had in previous series. Glenn McGrath had stated that he was targeting myself and Vaughan, and that the result was likely to be 5–0. Warne was firing off verbal volleys to anyone who would care to listen, and the media were lapping it all up. We had to assess what the right way to deal with these taunts was. Despite the temptation to meet fire with fire, it was decided that at all time we would try to be 'classy' with the media. In some ways that meant going down the boring route of not saying anything controversial, but we all felt that it was important not to give the Aussies any more incentive than they already had to win the series. We would let our cricket do the talking.

The other conclusion that was drawn in the build-up to the first Bangladesh Test, was how we could deal with the inevitable Aussie bullying tactics. England sides in the past had been intimidated by the brash, in-your-face style of Australian cricket, and we had to make sure that this was not repeated. We had to show them right from the off that we were not going to be overawed. If we were going to let them do all the talking off the pitch, it was on the pitch that we had to do our talking. This included making sure that we never let them get to any one player. It was decided that if the Aussies got stuck into anyone, then it was the responsibility of all of the rest of the team to both support him, and to give it back to them. This was to have greater significance later in the summer. The great advantage of focusing our cricket on the Ashes so early was that it also helped us first concentrate on what was essentially an almost meaningless series.

For me, there was the added incentive of trying to rediscover my game after a horrendous patch of bad form for Middlesex. Under normal conditions I might have displayed more apathy towards a series against Bangladesh. I would have been concerned about getting myself up for the games, and missing out because I wasn't switched on enough. This time it was different. Because my confidence levels were so low, I was far from certain that I was going to get runs against them, and also I knew that I had so much work to do prior to the Ashes that I really welcomed the businesslike environment that accompanied us meeting up. Duncan Fletcher was eager to work with all the batsmen in ironing out faults that might have appeared during our time apart, and for me it was fantastic to talk about what lay ahead, rather than concoct excuses for what had gone on in the weeks before. Mentally it was like turning over a new leaf, and suddenly I felt refreshed and reinvigorated.

The First Test against Bangladesh went almost completely according to plan. The young, impetuous Bangladeshi batsmen struggled against the pace and bounce of our bowlers. Brought up on the low, slow wickets of home, they found it difficult to leave the ball enough, and almost inevitably started edging length balls to the expectant slip cordon. Trescothick and I, despite having only scored 200 first-class runs between us in the season up to that point, managed to get through a few searching deliveries from their opening bowlers before taking advantage of the placid Lord's pitch as the ball got older. As I reached 50, I remember mentioning to Trescothick that the last time I had got a score of over 50, it was against South Africa in Johannesburg, nearly four months previously. It had been a long drought.

Trescothick and Vaughan went on to get hundreds, Ian Bell got an unbeaten fifty, and we wrapped up the game with another clinical bowling performance. Despite having to take part in one of the hardest fitness sessions I have ever done straight after post-match presentations, when normally a few beers would be flowing, we sat down in the dressing-room after the match satisfied with the start of our summer. Playing against Bangladesh before Australia seemed to be having some unforeseen benefits. Firstly, it was an opportunity for us to get cricket under our belts without the normal mental pressures that accompany Test matches; secondly, it was the perfect opportunity for us to gain rhythm after our forays into county cricket and thirdly, there is no substitute for winning. An Olympic athlete prefers not to have to put in their peak performance en route to the final, but instead save it until it really matters. In a sense we were the same. There were going to be plenty of occasions in the coming months where we would have to bat as if our lives depended on it, or bowl with every last ounce of energy. We didn't need to be over-exerting ourselves at this stage.

The Second Test followed the same predictable route, with Bell scoring his first Test hundred, and Trescothick making the most of his return to form with a century of his own. Graham Thorpe played his hundredth Test match, and looked very much in control of his game. Little did we know that it was going to be his last game for England. Kevin Pietersen had made an almost irresistible case to be included in the team by overcoming the animosity of both crowds and players in South Africa, before joining his new county Hampshire, and also joining the long list of England batsmen who couldn't score a run in the early part of the season. There was a feeling amongst the players that his in-your-face type of cricket would be ideal for the Ashes series, but 12 into 11 didn't go. Thorpe was our most experienced player, whose record against the Aussies was excellent, and Bell had made the most of the early season by scoring runs at will. The selectors had a very difficult decision to make prior to the Bangladesh Tests, and Kevin was the one to miss out. Whether the team would remain the same for the First Ashes Test depended on KP's performance in the one-day series that followed. He was under pressure to perform, and by the looks of his career up to that point, that is when he performs at his best.

By the end of May, the Aussies had arrived in town. With every passing day, the Ashes drew nearer, but for both sides, the one-day series was going to play a very significant part in drawing the battle lines for what followed. For both batters and bowlers it was a chance to strike first blood, and even though each of the one-day encounters we had with Australia were vitally important games in their own right, no one could help but feel that there was an underlying script to these games, the conclusion of which would not become apparent until September.

As with most good books, the introduction to this script was short, sharp, and grabbed attention straight from the word go. It was, of course, the inaugural Twenty 20 international held at the Rose Bowl. On a beautiful early summer's day a festival atmosphere awaited us as we arrived at the ground. Twenty 20 had long since taken the county game by storm. Thousands of people who had no interest in watching counties lock horns in four-day cricket were willing to have a few beers on a summer's evening, and watch the ball being smacked around for a couple of hours. The game is fast, frenetic, full of action, and without doubt the best way to attract new audiences to cricket. The players love being able to shed inhibitions, and play the way they always wanted to before coaches started talking about 'taking responsibility' and 'playing the percentages'. Over the couple of years it has been played, the game has developed from a slogging contest into a complex tactical battle in which spin plays a surprisingly significant part, but the underlying attraction to it still stands. Spectators see the ball being smacked out of the park, and wickets being shattered, all in minutes rather than days.

Having endured such a long build-up to the Ashes summer, excitement was already considerable throughout the team long before we arrived at Southampton for the encounter. As we pre-pared for the game, this mixture of nerves and excitement at what lay in store over the next three months, gave us an extra energy that everyone could see. We were pumped up for the game. This was the first opportunity for this new England side, a side which had won consistently over 18 months, to show what we could do against the best side in the world. After all the meetings and preparation there was a real feeling that we had to hit this side as hard as possible right from the start, and the format of Twenty 20 cricket was perfect for the task. Trescothick and Geraint Jones set the tone by getting stuck into Lee and McGrath, before Pietersen and Collingwood, in particular, upped the ante by propelling us to a very competitive score of 180.

The Aussies, who had entered into the festival spirit of the game by not looking to take it too seriously, were then surprised by the pace and hostility of our bowlers. Wickets were tumbling as Harmison, Gough and Flintoff attacked their batsmen, and once they had reached 31/7 there was no way back. My one abiding memory of the game was that of Darren Gough, a bowler who had spent the whole of his career watching England capitulate against the Aussies, steaming in at Andrew Symonds. He had removed

Gilchrist and Hayden in the two previous deliveries, and was on a hat-trick. The delivery did not take a wicket, but the venom in the bouncer he bowled showed exactly what it meant to him to beat Australia. This was his chance to play a part in the Ashes summer, and he was determined to make the most of it. It said a lot about Darren's stomach for the fight, and went a long way to explaining to me why he has been such a fantastic bowler for England.

If the game had managed to send out signals to the Australian dressing-room that we were a different side to the one they had played previously, then it was vitally important to keep the pressure on for the seven ODI encounters that followed. The one-day series gave either side a golden opportunity to grasp the momentum of the summer long before the Tests got under way, and if we wanted to win the Ashes, we could not afford to be outplayed and outclassed in this format.

Given that Australia were the world champions in the shorter form of the game, famed for their preparation and attention to detail, we all found it slightly strange first to watch them get beaten by Bangladesh in their opening game, and then only arrive at the ground at Bristol 45 minutes before our first encounter was due to start due to problems with the traffic. In addition, Andrew Symonds was banned for the game due to a night of excessive drinking. It seemed on the outside that the Aussies were in a bit of turmoil. They had expected a light, relaxed opening to the tour, and everything seemed to be going wrong for them. When individuals get stuck in a rut, it can be hard to get out of; the same is true for teams also. What both Australia and we knew, however, was that it was not going to last forever. They had far too much quality in their side to stay down for too long, and we had to make sure that we took advantage of the situation while a few of them were struggling for form.

The game itself proved to be an absolute thriller. Australia managed a par score of 250, thanks largely to Mike Hussey, who proved to be as difficult to get out wearing the green and gold as he had wearing the dark red shirt of Northamptonshire in years past. It was a score we backed ourselves to chase, and got off to a decent start before being pegged back in the middle overs. The equation became more and more difficult as the game reached its climax and without Kevin Pietersen we would have got nowhere near their score. His was an unbelievable innings, in which he combined his two greatest assets, immense power and a cool head under pressure. Despite needing over eight an over, he still backed himself to get the runs, even if he had to get most of them himself, and his assault on Gillespie in particular was about as violent as you can get.

It was a match-winning innings in the true sense of the word, and underlined the value of having two players, himself and Flintoff, who could play that sort of innings, rather than just one. The rest of the batsmen had our blushes spared a little by his innings, but we couldn't help feeling that we should have chased the score down more clinically. Too many of us got to 20 or 30 before getting out, and it would only have taken one of us to stay around with Kevin for us to reach the target easily. Despite our failings, the fact of the matter was that Australia had been beaten for the second time in two days, and we had got off to the perfect start in the quest for our holy grail, the Ashes urn.

Although Bangladesh had beaten Australia at Sophia Gardens, and also took them close in Canterbury, it was easy to forget that there were actually three teams taking part in the competition.

Everyone knew that the final was going to be contested between Australia and England, it was just a matter of getting through the Bangladesh fixtures without taking them too lightly and suffering an embarrassing defeat. Yet again we were experiencing the 'easy runs' conundrum, but this time the format was limited-overs cricket. For once I did manage to fill my boots, by scoring 82 not out, 152 and 98 in the three games against the Bangladeshis. I can honestly say, however, that they were three of the least satisfying innings I have ever played. They meant nothing, they didn't influence the direction of the game, and I couldn't rest my head on the pillow at night knowing that I had overcome a significant test; I hadn't.

Looking back, the three innings did help to get me used to spending time in the middle again. After six weeks spent with Middlesex, my pads were still pristine, I had not even thought about wearing more than one pair of gloves, and my bats were more damaged from being flung around dressing-rooms in rage than from meting out punishment on cricket balls. Even though I had got a 50 at Lords, and an 80 in the one-day warm-up game against Hampshire, I still had to experience that comforting feeling of being in control in the middle. When a batsman is in form, he feels that he is the master of his own destiny. Any dismissal is likely to be his own fault – a lapse in concentration, or a foolhardy shot – but when out of nick, the roles are reversed. Somewhere in the back of his mind the player is counting down the balls until the one with his name on it comes down. He feels as though he has little control over events, and is desperately clutching to remain in the game before being subjected to the long walk back to the dressing-room. His wicket is no longer the main event, but a minor insignificant fillip for the opposition.

After the Bangladesh matches, I felt much better about my game. I hadn't scored too many against the Aussies, but the idea of spending a few hours in the middle was not completely alien to me either. I felt as though things were coming right just in time for the Ashes.

The Ashes, however, were still a few weeks away. Although we were getting used to playing against Australia and everything that went along with it, the intensity of each game was not diminishing. After their twin defeats, they came back strongly against us in Chester-le-Street, beating us comfortably before meeting us again at Edgbaston for our last group game.

The game ended up being rained off after we had barely started our reply. In a cricketing sense it hardly deserves a mention. In a psychological sense, it is hard to know how important one incident in the game was in deciding the outcome of the Ashes. The incident started with Matthew Hayden driving a full-length ball from Simon Jones straight back at the bowler. Simon picked the ball up, and in a typical show of aggression from a fast bowler, threw the ball back at Hayden's stumps in the hope that he might possibly run him out. The throw was a little high and, instead of hitting the stumps, it hit the rather larger target of Hayden's barrel chest. Hayden took instant exception to this and started hurling abuse in Jones's direction.

Events moved pretty quickly, but from my view at mid-wicket, I immediately thought about the vow we had taken, when planning for the series, that we would always come to the aid of our team-mates if the Aussies targeted them. This was our hypothetical situation happening. I walked towards Hayden, and by the time I got there, Paul Collingwood was already in the mix, telling the Australian where to go. I added a couple of words myself, and both Michael Vaughan and Andrew Flintoff also got involved. The situation was defused quickly by the umpires and Ricky Ponting, who was standing at the other end. It would have done the game of cricket no good whatsoever for it to have gone any further. For us as a team, though, it was a pivotal moment. We had sent out a signal to the Aussies that we weren't about to be intimidated by them as previous sides had been. We still expected to get some stick from them in the coming months, but it was not going to be one-way traffic. It may just be coincidence but the Aussies didn't seem to take us on verbally nearly so much after that game. It was as though they had probed to find a weakness, found none, and so decided to concentrate on other areas.

The final of the NatWest series proved a nail-biting finale to a very evenly matched series, with us scrambling a two off the last ball to tie the game. Ashley Giles usually runs a two in the same time that it takes most batsmen to run a three, so we were all a little surprised that he was able to complete the run. As he made his ground we didn't know whether to celebrate or commiserate about our performance. Restricting the Australians to 196 meant that we should have won the game comfortably, despite a tricky two-paced wicket, but after subsiding to 70/6, we had to be grateful that Collingwood and Geraint Jones were able to get us back on track to win. A couple of wickets falling at important times as well as Mike Hussey, of all people, bowling well at the death enabled the Aussies to get back on top, before a McGrath no-ball and a couple of lusty blows put us in the position to get three off the last ball to win.

On reflection, it was probably a fitting end to the series. In the group stages, we had each beaten each other once, there was one no-result, and the final was tied. We couldn't help feeling, though, that they had not played their best cricket at all, and we had squandered the chance to gain valuable momentum before the Test series started. If there was one thing that we couldn't afford to do later in the summer, it was to let them off the hook, and in some ways that is what we had done.

Both sets of players were starting to get weary of the endless travel required in one-day cricket. A pattern of play, travel, practice, play had been taking place for over four weeks, and it was hard to keep putting the same intensity in to each performance time after time. The NatWest Challenge, a set of three one-day games against Australia straight after the final of the previous series, seemed to be a case of overkill, and certainly had a greater appeal to the money men at the ECB than to the players. But with the Ashes only a couple of weeks away, we could not afford to lose ground to Australia and so reacquainted ourselves with the M1 motorway for the umpteenth time and made our way up to Headingley.

We won the game at a canter, chasing down their score of 230 only one wicket down, but the game was totally overshadowed by the bombings in London on the same day. News of the atrocity filtered through to us as we were fielding. The 12th men were giving us a running commentary at each drinks interval, and as I was grazing in the outfield, all I could think about was whether my sister, who lived near Kings Cross, was one of the unlucky ones. The game of cricket, to which we give so much of our energy and commitment, was very much put into perspective that day.

The final two one-day encounters were one-sided affairs, where Ricky Ponting and Adam Gilchrist both got themselves back into form with centuries at Lord's and The Oval respectively. We seemed to have run out of steam a little, and the only real highlight of the twin defeats was Kevin Pietersen's violent 70 in the last game. He was playing for a spot in the Ashes, and had got his timing absolutely right. Once again the selectors had a difficult decision to make. Would it be Thorpe, Bell or Pietersen that missed out? All three deserved to be involved in the series, but there was only room for two. In a way it was fantastic to be in that position, but I am sure the selectors had a few sleepless nights, knowing that their decision could be pivotal in deciding the destination of the Ashes.

The preliminary skirmishes were over. Neither side had gained a significant advantage over the six-week period. The Australians had beaten us three times, we had beaten them twice, there was one tie, and we had won the Twenty 20 international. Batsmen from both sides had scored a few runs, bowlers had taken wickets, and only Jason Gillespie had been really short of form. The run-up to the Ashes had the potential to give one side an important momentum heading into the series, but it had not happened. We were satisfied that we had taken on the Aussies and had gained some success. They were happy to have won the NatWest Challenge, and got their tour back on track after a dodgy start. Both sets of players were itching to get involved in the Ashes. There had been too much talk.

10

TIME FOR PLAN B

I have no memory of the last time England won the Ashes. I have heard plenty of stories about the tour, both from Mike Gatting, and others who were part of proceedings, but for some reason, maybe I was just too young, or too involved with other sports over that winter, I can't remember at first hand any news reports or highlight of the games. You only have to see how some of the players on that tour, including Gatting himself, have been immortalised on their showings in that series to realise how important that victory was, but in the 1980s, it was the West Indians who ran the show. The Ashes was important for its history, not necessarily for the quality of the sides on offer.

Over the years, however, the series has become more than just a battle between two old enemies. It has become increasingly a test of the England team against the best. Australia has been widely recognised as the dominant team in the world since the mid-1990s, and every two years or so, England have had the opportunity to test ourselves against that benchmark. Viewing each series has been so riveting that it doesn't take any real effort at all to generate a highlights package in my head: the 1993 Ashes, when a young tearaway opener from New South Wales called Michael Slater brought a full house at Lord's to its feet, and the England team to their knees; the 1997 series, when a 3–0 one-day whitewash, added to a remarkable First Test victory, had everyone hailing what turned out to be a false dawn. The 1998/99 tour to Australia lives very clearly in the memory. My first winter away from home, playing grade cricket in Sydney, became increasingly tough as England got blown away early, before Dean Headley's remarkable spell at Melbourne allowed me some comeback to the taunts I was getting from my Aussie team-mates. Feeling buoyed by the victory, I made my way to the SCG for the final Test, hoping for a 2–2 series draw. Despite Darren Gough's hat-trick, Michael Slater scored another brilliant hundred, and I had to return to my team-mates the following weekend with my tail once more firmly between my legs.

I felt more involved in the more recent series between the sides, probably because I was playing first-class cricket, and those representing England were no longer back-page heroes, but work colleagues. Steve Waugh's hundred on one leg in the Oval Test in 2001 will always be remembered for him showing everyone the depth of his desire to play and win. Finally there was the last series in Australia, where England struggled with injuries prior to going, got beaten comfortably, but where everyone watched in awe as Michael Vaughan took the game to them and cemented his position as one of the game's great players.

Every time I let myself think about what had happened in previous series, it brought a shiver to my spine. These memories had motivated me to pick up a bat in the first place, and now the summer's main event had finally arrived. The 'A' word had been on everyone's lips ever since our record-breaking summer in 2004 brought a realisation to a public, starved of cricketing victories over Australia for decades, that this series might just be different. Newspapers all over the country had been providing their own insights into each of the teams, highlighting strengths and weaknesses, anticipating the key battles. TV stations, radio stations, magazines, they all seemed to be clambering over each other to build up a series which in truth didn't need any building up.

As players it was not difficult to imagine what lay at the end of the rainbow. The Rugby World Cup victory, and the celebrations that followed, provided the precedent. We had the opportunity to put cricket back on the map. For once there was no competition with other major sporting tournaments. Cricket was the main event.

With anticipation came a certain amount of pressure. We were fully expecting the series to be closely fought, but we didn't know how we were going to handle the expectation. The only question that we had not answered yet in our record-breaking run of victories was, 'Could we do it against the best when the pressure is really on?' It was a question that journalists had been asking all of us more and more as the series approached.

During the build-up to the game, Duncan Fletcher organised a motivational speech from a guy called Alan Chambers. He led the first successful British attempt to get to the North Pole against the current, and gave us some great insights into how to prepare yourselves for huge challenges, how to motivate others around you, and how to overcome major setbacks. His expedition finished with only two of the original four-member squad making it to the Pole, having not eaten anything for days on end, and having succumbed to frostbite in the −50°C conditions.

He stressed the need for thorough preparation, but what stuck with me most was one phrase he used − 'Never put your body in a place that your mind hasn't been first.' If we wanted to achieve our challenge of winning the most important series of all, we had to put ourselves mentally into the situation first. We had to visualise what it was going to be like to take on Shane Warne, or bowl at Adam Gilchrist when in full flow. We had to expect the unexpected, and be ready to deal with whatever came our way. We could not afford to be hesitant in anything we did, or to take time to adapt to game situations. We had to be ahead of the game. Our minds had to have played out the series first.

By the Monday before the Lord's Test, the selection dilemma was finally answered. Kevin Pietersen had done enough in the one-dayers to be assured of his Test debut. Graham Thorpe was the man to miss out and, in a lot of people's eyes, that left us very short of experience. Of the main batsmen only Trescothick and Vaughan had played more than 50 Tests. I had played 14, Bell three, Pietersen none. There was definitely the potential for us all to be lambs to the slaughter. One thing we were short of, though, was the experience of losing to Australia. Graham Thorpe, great player that he was, had experienced nothing but defeat against the Aussies, and by the end of their careers the likes of Thorpe, Atherton, Stewart and Hussain must surely have doubted that it was possible to beat them. We didn't have that mental baggage, but we didn't have their wise old heads either.

On 21 July 2005 our date with destiny finally arrived. All the build-up was over. The one-day results were irrelevant. We could no longer talk about being up for the challenge, and determined to take these guys on. Now was the time to walk the walk.

A look outside my window after a fitful night's sleep confirmed what the weather forecasters had predicted. It was going to be warm and sunny. We had breakfast in a specially cordoned off area in the luxurious Landmark Hotel in Marylebone. The guys were chatty, but it wasn't difficult to see that we all had that sickly feeling that nerves being on. We made our way out to the back of the hotel, waiting for taxis to turn up.

One of the by-products of there being so much interest in the series was that the players' car park at Lord's was turned into a large marquee for corporate guests of the MCC and as a result Phil Neale, the team manager, had to somehow convince suspicious London taxi drivers to take us on a five-minute ride from the hotel to the ground, when there were far more lucrative fares on offer from the many commuters arriving at Marylebone Station. The situation became almost farcical as we waited, on this the most important day of our careers, for a few cabs willing to take the fare. Finally one or two of us, including the captain himself, decided to walk and arrived at the ground 15 minutes later, having been subjected to 'good lucks' and 'all the bests' all the way from England supporters. It was definitely one way of sampling the atmosphere, but none of us could imagine the England football team turning up to a ground in the same way. It wasn't a great start to the week.

As we settled into our pre-match routine, we could hardly fail to notice that the ground was almost completely packed well before the captains had tossed. Eager TV commentators were all peering at the wicket, which looked drier than normal, and all agreed that it was a wicket on which to bat first. Michael Vaughan, hardly famous for his ability to win tosses, duly lost the spin of the coin, and we were consigned to a day in the field.

The reception, as we walked down the stairs and into the Long Room, was like nothing I had ever experienced before. MCC members, normally not the most vocal of people, were crammed into the room like sardines, and screaming at the top of their lungs, 'Come on, England.' It was enough to make the hairs on my neck stand bolt upright, and it was almost impossible not to feel a little emotional. So this is what Ashes cricket is all about, I thought to myself.

In the team huddle Vaughan reminded us to keep being positive at all times, and to enjoy the experience, but he didn't need to say anything. We were all completely pumped up. The Aussie openers, Langer and Hayden, ran out to the middle to join us, and it was obvious that they were up for the challenge also. In previous series between the sides, the Australians had made a point of coming out hard, and trying to dominate the opposition bowlers straight from the start. We expected them to try and do the same.

Steve Harmison ran in to deliver the first ball. Everyone at the ground was screaming at the top of their lungs. In the slip cordon, we were all trying to keep as still as possible in case an edge came our way, but the excitement generated by the occasion made it incredibly difficult to do so. The ball was a beauty, right on a length, and impossible to score off. Langer let it go. Second ball, Harmison unleashed a beauty that bounced from just short of a length, and hit Langer squarely on his right arm. Langer had played an important part in my development and it looked nasty, but at this moment I didn't care. Harmison had just made a statement for England.

The first half hour was intriguing cricket. Langer and Hayden played shots, our bowlers bowled with real venom, and we all knew that something had to happen. Either they were going to wrestle the initiative away from us, or wickets were going to fall. After seven overs, Hoggard got the breakthrough. Hayden aimed to hit a booming drive down the ground, and was comprehensively bowled. Ponting, having been hit hard on the helmet by Harmison, followed five overs later, before Langer, who had made 40 at a run a ball, was deceived by a Flintoff bouncer.

Almost immediately Martyn edged a ball from Simon Jones behind, and Australia were in real trouble. Everyone at Lord's was a little stunned. Here was the pride of Australian batting, all of which were averaging around 50 in Test cricket, and they were all back in the Pavilion well before lunch on what looked like a good wicket. This was the start we had all dreamt about. Michael Clarke was lbw for 11 soon afterwards, and at lunch the Australians were standing on the edge of a precipice at 97/5.

After the initial euphoria, back-slapping and congratulations had finished in the dressing-room, our lunches were increasingly being disturbed by the thought that Adam Gilchrist was still at the wicket. He has long been famous for his ability to dig Australia out of holes, and there is nothing more demoralising for a side than to do all the hard work to get Australia five wickets down early, and then proceed to watch it all being undone by Gilchrist in a matter of minutes. Although Flintoff seemed to have got the measure of him to a certain extent in the one-dayers by bowling around the wicket, we were still nervous. One session of Gilchrist fireworks and the game could be turned on its head.

In the event, he did manage to get a few of his trademark drives and cuts away, before Flintoff did the business against him again, getting him out caught behind. It was left to Simon Katich to add a little bit of respectability to their score, but some magnificent work by Harmison against the tail saw the Aussies bowled out for 190. He ended up with five wickets, and underlined once again how important it is to have genuine strike bowlers in your side.

No one likes balls flying around their noses at 90 mph, not even the much-vaunted Australians.

Trescothick and I hurried up the stairs to get our pads on and prepare ourselves for the challenge of Brett Lee and Glenn McGrath. As I was strapping on my pads, I couldn't help but think about what a magnificent opportunity we had in front of us. If we could just get through the new ball, the pressure would be fully on Australia. They would need to go searching for wickets, and in doing so would provide scoring opportunities. It all hinged on getting through that new ball.

We managed to get through the tricky 20-minute session prior to tea without any mishaps, despite Lee hitting me on the shoulder with one of his thunderbolts. (It was not to be the last time in the series that he inflicted damage, and I can safely say that when a cricket ball hits you at 95 mph, it hurts.) At tea all the talk was about hammering home our advantage, taking one ball at a time, and being positive. Unfortunately neither Trescothick nor I had any time to get those clichés out of our heads before we were back in the dressing-room with our team-mates. Trescothick went first ball after tea, giving McGrath his five hundredth Test wicket and he got me, too, early the next over. Things went from bad to worse when Vaughan, Bell and Flintoff were all bowled by the same man, and suddenly we were 21/5.

The atmosphere in the dressing-room had changed from light-hearted and buoyant to a morgue-like state. Lower-order batsmen were rushing around in a panic, trying desperately to get padded up before their turn came, while those of us who were out were staring into space as though we had just lost a close relative. In truth, we were being subjected to one of the best spells of bowling that I have ever experienced. McGrath could do no wrong. He was putting the ball on the spot in his normal metronomic fashion, and it was either nipping away, keeping on going straight or, in most circumstances, going down the slope on to the batsman's off stump. By the end of play the stump had far more damage inflicted on it than any of our bats. We simply couldn't get anywhere near the ball.

Glenn McGrath provides a unique challenge for a batsman. In a world where fast, entertaining cricket is the vogue, he is there to remind us that the old virtues of line and length remain the key to taking wickets. While other bowlers whirl the ball around batsmen's heads at 100 mph, and look as much at the speed gun as their figures, he realises his limitations, and bowls to his strengths. Any opening batsman wants three things when he goes to the wicket. He wants to be able to leave as many balls as possible, he wants some loose deliveries to score off, and he wants to see no lateral movement. When facing McGrath he gets none of these things. Every ball McGrath bowls is in the business area. Batsmen face anguish over which balls to play and which to leave because his line is so good. Also he hits the seam more often than just about any other bowler. Even if there is very little moisture in the wicket, the ball is likely to deviate. As batsmen, we can just about handle it when the ball swings; we have time to adjust to it. But when the ball seams, our stay at the wicket is in the lap of the gods. We don't have enough time to react.

Batsmen over the years have tried all manner of schemes to overcome McGrath's nagging accuracy. Standing outside your crease, getting a big stride in, going down the wicket, and even complete slogging have been tried, all with very little success. Those that have scored lots of runs against Australia have generally given him the respect he deserves, and gone hunting for their runs elsewhere.

Kevin Pietersen, despite making his Test match debut, managed to work out a plan to handle McGrath faster than the rest of us. By getting a large stride in to the ball, he managed to negate to a certain extent the low bounce that was causing us all trouble. Under very difficult circumstances he showed us all yet again how much he enjoyed being centre stage. He also displayed a stomach for a fight that he had never had to prove in ODI cricket. At the end of a tumultuous day, he was still there on 30, but Ashley Giles was out to the last ball of the day to leave us at 92/7.

As we wandered back to the hotel, we were all completely exhausted. Day one of the Ashes series had lived up to its billing. It was frenetic, compulsive viewing, and full of highlights. Unfortunately, too many of those highlights were dominated by Australia, and one man in particular, Glenn McGrath. It was devastating to have had such a great start to the series wiped out by one inspired spell of bowling. Our tails were firmly between our legs, Australia had grabbed the momentum, and we knew that we had much work to do if we wanted it back.

One way to grasp back that momentum was to come out on day two, keep the Aussies in the field as long as possible, and get as close to their score as possible. Kevin Pietersen was the danger man, and he attacked right from the moment the players went out on to the field. McGrath was hammered for one of the biggest sixes I have ever seen as KP brought up a maiden Test 50. McGrath suddenly didn't look the same bowler as he had the night before. The ball had lost much of its hardness and as a result the extravagant movement was no longer there. From being 92/7 we did well to get up to 155, only 35 runs short of Australia's score. The problem was that the wicket was only going to deteriorate as the game progressed. Shane Warne was likely to play a far greater role in the second innings than he did in the first. We could not afford to be chasing anything much over 300 if we still wanted a realistic chance of winning the Test. In order to do that, our bowlers, who had only had about 60 overs' rest, had to bowl out Australia for under 270 runs. A tall ask.

Things started pretty well. Another capacity crowd at Lord's did everything they could to lift us, and we came out all guns blazing. Langer was run out by a sharp piece of fielding by Pietersen, Hayden was out pulling, and Ponting was out for a quickfire 42. The game was very much in the balance, with Australia 100/3, a lead of only 135.

Michael Clarke arrived at the crease under some real pressure. He was struggling for form before the series, and there were already some calls for him to be dropped. Here he was in a pressure situation, and he had to come up with the goods. He started a little nervously, and he was hardly into his stride when he went after a length ball from Simon Jones and hit it straight to cover, only for the catch to be put down by Kevin Pietersen. We all drop catches, and there is no way that I would ever blame a team-mate for putting down a chance but, in the end, it proved to be the pivotal moment in the game. Clarke went on to get a rapid-fire 91, Damien Martyn got 65 at the other end, and by the time Simon Katich brought up his own half century, Australia were almost out of sight. After three days of the most intense cricket I have ever played, we found ourselves in a position that so many England teams had been in previously, trying to play catch-up to the best side in the world.

After finally bowling out the Aussies for 384, we were faced with getting 420 to win the game. As Trescothick and I strapped on our pads for the second time, there was a realisation within the team that in all likelihood the task was going to be beyond us. Individually, however, we all had much to prove. Australia were full of confidence, and McGrath, in particular, was revelling in his first-innings performance. We had to show that it was a one-off, and that he had not created any psychological damage to exploit in the coming Test matches.

Things went pretty much according to plan, with us reaching 83 without loss. Suddenly there was just a slight scent of victory on the horizon if everything went our way. Unfortunately, as has been the case so often in previous series, it was Warne who scuppered all our hopes. He bowled brilliantly on a wearing pitch to get rid of Trescothick, Bell and Flintoff and, after a brief moment's respite when the heavens opened on the fourth morning, Australia cleaned up our tail to earn a thoroughly deserved 239-run victory.

We sat in our dressing-room after the presentation ceremony as dejected as it is possible to be. We had thrown so much preparation, emotion, toil and will into the game, and had come off comfortably second best. We could draw some comfort from the fact that we had competed with them for large periods of the game, but as we made the journey back to our hotel one final time, it was very difficult not to feel as though we had let the nation down. So much anticipation had come alongside the game and we hadn't reacted to it very well. We were fully expecting to receive a hammering in the papers the next day, and not surprisingly that's exactly what we got.

Dear Australia,
Congratulations on winning the first Test match by 239 runs. You
were great. We beg to remain, sirs, your humble servants,
The England cricket team.

ENGLAND concluded this match in a mood that was not so
much quiescent as downright sycophantic. When rain robbed us
of two entire sessions at Lord's yesterday, England had the
remotest of remote chances of saving the game; admittedly one
that involved hanging on yesterday and then performing an
all-night rain dance.

It was a grim scenario and it required consequent grimness
from the England batsmen, resuming on 156 for five. But England
came out in holiday humour and went on a cheerful splurge,
blowing the last five wickets in 61 balls. Oh colonial masters, you
are great, great is your wisdom, great your cricket, and we bow
down to you to acknowledge your infinite superiority.

Simon Barnes in *The Times* summed up the mood of the nation
when he wrote this article in the aftermath of the game. After
reading it, I used it as motivation for the rest of the series. I was
angry with my own performance, out for 2 and 37, I was angry at
the team's performance, and I was also angry at the way the press
had reacted to the defeat. We had played near-perfect cricket for
18 months, and in the space of one game we were being written
off. If we needed any further motivation to pick ourselves up and
come out fighting for the Second Test, now we had it.

First, however, we all needed to get away from the ridiculously
intense atmosphere that accompanied the Ashes series, take a week
off, and regain some perspective. In just ten days we were going
to be in make-or-break territory. If we could win at Edgbaston,

our quest for the urn was well and truly back on track; if we lost, then it was almost certain that our dream of holding the Ashes would remain exactly that: a dream.

11
DOWN TO THE WIRE

For me it was a chance meeting with Stephen Fleming, the New Zealand captain, that finally enabled me to get rid of the demons of that first demoralising defeat. In an effort to spend some time away from the cricket pitch, I had joined up with my Middlesex team-mates for a game of golf during the week in between the Tests. As I arrived at the golf club, I was more than a little surprised to see Fleming, and most of his team hurriedly putting on their golf shoes in the locker-room.

'Hi, Flem,' I said, trying to take in exactly what the New Zealand cricket team were doing at a golf course in the UK. 'Are you lot not meant to be on tour somewhere?'

'Actually we are on our way to South Africa, and they have cancelled our flight for some reason. You don't mind if we join in with the golf, do you?' came the reply. Anyone who has seen Fleming play golf would never refuse a chance to take such easy money off the man, and both myself and the Middlesex boys were delighted to have a round and a couple of beers with the New Zealanders.

It was in the clubhouse at the end of the round that the inevitable subject of the Ashes came up. 'How are you guys feeling after the Lord's game?' he asked, in a surprisingly serious tone. 'Well,' I replied, 'pretty gutted, to be honest. We felt that we were on a bit of a roll during the one-dayers, but we have had to come back down to earth.'

His reply really surprised me. 'You don't know how close you are. The Aussies are definitely ruffled by your quick bowlers; a few of their key players are out of nick, and they were flattered by the result. If you guys keep playing the way you are, you have got a real chance.'

He was the first person to put some real perspective on the situation. For six weeks now we had been fighting with the Aussies tooth and nail, both in the Twenty 20 match, and the one-dayers. The results had shown two very evenly matched sides. One bad Test match did not change things. Also Fleming had gained his reputation as one of the world's best captains largely by getting his team to perform well against Australia. He knew what it took to beat them, and it was incredibly reassuring to hear those words. From that point on I felt a renewed sense of purpose as I prepared myself for the Second Test match. We had surprised the Aussies by our aggressive play and we had to keep playing that way if we wanted to match them.

The build-up to the Second Test was overshadowed a little by the furore created by Ashley Giles, who had accused some former players, and members of the media, of failing to back us after the First Test. I think one journalist had written something along the lines of: 'England may as well play with 10 men if Ashley Giles is playing, he is not going to contribute.' Ashley was well within his rights to feel aggrieved, especially as the First Test was completely dominated by seam bowling. He could hardly be blamed for our defeat.

The reaction of the press to his comments taught us all a valuable lesson. No matter how unfairly we felt we were being treated, there is no point in having a go back at them. There is only one winner. Also, I have to say that most of the media were firmly fighting our corner. Most of the negative stories about the series so far had been focused on the Australian squad. If we could perform well in the coming Test, we knew that the press were itching to get behind us.

The other headline-grabbing news in the lead-up to the game was about a mini-tornado, which had narrowly missed the Edgbaston ground a few days prior to our arrival. It had de-roofed a few houses in the area, and dumped a load of unexpected rain on the unprotected wicket. The groundsman, Steve Rouse, was concerned about the effect it would have and, when we looked at the wicket after our first practice, it did look much greener than usual.

In the final preparation for the game a really honest team meeting saw us dissect the defeat in the First Test, and vow to keep positive in everything we did. We knew that it was the only way to beat them, and resolving ourselves, as a team, to continue these tactics helped to focus the minds ahead of what was already a must-win game. The morning of the Test was a tense affair. The commotion outside the ground, where excitable spectators, many in fancy dress, were waiting to be let in to the stadium, was in marked contrast to the feeling in the dressing-room. We all had a frisson of excitement pulsing through our veins, but there was not much laughing and joking. We were all focusing on the job in hand.

As we finished our warm-up, and were making our way over to the nets, I heard one of the players saying, 'McGrath's gone over. It looks serious.' We usually try not to spend too much time looking at what the opposition is up to on the day of the game – it can be quite distracting – but this news had all of us, without exception, peeking over to the Australian warm-up area. From an

Australian point of view, the sight was not a good one. McGrath lay prostrate on the ground, obviously in a lot of pain. Their physio and a few of the players were trying to help him on to his feet, but the task was proving difficult. It was obvious that he was not going to be fit to play. What a strange quirk of fate. Glenn McGrath, their chief architect of destruction, a player who never seems to get injured, had severely twisted his ankle by inadvertently standing on a cricket ball while warming up. Although no player likes to see another get injured, it did look like the omens were in our favour.

The situation was compounded by the toss. Despite the effects of the tornado hitting the ground, the wicket had dried out considerably by the first morning. Anyone who has played at Edgbaston knows that it is very much a bat-first wicket. I knew that to my cost, as I had decided to have a bowl when Middlesex fielded first a couple of years earlier and I led my team to an early defeat. Although the wicket was likely to do a little in the first hour of the match, the increasing variation in the bounce as the wicket deteriorated would more than make up for the tricky period that the team batting first would have to go through.

When Ponting won the toss, we were sure that the Aussies were likely to bat first, especially as their leading seam bowler had just been injured, and their remaining match-winner, Shane Warne, would have wanted to bowl last, when the wicket was wearing. Trescothick and I were gobsmacked, therefore, to be strapping on our pads five minutes later. Ponting had put us in, and we couldn't understand why. Perhaps the Aussies felt that our batting line-up was fragile after the performance in the First Test. Whatever the reason, they had presented us with a gilt-edged opportunity to grab the momentum of the game.

After the first over came and went, it soon became apparent that the wicket was a belter. Trescothick was easing Brett Lee and Jason Gillespie through the covers, and the lightning-fast outfield meant that we didn't have to trouble ourselves by doing any running. After ten overs we were 50/0, and it was clear that our positive intent was paying dividends.

Shane Warne came into the attack to do some damage limitation work. He had extracted a huge amount of turn during the Lord's Test and, as he came in to bowl, I was concerned about what he was going to get out of this wicket. After three fairly unthreatening deliveries, I had a choice to make. It was clear that this would be the moment to attack if ever there was one, but it was still a little difficult to do so early in the match. I thought back to our team meetings, and decided to try and go after him. The next ball was well flighted, and provided the perfect opportunity to get down the track. I got down to the pitch and hit the ball straight over his head. It signalled our intent, and from then on, things became much easier against the legspinning maestro.

Warne, being the bowler he is, relished the challenge, and eventually bowled me for 48 shortly before lunch. Trescothick continued on, and even had the audacity to hit Lee for 16 in the over before the break. At lunch we were 130/1, and the momentum had been seized.

Things continued in the same vein after the break. Trescothick played magnificently to get 90, Flintoff got a well-earned fifty, and when we were finally dismissed just before the close, we had scored 400. Some pundits and commentators were disappointed that we didn't show more application, and go on to get a much larger score, but I believe they missed the point. Australia, as a side, has very rarely lost control during a match in the last decade.

Whenever a team was starting to get on top, the captain was able to turn to McGrath and Warne to put a lid on things. In this match, without McGrath, Ponting had difficulty in stemming the flow of runs. For an English side, used to being on the receiving end of Australian onslaughts, it was fantastic to watch, and showed more than anything that we weren't prepared to roll over and die.

The key to the game, however, lay with the bowlers. We needed to have a lead going into the final two days, as Warne was likely to figure more and more as the game progressed. As Vaughan gave his final instructions in the dressing-room, it was clear that they were all pumped up. When you have three bowlers in the side capable of bowling over 90 miles an hour, and you see them raring to go, then you know that it is going to be difficult for the opposition.

We got off to the perfect start, Hoggard removing Hayden first ball, caught at short-cover. It was one of a number of unconventional field placings that Vaughan employed against the Australian batsmen. Duncan Fletcher has the uncanny ability to dissect a player's technique better than anyone else I have known. He looks at the fundamentals, grip, stance, backlift, and then figures out which shots a player will find difficult to play, and which deliveries he is likely to struggle against. It means nothing if the bowlers are unable to exploit those plans, or if the batsman enjoys a lot of fortune, but over the couple of years that I have played for the side, he had very rarely been wrong about any player's technique. Over the course of a series, the weaknesses that he identifies will lead to their downfall. Hayden's hard hands, and willingness to drive on the up had led to his downfall here, and the Australians were under pressure.

Ponting and Langer frustrated us to get Australia to the relative safety of 88/1, but it was to be the turn of Ashley Giles to dictate proceedings. The wicket of Ponting, who was caught sweeping, was a brilliant moment for Ashley, who had been on the receiving end of so much stick from the press, and the whole team rushed to embrace him. We could all appreciate what he had been through over the last week, and it was a great opportunity for us all to show our support. He went on to take the wickets of two of Australia's most dangerous stroke-players, Clarke and Warne, and finished with figures of 3/78.

Flintoff bagged three wickets of his own, and Australia were bowled out for 308, giving us a lead of 99 runs. With the pitch likely to deteriorate over the last three days, we knew what a fantastic position we were in. All we had to do was negotiate the final few overs of the second day, and then work hard to build a sizeable lead. Things did not happen as we envisaged.

The day ended badly when Warne bowled me for the second time in the match on 6, offering no stroke to a ball that pitched a yard outside off stump. On TV it looked like an unplayable delivery, but as I reached the dressing-room, I was furious at myself for getting out like that. My team-mates gave me the customary five minutes to cool down, before Pietersen chirped up with, 'Not sure that you should have left that one, Straussy.' I had to laugh. Warne had bamboozled me, like he had so many other players, and I would have to work hard in the days before the next match to counteract his ever present danger.

The next morning started even worse with Trescothick, Vaughan and Pietersen all back in the hut before lunch. Warne was doing his magician's trick, conjuring up sleights of hand to dismiss uncertain batsmen, and by the time we reached a hundred, we were already seven wickets down. Australia had clawed their way back into the match. Thankfully, Flintoff was in no mood to simply lie down and die. He counter-attacked brilliantly and, with the help of Simon Jones, managed to put on 51 for the final wicket, taking us up to 182, and leaving Australia 282 to win.

The mood in the dressing-room was one of quiet determination. We knew that we had lost the chance to bury the Aussies, but we were still encouraged by the way the wicket was playing. It looking like it was hard work to bat out there, and if we did everything right with the ball, it was going to be difficult for Australia to reach the target. This was do or die time. We had to take ten wickets in order to keep our hopes of winning the series alive, and our bowlers ran in accordingly.

Hayden and Langer weathered the storm well to reach 47 without loss, before Flintoff – who else – provided the inspiration we needed. In what was probably the best over of the series, he bowled Langer via his elbow, and then proceeded to send down three unplayable deliveries to Ponting, before finding his edge with the final delivery. The ball was starting to reverse, and with Australia already two wickets down, we knew that we held all the aces.

In what turned out to be a bit of a procession, Hayden, Martyn, Katich, Gilchrist and Gillespie all followed each other back to the pavilion. Australia had gone from 46/0 to 137/7 in a crazy hour and a half. The victory target of 282 seemed a mile away, and when Clarke was deceived by a Harmison slower ball to finish the day, we knew that the game was as good as won. With Brett Lee at the crease alongside Shane Warne, and only Michael Kasprowicz to come in, it would take them a miracle to score the remaining 107 runs. From previous experiences against Australia, we were aware it was dangerous to count our chickens before they hatched, but that evening, sitting in a trendy restaurant in the middle of Birmingham with Vaughan, Giles and Trescothick, I relaxed for the first time in the series. Talk was about going out and winning the Ashes. Mentally the match was in the bag.

Casting my mind back to that final day at Edgbaston still fills me with the same kind of dread that you feel when you realise you have just missed an important meeting, or locked yourself out of your house. For us, though, that feeling didn't come as a shock, but a gradual swelling, before reaching an unbearable crescendo when Australia got closer to the finish line. The day started in good humour, with thousands of England fans turning up to watch the landmark victory procession. A few die-hard Australian fans started singing, 'Ninety-six runs to go, ninety-six runs to go' to the tune of 'Hi ho, the diary oh', starting again with every single taken. They weren't expecting to get close, but they were determined to enjoy the day nonetheless. After an hour, however, things were just starting to get uncomfortable. Whereas every ball seemed as if it was going to take a wicket the evening before, during that morning two of their less talented batsmen didn't look like they were in any trouble against the pride of English bowling. A few boundaries at the start of play from Warne could be appreciated by the fieldsmen, and the endless chants from the Australian fans, 'Seventy-six runs to go, seventy-six runs to go' even raised a few smiles, but by the time they got within 65, we were beginning to get a little disturbed.

Our nerves were calmed by Warne getting out with 62 still needed and, with Kasprowicz striding nervously out to bat, we could once again cast our thoughts forward to having a couple of beers and a night out in Birmingham. Brett Lee, however, had other ideas. He saw the dismissal of Warne as his cue to take a few risks, and tucked into Ashley Giles in particular. With every ball that hit the middle of his bat, we could all sense that his confidence was growing, and much of it was rubbing off on Kasprowicz at the other end.

By the time the Aussie fans got their countdown below 25, things were starting to get out of hand. Gone was the swagger and confidence of earlier in the day. Vaughan had tried all our bowlers and, with the exception of Flintoff, who was still threatening with short deliveries, they were struggling to stem the flow of runs. Standing in the slips was torturous. On the one hand, we had little control of events, and had spent most of the last hour watching the ball being retrieved from the boundary, but on the other, we knew that at any moment we could be called on to take a difficult catch to win us the game. Drop it, and there was every chance that whoever the lucky man was would see his picture in the papers the next morning with a turnip on his head. None of us wanted to be that man.

Unfortunately, Simon Jones was the man that the cricketing gods picked out to take a difficult catch at third man when Australia still needed 15. His athletic dive forward enabled him to get his hands under the ball, but he was unable to hang on. The moment the ball dropped free from his hands was like a dagger through the heart. It was clear it was not our day. Fielders who had spent all morning clapping and encouraging the bowlers started to go quiet, thinking about the ramifications of clutching defeat from the jaws of victory, and Vaughan was suddenly a very lonely man. We had all run out of ideas.

As the Australian tailenders neared the finish line, with only a few runs needed, it was clear that they were starting to feel the pressure more. When they came together they were not expected to get anywhere near, now their team-mates were thinking that they should go on and finish the job. We, on the other hand, got a second wind. Even if they only needed two to win, we still had a chance, as we only needed one wicket.

As it happened, they needed three to win, when Harmison surprised Kasprowicz with a short ball which hit the glove and carried to Geraint Jones behind the wicket. It was obvious to all of us that it was out, and the moment we saw Billy Bowden raise his finger, all hell broke loose. We all started jumping around completely uncontrollably. Geraint Jones ran off to show some of the Aussie fans what he thought of their heckling throughout the last day, Flintoff grasped Vaughan in one of his giant bear hugs, and the rest of us just jumped up and down in a circle. It was madness, and the fact that I can remember very little of it speaks volumes. We were lost in the emotion.

I am not ashamed to admit that the plight of the two mortified Australian batsmen was the last thing on my mind as we walked off the field. I should have felt for them, as Warne, Lee and Kasprowicz had done an incredible job in getting them so close to the target, but I was still coming to terms with the fact that we had won the game. It says much for the character of Freddie Flintoff that he had the presence of mind to put a consolatory arm around Brett Lee's shoulder. It was a great sporting gesture, and single-handedly brought the players of both teams much closer together after all the posturing of the previous couple of months.

In the dressing-room in the hour that followed, there was very little of the wild celebrations that you would expect from a win like that. We all felt a bit hollow, as if we didn't have any emotion left to celebrate with. I remember vividly staring at Giles and not having a thing to say apart from just shaking my head slowly. He did exactly the same in return. It was a little like just avoiding a head-on collision on a motorway. Words could not express the terror and relief. We had levelled the series.

Three days was not a lot of time to get over the horrendous hangover after a great night out in Birmingham, put the momentous events of Edgbaston to the back of our minds, and prepare fully for the Old Trafford Test match. For me, those three days were made even shorter because I had to come up with an improved game-plan against Shane Warne in that time.

Shane Warne is, without doubt, the greatest spin bowler of all time. In due course it is likely that Muralitharan or someone else will take more wickets than him, but no one has the unwavering confidence in his ability, and the iron will to affect the course of a game by his own actions that Shane Warne has. As you square up to him as a batsman, you know that he will be continuously probing for weaknesses from ball one. He will use variations in pace and spin to test whether you can read his hand, and then he will bowl from different areas on the crease, and use the rough outside the left-hander's off stump if you pass that first test. He doesn't mind going for the odd boundary, as often he is trying to set you up for one of his faster or viciously turning deliveries. He gives the impression that he has already bowled the over to you in his head long before the first delivery comes down.

What sticks out is his immense will to win. There were times during the summer where Australia was dead and buried. Either with the bat or the ball he would then grab at any thread that we left dangling for them, and contrive to claw Australia back into the game. He does not and will not ever rest on his laurels, whether it is for his club side in Melbourne, for Hampshire, or for Australia in an Ashes Test match. I don't know whether he continuously feels the need to prove himself or whether he just enjoys the personal duels between batsman and bowler so much, but every time you face him, you know that you have a real battle on your hands. It is incredible that he has managed to play Test cricket for 15 years, overcome a few potentially career-threatening injuries, and yet still be able to perform at the very highest levels. Anyone who is capable of doing that must have a real deep-rooted motivation to compete, and that is the secret of his success.

Although he lets the opposition feel very inch of that competitive fire out in the middle, he is the first one to chat to youngsters, and spend valuable time after the game chewing the fat with opponents, talking about anything to do with the game. I think that he is genuinely in love with the game of cricket, and will keep playing as long as he possibly can.

That thought was not of particular comfort to me as I walked out to the practice area at Old Trafford the day before the Third Test. Nor, for that matter, were memories of the previous Test where he had got me out twice. I had to come up with some sort of a plan pretty quickly if I wanted to keep him at bay on one of the most spin-friendly wickets in the country. We were fortunate to have a prototype bowling machine travelling around the country with us called Merlyn. It had taken its inventor a decade to get it fizzing out balls with a similar spin and trajectory to Warne, and it became increasingly invaluable to us as the series progressed. That day I spent close to three hours playing correct shots, incorrect shots, and shots that even my mother would be embarrassed to play. The idea was to work out which balls I could score off without taking a massive risk, and which shots had to be kept in the locker. The key to playing someone like Warne is to have a method of getting off strike. If you allow him to bowl six balls at you over after over, eventually one will misbehave and you will get out. As Mike Gatting used to say to me, 'The easiest way to play world-class bowlers is from the other end.' With Warne this is very much the case.

I felt far more certain about my method as I went to bed the night before the game, and a restful night's sleep was only ruined by a dream in which Australia managed to score those winning runs at Edgbaston, and I was the one to drop the catch. It would take more than a few days for us to get that game out of our systems.

The build-up to the Test had been dominated by the fitness of Glenn McGrath and Brett Lee, Australia's main fast bowlers. Lee had picked up a knee infection during the course of the Edgbaston Test and McGrath was making a miraculous recovery from the ankle injury he sustained a week earlier. From England's point of view it was best to prepare for them both playing and, in the end, they both did. The toss at Old Trafford is always crucial, and even more so with the opposition having Warne in their ranks. Vaughan, who was developing a useful habit of winning them after a horror run the previous summer, had no hesitation in batting first. Our bowlers were still feeling the effects of the monumental efforts during the previous Test, and the wicket looked like a belter to bat on.

Despite me being cleaned up by Lee early, things went very much to plan that first morning. Vaughan was at his imperious best, clearly enjoying the pace and bounce that the pitch offered.

He had not had the most productive of starts to the series, but his back-foot drives and pulls reminded everyone of his class and put the Australians on the back foot again. It was important to prove that the Edgbaston victory was not a fluke, and at 290/2 shortly after tea we were once again in charge of the game. A flurry of late wickets, including Vaughan and Pietersen, brought the Aussies back into the game, but at 341/5 we were still well placed, especially as Flintoff was yet to come in. We would only find out on day two how much the Edgbaston Test had taken out of our bowlers. We needed to get well past 400 to give us some breathing space.

Our final score of 444 gave us the perfect platform to be aggressive at the Australian top order, many of whom were showing increasing signs of being out of nick. Hayden and Langer weathered a testing new-ball spell before Giles once again proved his class by removing both the openers, and Damien Martyn with one of the balls of the summer. He has been criticised for bowling too often over the wicket to right-handers, but many people do not realise that he doesn't do it for negative reasons. He has the ability to get very close to the stumps, so that he is still able to get lbw decisions, and when one turns and bounces out of the rough, as was the case with Martyn, there is a chance of getting players out bowled or caught at slip. The fact that he is harder to score off from over the wicket is a useful by-product, but he does it mainly to take wickets.

Katich and Gilchrist both succumbed to the seamers, and suddenly Australia were 186/6, and facing the prospect of not making the follow-on. I doubt strongly whether Vaughan would have enforced it, largely due to the unsavoury prospect of facing Warne on the final day, but it was the legspinner himself who put the issue beyond doubt. Over the course of the evening, a short session on day three, where the weather restricted play to only 14 overs, and the morning of day four, he flicked, flayed and muscled our bowlers to all parts of the ground. It was a one-man effort to haul the Aussies back into the game, but just when it looked like he was destined to make a century, a full-blooded hook shot managed to find its way straight into the arms of Giles at deep mid-wicket. Simon Jones snapped up the final two wickets, giving him six for the innings, and the Aussies were out for 302, 142 short of our first innings.

The approach to our second innings was very much one of initial caution. We knew that we had a limited amount of time to get enough runs in order to declare, but our over-attacking start at Edgbaston in the second innings had left us reeling and had brought Australia back into the game. Despite a more cautious approach, Trescothick was smiting the ball to all parts, and I, feeling a little out of form, and battling against the pace of Lee, was very much the junior partner. Despite telling myself time and time again not to try and hook the Aussie speedster on the fast bouncy track, I still managed to get hit twice by him attempting that very shot. When you have such a short amount of time to make a decision on how to counteract a ball, it is easy to premeditate a shot, and my instincts said hook rather than duck. I got an incredibly stiff neck and bleeding ear for my misjudgments.

My main concern, though, was the thought of playing Warne on a wicket taking increasing turn. In some ways it was lucky that we were forced to be positive, due to the game situation, but it was very satisfying to see that some of the methods I had worked on prior to the game were coming off. In the main, Ian Bell, who joined me with the score at 97/2, and I contented ourselves by taking singles off the maestro, and scoring off the seamers at the other end.

As the day wore on, I neared a hundred, and England neared a declaration. I remember Matthew Hayden at slip saying to me, when on 80, 'You must be loving this, there is nothing better than batting with no pressure during an Ashes Test, as an opener.' He should know, as he has opened for Australia many times with them completely in control of a game, and winning the series. The truth was that he was right. Without the pressure of knowing that your dismissal could get England into a huge amount of trouble, I flew through the 90s, hitting Warne for a six, and then despatching McGrath to mid-wicket to bring up the hundred. I had scored my first Ashes century, and it was an exceptionally proud moment. As I took off my helmet, unveiling a ridiculous-looking plaster which was holding together my damaged ear, and raised my bat, I revelled in the fact that I had overcome some demons in reaching the score, had contributed to England being in a position to win the Test match, but at the back of my mind, I also realised that they were likely to be the easiest runs I would score against Australia, certainly in the series, but in all probability in my career.

A second 50 in the match for Ian Bell, and some lusty hitting from Geraint Jones, meant that the skipper could call us in 30 minutes before the close of play, setting Australia 423 to win. To me, it looked like a great declaration. We had over a day to bowl them out, and it was unlikely that they would get close to the runs, although if two of them really got going, that carrot might just lead to their downfall. The final day was going to be full of exactly the same drama and suspense that had characterised the series so far.

The suspense started well before the match got underway. Spectators were able to buy tickets for the final day's play in the morning and, such was the interest in the potential drama, that well over 30,000 members of the public turned up searching for 20,000 elusive tickets. While it was bizarre to see so many people milling around the gates of Old Trafford at 9 a.m., and gave us our first real glimpse of the cricket mania that was sweeping the country, it soon became clear that it wasn't going to be easy for us to get into the ground. There was a queue of cars well over a mile long in front of me as I approached the ground, and there wasn't much time to spare before we were due on deck. A peek out the window, and a couple of frantic calls to team-mates later, I realised that the police had shut down the roads, because there were so many pedestrians around, and I was forced into a potentially dangerous, and highly illegal manoeuvre of driving down the wrong side of the road to cover the distance to the police blockades, before sheepishly asking the PC on duty, whose face was crimson with rage, whether I might possibly get through in order to play the game. He grudgingly agreed before bracing himself for six or seven other cars carrying players to come roaring up the right-hand side of the road. In short it was mayhem.

In due course, Australia faced mayhem too, when Langer was out to the first ball of the day, and Flintoff uprooted Hayden's leg stump, but they were to be our only successes before lunch. Ponting was looking increasingly certain on the final-day wicket, and we weren't getting the amount of turn we expected. This one was again destined to go down to the wire.

During the afternoon session it kept looking as though the chance of victory was slipping away from us, before a wicket would bring us back into it. Harmison dismissed Martyn, and Flintoff got the two key wickets of Katich and Gilchrist shortly before tea. Australia were five wickets down, Michael Clarke was carrying a back injury, and we were only one wicket away from exposing the tail.

As we munched on our sandwiches, and sipped on our energy drinks, the atmosphere was unbelievably tense. Our bowlers were exhausted, Simon Jones was receiving treatment for cramp, and we knew that the final session was likely to be in the lap of the gods, with the game going down to the wire.

The session started brightly enough with Simon Jones reverse swinging one back to take out Clarke's off stump. Gillespie, who had an annoying knack of hanging around was trapped lbw, and the Aussies were seven wickets down, with 30 overs still to be played. Warne's style of batting is not ideally suited to blocking out for a draw, but with Ponting having reached a brilliant hundred at the other end, he decided that attack was the best form of defence, and for 20 overs their combined aggression blunted our attack, and also raised the slim prospect of an Australian victory.

With a hundred needed and under ten overs to be played, the prospect of defeat was far-fetched, but three wickets seemed like too many to get. Flintoff was getting some extravagant reverse swing, and Marcus Trescothick, standing at first slip, turned around to me and said, 'Warne is nicking this ball, and it is going to you.' 'Right,' I muttered sarcastically in reply, before witnessing a flashing blade, and a ball travelling right at me. I saw it all the way, got in the perfect position to take the catch, and suddenly whack, the ball hit me on the thigh. Don't ask me how, but it had missed my hands completely, hit my leg and had looped up in front of Geraint Jones. Fortunately his reactions were far better than mine, and he dived sideways and scooped the ball just before it hit the ground. Australia were eight wickets down, and I hobbled to Flintoff with a sheepish look on my face, talking defensively about the difficult background and dodgy light conditions.

The scriptwriter in the sky added more drama to the situation by ensuring that Ponting gloved one down the leg side with four overs still left in the game. He had played a monumental innings, seen Australia all the way to the brink of safety, and had fallen at the final hurdle. It was a cruel blow that he didn't deserve.

Four overs at McGrath seemed like more than enough, but our bowlers were completely exhausted, and Lee at the other end was farming the strike, so that he faced most of the balls. We could not believe that we were in such a tight situation again, only a week after the famous Edgbaston win. With the last over about to be bowled, a message was sent out to McGrath to bat out of his crease, so as to take the lbw out of the equation. The first ball of the over was down the leg side, and Geraint Jones quickly under-armed the ball back to Ian Bell at short-leg, to prevent Brett Lee from getting on strike. Bell collected the ball and seeing that they were not attempting the run, casually threw it back to the bowler. We thought nothing more about it, until sharing a beer with the Aussies after the match; they brought it to our attention that McGrath had never got back in his crease. He was out of his ground, and if Bell had dislodged the bails he would have been out. I don't know if there were any cameras that picked it up, so I can't be sure if it was the truth, but I suppose the game didn't deserve to finish in that way.

Brett Lee got his bat on the final delivery from Steve Harmison, the ball rolled safely away for four and Australia saved the game. Vaughan called his fatigued and dejected troops together, told us to look up at the Australian dressing-room, which was full of high-fives and slaps on the back, and told us how proud he was of us as a team. Who had seen the Australian cricket team ever celebrate a draw before?

12
HOLDING THE URN

Following the two unbelievably tense Test matches, the country was well and truly gripped by cricket. Football stars were being asked about their thoughts on the Ashes, and I even remember Arsene Wenger having to fend off a few cricket-related questions in one of his pre-season press conferences. Streets up and down the country, including my own heavily sloped one, were acquiring makeshift wickets, and enthusiastic youngsters, trying to emulate the incredible feats of Flintoff and Pietersen, were smacking tennis balls in all directions.

Everywhere I went during the week off in between the Third and Fourth Test, I was met by people who wanted to give us their best wishes, and most sentences usually included the phrase, 'You have to beat those Aussie bastards.' It was brilliant to feel as though we were part of something important, but it also made it a little difficult to get away from the cricket. On the morning following the Old Trafford Test, for example, I was enjoying a bowl of cereal, listening to Radio 1, when Chris Moyles started replaying one of the interviews I had done for radio earlier during the week, and comparing my voice to *Big Brother* contestant, Eugene, who was rapidly becoming famous for his geekiness. I thought it was a bit harsh, but judging by the number of text messages that came through from my team-mates, the rest of the boys loved it.

Surprisingly, the ECB had received a bit of stick during the week off about some of the players being unavailable to play for their counties in the Cheltenham & Gloucester semi-finals. I can understand the counties trying to make the most of cricket's new-found popularity, but even the most parochial of county chairmen surely understood that a week of rest was the best way to prepare for the all-important Fourth Test, especially after all the tension of the previous two. It seemed like a strange time to be finding fault with the ECB's management of players.

Despite all the goings on, we headed into the Fourth Test feeling refreshed and confident that we had Australia on the ropes. In a two- or three-Test series there is not really enough time for players to take a psychological hold on members of the other team, but it was clear that the Australian batsmen were not enjoying the reverse swing that Jones and Flintoff were able to get. Reverse swing is a mysterious art at the best of times, and asking a batsman to talk about it is a little like asking mink about fur coats. We are the ones that it is done to, and as a result know very little about it. It is, however, the hardest type of swing to counter. For a start the ball seems to move later in the air, causing last-second adjustments, and also, good exponents are able to get it reversing both ways, something that is more difficult with conventional swing. Batsmen have to look very carefully at which way the ball is put into the bowler's hand to get an indication of which way it is going to swing. It is a dangerous game of Russian roulette, as bowlers can change grip while running up, and sometimes it is better just to react to what is coming down at you.

The real mystery with reverse swing is how to get the ball in the right condition to swing properly. There are an unbelievable number of theories as to how it is done, and there is no doubt that the easiest way is to rub one side of the ball against concrete for half an hour. As Angus Fraser, my former captain at Middlesex, once observed: 'The one thing to be said about ball tampering – it works.' Unfortunately, we can't do that during a game, so most of the time you are relying on keeping one side of the ball dry, and hoping that the ground conditions help to rough up the ball. The days of using bottle tops and other illegal means to get the ball in the right condition have gone, but our bowlers showed how important it is to get the old ball swinging around. Looking back, it could have been the most decisive factor in our Ashes victory.

The one difficulty we faced was with the Trent Bridge wicket. Although the pitch itself looked like a good batting wicket, the outfield was green and lush. This meant that the ball was unlikely to reverse swing nearly as much as it had done in the previous two Test matches. We would have to rely on other methods to prise out Australian batsmen. One of those would be with conventional swing. For some reason, and don't ask me to explain why, Trent Bridge helps genuine swing bowlers, and Matthew Hoggard, who had done his job, but had not taken too many wickets leading up to the game, was expected to play a pivotal role. For Australia, Glenn McGrath looked as if he was going to be unfit, and the uncapped Shaun Tait was expected to make his debut. The only footage we had of him was from the previous season, where he had played one game for Durham, and had gone for a hundred off ten overs, including a host of no-balls. But he had a low slingy action that looked difficult to pick up, and with the sightscreens at Trent Bridge being small, and usually decorated around the edges with very beautiful baskets of multi-coloured flowers, he had potential to cause problems.

This Test match will always be ingrained in my head as the 'Rocket Man' Test. We travel around the world with a huge number of gadgets, many of which are of little use in places like Pakistan. The one gadget that never seems to fail in lifting spirits is the iPod and speakers that accompany us to every ground. For some reason, at Trent Bridge, Freddie Flintoff assigned himself as the unofficial DJ, and from the moment Trescothick and I walked out to bat on the first day, to the final dramatic moments where Ashley Giles and Matthew Hoggard were seeing us to victory, the tunes of Elton John were never far away.

The match itself followed a similar pattern to the previous two. Vaughan won the toss, Trescothick and I put on a hundred runs quickly on a flat wicket, against the McGrath-less attack, and Australia pegged us back a little towards the end of the day, especially when Vaughan got out to his opposite number, Ricky Ponting. It was Flintoff, however, who took the game away from Australia. Listening to him bellowing out 'Rocket Man' just as the Australian team was walking on to the field on the morning of his innings left no one in any doubts as to his mood. He was relaxed, confident, and keen to take centre-stage. His century was an awesome innings from a man who had done more than anyone this series to wrestle away the initiative from the Aussies. Flintoff has had to deal with some difficult times over the course of his career, none more so than living with the label of the 'next great thing'.

How many times has a child prodigy been handed that label in a particular sport, only for them to fail to live up to the massive expectations they have been burdened with, find it hard to deal with the failure, and slowly fade into the background, to post-mortems about where they went wrong, what they lacked, and whose or what influences they should have stayed clear of. Cricket has seen more examples of this than most sports. Maybe it is because there has been a collective longing from the media and the public for England to produce a genuinely world-class player to take over the heavy mantle worn by Ian Botham for so long, or maybe it was just desperate attempts by selectors to find a player to provide new impetus to an ailing England side. Mark Ramprakash, Graeme Hick, John Crawley, Dominic Cork, and latterly Ben Hollioake, all were forced to deal with these pressures and struggled to contend with the expectation.

A few years ago, another player seemed in danger of joining the casualty list. Freddie Flintoff always looked like the ideal candidate to be a world-class allrounder. I remember playing against him for Durham University, when he was representing England Under-19, and being astounded by how hard he could hit the ball. His progress, however, was hindered by back injuries, which curtailed his bowling, and by a difficult transition into the professional ranks. But even when he was struggling, his blistering power still managed to turn heads. With the England side longing for new blood, he was rushed into the team at the tender age of 20 by selectors who hoped that the intensity of Test cricket would bring the best out of him.

The next three or four years followed a fairly similar pattern. The odd brilliant performance to remind everyone of his immense talent was intermingled with periods where he found it difficult to adjust to playing at the highest level. Some were already sharpening their pencils in order to write the post-mortems when he finally found the consistency in both his batting and bowling that turned him into a solid international performer. By the time I came into the England side in late 2003 he had definitely turned the corner. In ODI cricket he was undoubtedly our best bowler, and most dangerous batsman, while in Test cricket he was starting to take the wickets he had deserved for a couple of years. He played brilliantly throughout our 7–0 summer, and looked every inch the world-class allrounder that everyone had thought he could become all those years before. With the Ashes just around the corner, everyone wondered whether he could repeat those performances against the best. That was where the real test lay.

The public perception of Freddie is that he is a very laid-back character. He goes out, hits the ball as hard as he can, bowls his heart out, then comes back to the hotel, doesn't think about the cricket at all, enjoys a beer, and then does it all again the next day. In some ways he seems to be a relic from the past. Last summer, against the Aussies, that image was completely transformed. The start of the series was difficult for both him and the team as we surrendered the First Test at Lord's. It was hard for all of us to deal with the expectation, but Freddie, more than any of us, had the hopes of the nation resting on his shoulders. The way that he reacted to that pressure assured us in the team, and everyone watching the cricket, that he was not going to fail in this ultimate test.

After Lord's, he did the right thing in getting away from all the attention, took stock of the situation, and turned up at Edgbaston determined to take the game to Australia. Anyone who saw the passion on his face every time he took a wicket could tell that something was different with Andrew Flintoff. Here was a man who was facing his ultimate test against the side in comparison with which all England players are ultimately judged. Not only was he starting to succeed personally, but he also was pulling the rest of the side along with his gargantuan efforts. Michael Vaughan deserves much credit for instilling a belief in the team that we could beat the Australians, but Freddie did more than anyone to show us that our belief was not misplaced.

Gone were the days of idle banter in the slip cordon. Suddenly he was thinking up ideas on how to get opposition batsmen out. Gone were the days of a quiet kip in the dressing-room when he was not involved in play; instead he was geeing up those who were down on confidence and form. Gone were the days of a quiet beer after play. He was in the ice-bath as quickly as anyone else in order to get himself prepared for the next day's play. Some people may see this as a conscious effort to change his attitude, or a sign of Flintoff maturing as a cricketer, but I don't think it was. I think it was Flintoff showing everyone that underneath his laid-back image there is someone who cares deeply about his performance, his team-mates, and takes great pride in representing his country. It is these traits that really make a world-class cricketer, just as much as having the ability to hit the ball a long way, or bowl at 90 mph.

By the end of the second day we had Australia on the ropes. Flintoff's inspired batting had put us in control of the game, and in reply the Australians were unable to adjust to Hoggard's swing bowling, and were standing on the edge of a precipice at 99/5. All we had to do was wrap up the Australian tail the next morning and we would be in an ideal position to enforce the follow-on and push for an innings victory.

Generally, I am not a great fan of enforcing the follow-on. Bowlers and fielders are tired after bowling a side out first time around, and it is never as easy the second time. Also, the side that are following-on know that they have a slight chance of forcing an unlikely victory if they bat really well. Fourth-innings chases are notoriously difficult, especially if you have a good spinner in your side. The follow-on is only really a good idea if you have little time left in the game, or you are certain that the wicket is sufficiently bad that you won't have to bat again.

By lunchtime on the third day Vaughan had that difficult choice to make; we had bowled out Australia for 217 with some sensational bowling and catching. After the catch that I parried to Geraint Jones in the Third Test, it was incredibly satisfying to feel the ball nestle into my left hand as I dived to catch Adam Gilchrist. It was without doubt the best catch of my career, but it is difficult to remember exactly what happened, let alone describe it. You rely completely on reactions to take slip catches, and in this case all I remember is seeing a ball flying somewhere to my left, and then having it in my hand. I don't remember the dive, or the attempt to get two hands to it, or the last-second change of mind to go at it with one hand. Thankfully Patrick Eagar managed to capture the moment perfectly on film, and if ever I need any help remembering it, I can see the framed print on my wall at home.

At the end of the innings, Vaughan gathered us all around, and asked all the bowlers how they felt about sending the Aussies back in. It was a rushed affair, as we didn't have much time to make the decision, and the feedback from the bowlers was positive – we backed ourselves to bowl them out again. Simon Jones, however, only made it into our huddle later than everyone else, as he was getting his water bottle from the other side of the ground, and during that brief chat did not have the time to tell Vaughan that he was struggling with his ankle. It was to rule him out of bowling in the second innings, and made the task of bowling Australia out again much, much harder.

Langer, Ponting, Clarke, Katich and Warne all reached 40 in their second innings, and as their score went over a hundred beyond ours, Trescothick and I started to become nervous. This was not going to be a case of a couple of boundaries and the game was ours; there was going to be a huge amount of pressure on us and the rest of the team to make sure we crossed the finish line. By the time Tait was last man out, we had a target of 129 to chase, and we knew what to expect – a full-on barrage from Brett Lee and Shane Warne. This was not going to be easy.

129 to get: things start off well enough. Trescothick tucks in to Kasprowicz, and before we know it we have reached 30. I am having a less enjoyable time fending off Brett Lee, who is bowling at 95 mph. Although I am trying to be positive, I know that I can't take on the short stuff, and will have to bide my time.

97 to get: Warne comes into the attack. I can feel my heart beating slightly faster. If Australia are going to pull off a victory, he is likely to be the man to do it. He walks to his mark, flips the ball in the air a couple of times, turns around and walks in to bowl. From the non-striker's end I hear a faint 'Come on, Shane' as he prepares himself yet again for the challenge of doing the remarkable. The ball is perfectly pitched, hits the edge of the footmarks, and clips Trescothick's bat before hitting his pad and nestling in the hand of Ponting at silly-point. We are one down; Warne has struck with his first ball. Australia are still in the game.

93 to get: Warne strikes again, this time getting Vaughan out for a duck with one that finds extravagant turn and bounce. I can feel the tension more now. Australia is beginning to believe.

72 to get: things have calmed down a bit, and I have scored a couple of boundaries off Lee and Warne. I get the sense that they are striving for wickets, and that provides scoring opportunities. Warne comes in to bowl. The ball is straight, and I try to flick it

legside for a single. I get it too fine and it's in the hands of Clarke at leg slip. I didn't see him catch it so I stand my ground. The Aussies tell me where to go. The umpires meet and send the decision to the third official. I look at the big screen, awaiting my fate. Shit, we are three down. Warne has had all three, and my involvement in the game is over. I no longer have any control over events. Next over, Ian Bell is out, caught at fine leg. Our fourth wicket is lost and things are looking extremely bad. Surely we can't lose this game?

26 to get: Pietersen and Flintoff have soaked up the pressure to put on 46 runs. Australian heads are dropping, and excitement levels are rising in the dressing-room. We are nearly there. Lee gets one to move away and Pietersen nicks it. Should be okay though, as long as Flintoff stays in.

18 to get: Lee comprehensively bowls Flintoff. Things are getting tight again. Australia need four wickets, but we still feel just about in control. Watching from the dressing-room is becoming unbearable.

13 to get: I can't believe this. Geraint Jones has just holed out to long-off. Eleven runs suddenly seem like a long way off, and I am having trouble calming down Flintoff, who is alternating between hugging and punching me as a way of controlling the nerves. We are now down to the tail. Hoggard doesn't score too quickly, so much of it is going to be down to Giles.

8 needed: Hoggard and Giles have had some difficult moments against the extreme pace of Lee and the genius of Warne. Lee runs in and sends down a yorker. It is over-pitched and Hoggard drives it away to the boundary. I have never seen him play that shot before. I get another bear hug from Flintoff. We are almost there.

2 needed: we are all arm-in-arm in the dressing-room. One shot

and victory is ours. Everyone is emotional. We have been in turmoil all day. Warne bowls on leg stump, and Giles swats it through mid-wicket for the two runs we need. Absolute pandemonium breaks out. Everyone is jumping around the room without really knowing what to do. We rush downstairs to welcome back our batting heroes, Giles and Hoggard. We shake the Australians' hands and spare a thought for the way they came back at us today. They never give in. It's time for the team song and lots of beer. We are ahead in the Ashes.

The non-stop effort, tension and pressure had taken its toll on everyone by the time we met up for the final Test at The Oval. During a supposed week off I had to do a huge number of interviews, a couple of appearances, a charity golf day, and a benefit dinner. I was beginning to understand what it was like to be a celebrity, and I wasn't particularly enjoying it. It wasn't so much the fact that there were a large number of demands on our time, but more that we had some very important unfinished business to attend to and, even in the most relaxing of situations, the thought of the final series-deciding Test was never far away.

I like to think of myself as a pretty laid-back, relaxed kind of guy. I generally don't get too caught up in what is going on around me, but in the days leading up to this Test match, I was having difficulty sleeping. There was so much riding on this one Test. Win, and we would be riding around Trafalgar Square in an open-top bus. Lose, and it would be the No. 37 bus home with dark glasses on so as not to be recognised by dejected England supporters. I know for a fact that the rest of the boys were feeling exactly the same. This was to be the most important five days of our careers.

The build-up did not go according to plan. Simon Jones, who

had got five-wicket hauls in the previous two Tests, was ruled out on the Tuesday, despite having 24-hour-a-day treatment for the previous week on his troublesome ankle. He was bitterly disappointed, and as he had done so much to get us in position, we were going to be much weaker without him. Paul Collingwood was his replacement, who could offer some batting resistance as well as some useful medium-pace bowling. We could not be sure which would be needed most over the final five days of the series, but every bit of his calm temperament and one-day experience would be needed if we were to succeed. His inclusion took the total number of players used by the England team in the series to 12. Never in recent memory had we had such a settled side.

The other aspect of the build-up that was different from previous Tests was that we could afford to draw the game and still win the series. This gave us a cushion, but also opened a potentially dangerous negative mindset. If we went into a game against Australia playing for the draw, the likelihood was that we would get beaten. It was stressed by both Fletcher and Vaughan at the team meeting that we could not afford to do that. We had to play the same positive, attacking cricket that we had all season. The match was destined to be a nail-biter.

I am awake long before my 7 a.m. wake-up call. Thoughts of what lies ahead made sure that I was tossing and turning for a couple of hours already. I don't know why, but when you are visualising what lies in front, you either see yourself getting out first ball or scoring a hundred. There is no in-between. I have played both these scenarios out many times in my head by the time I reach breakfast.

I don't feel hungry. The butterflies are already churning up my stomach, and I have to force myself to get a couple of pieces of toast down my neck, with some strong coffee to go with them. Trescothick is the designated driver for Vaughan, Giles and myself. He loves his cars, and is more than happy to be distracted for the twenty minutes it takes to reach The Oval from our magnificent hotel overlooking Tower Bridge. The traffic is light for a Thursday morning; and we arrive at the ground in plenty of time. A Sky News TV camera crew is hanging around the car park, and hurriedly starts getting themselves ready for the opportunity of talking to the players. The presenter is obviously not usually involved with cricket, and makes a complete hash of trying to interview the England captain. 'Matthew, what are your thoughts about the game today?' he asks. Vaughan politely informs him that his name is in fact Michael, and declines to comment.

We make our way up to the dressing-room, where we are met by Paul Collingwood. 'You'll never guess what just happened,' he says with a huge grin on his face. 'Some bloke from Sky News came running up to me and asked, "Geraint, what lies in store today?" I told him that my name was Paul!' He has obviously met the same reporter.

I spend a few minutes reading the papers before getting changed and making my way out to the pitch for warm-up. We all get the most incredible cheer as we start a gentle lap around the ground, and even our feeble footballing skills are applauded. Warm-up is followed by fielding practice, in which I join Trescothick and Flintoff for some slip catches. It is then left up to the players if they want to have a net or throw-downs. I opt for a gentle net.

Vaughan walks out for the toss. On a flat-looking wicket, we are dying for him to win it. None of us wants to bat last when it is wearing and spin-friendly. I am walking back to the pavilion as the coin goes up. I hear a huge cheer from the packed terraces and the camera crew moves to Vaughan. He must have won the toss. We are going to be batting. Trescothick and I try to appear calm as the minutes tick by. We have first use of a belter of a wicket, but we can't afford to squander the chance. I feel sick with nerves. Not even my debut felt like this. The bell goes, and we make our way outside. A huge roar greets us, and helps to calm the nerves. As we reach the pitch I feel much calmer. I am getting focused.

McGrath runs in to bowl the first over. I notice that he is running in much faster than usual. A look at the speed gun confirms my suspicions – 84.1 mph. Definitely quicker than earlier in the series.

We get through the first few overs without any real scares. The wicket is even-paced and does not hold any surprises. McGrath and Lee are both striving for early wickets, and in turn present us with a few scoring opportunities. I cut Lee for four, and then drive consecutive half-volleys from McGrath to the boundary. I am off and running, and beginning to calm down. Trescothick also gets off-drives away that race across the lightning-fast outfield. We are beginning to seize the initiative. The run-rate starts climbing. By 12 overs, we have reached 58, and things are starting to get easier. Ponting turns to his champion legspinner to bring some control to proceedings. It is clear that he is unlikely to get much turn at this stage, but that doesn't mean that he is going to be easy to play. We both get a boundary off his first over, and things look under control until Trescothick is brilliantly caught by Hayden with the score on 82.

Vaughan joins me at the wicket. 'What's going on, mate?' 'Not a lot, the wicket is good, and there isn't much turn. Let's get through to lunch,' comes my reply. We nearly do, but Vaughan

Brett Lee epitomises everything that is good in cricket. He plays hard and fair. I played in the same side as he did in Sydney when I was young.

I salute my team-mates and the crowd after scoring my second century of the Ashes series at The Oval in September 2005. It remains my most satisfying Test innings.

Head still, eyes on the ball – Kevin Pietersen hitting to leg during his unbelievable innings on the last day of the 2005 Ashes series.

I start on a beer as we begin celebrating the greatest moment in my cricketing life after regaining the Ashes from Australia in 2005. The champagne soon followed.

Feeling ropey and tired but very proud in Trafalgar Square on 13 September 2005 – next stop 10 Downing Street.

I still get goosebumps when I see pictures of us standing in Trafalgar Square with thousands of people sporting red and white, and dancing and singing.

Shoaib Akhtar wheels away in triumph after taking England's last wicket in our defeat at Multan against Pakistan in the First Test, November 2005. He bowled brilliantly during the series.

Inzamam-ul-Haq's manner suggests he should struggle against pace but he never seems rushed. Here he scores a century against us in Faisalabad.

Monty Panesar celebrates with delighted team-mates after taking his first Test wicket, that of the great Sachin Tendulkar at Nagpur in March 2006.

Anil Kumble, who has long been India's most consistent bowler, celebrates with his teammates after taking his 500th Test wicket during the match against England in Mohali.

Kevin Pietersen and I pile on the runs during the first innings at Mumbai in March 2006. We pulled off an unexpected victory to share the series.

In 47 degree heat at Jamshedpur dehydration was a major problem. After batting for 30 overs I was put on a drip to alleviate severe cramp. Here the resting Flintoff tries to cool me down.

Above left: Mahela Jayawardene, the Sri Lanka captain, showed that he is a world-class batsman by his performances in the Test matches and in the one-day internationals in England in 2006.

Above right: Chaminda Vaas once again proved himself to be a skilful bowler and a more than useful batsman in England in 2006.

Left: Muttiah Muralitharan always has a smile on his face. There again, I would be smiling too if I had taken more than 600 Test wickets. Here he celebrates another.

Signed stumps make good mementoes. Andrew Flintoff and Alastair Cook grab one each after our six-wicket victory at Edgbaston.

I sweep Sanath Jayasuriya on my way to scoring 55 in the Trent Bridge Test in June 2006. Sri Lanka won the match and the series was shared.

Trescothick looks on in awe as I boom another one straight down the middle – 'fore left.'

manages to pick out mid-wicket to become Warne's second victim with only three overs to go before lunch. Bell comes in with an awkward ten-minute session to negotiate. Warne produces one of his sliders to trap Bell in front. We have gone from 82/0 to 104/3. Lunch can't come quickly enough. Everyone is subdued in the dressing-room. I am feeling quite comfortable at the crease, on 42, but am aware of the perilous position we are in. Another couple of quick wickets and the match might be slipping away already. Hopefully Pietersen will come good.

I pass 50 shortly after the break with a cut shot from Brett Lee. Things are looking better. Pietersen seems to be getting himself in. Warne has other ideas, and bowls Pietersen off his pad for 14. We are back on the ropes, and I am not enjoying myself. There is too much at stake. I have to keep concentrating.

Flintoff walks to the wicket with an air of confidence. He is in great form, and clearly does not fear the situation. This is an opportunity for him to thwart the Aussies yet again. He announces himself with a couple of trademark drives through the offside. The great thing about batting with Flintoff is that the scoreboard is always moving. At the other end you don't have to worry too much about scoring yourself. I am able to lean on my bat and watch a huge array of shots. Flintoff is having no trouble on the benign wicket.

Before you know it, we have posted a partnership of 50, and I am nearing a century. Usually I would be a little edgy about trying to get to three figures before tea. I don't like stewing over it during the break. Today I have no such thoughts. We still have a huge amount of work to do, and my century is secondary to the fortunes of the side. This is not a time for personal glory. We arrive at tea with the score at 213/4 and I am on 92. As we take a well-earned break, we know that we have to keep going for at least another session to regain the initiative.

Lee opens the bowling after tea but his pace is a little down on earlier in the day. He gives me width, and I flay it square of the wicket for four. I am within one shot of a hundred. I wait patiently at the other end while Flintoff sees off Warne, and then prepare myself for another barrage from Lee.

The adrenalin is going now, but only because I want to get that single out of the way. There is still much work to do. Lee bowls a good-length ball, I watch it go through to the keeper. He has come around the wicket. I survey the field. If he gets a little straight, there is an area through mid-wicket that is not protected by a fielder. I must wait till the right ball arrives. He runs in, I pick it up early. It's straight enough to hit through the legside. I feel the ball hit the bat, and immediately know that it is going for four. I have reached a century on the biggest day of my career. A packed Oval cricket ground, full of patriotism and fervour, stands and applauds. Regardless of what happens in the rest of my career, I won't play a more important innings for England.

McGrath comes back into the attack to remove Flintoff for 72, and I am dismissed by my nemesis, Shane Warne, shortly after for 129. Our partnership of 143 has brought England back into the match, but we aren't dominating like we did in the previous three Tests. In the end our total of 373 is not as large as we would have liked. If Australia bat well enough, they can put us under some real pressure in the second innings.

The next two days of the Test belonged completely to Australia. Hayden shrugged off his poor form to get a century, as did his opening partner, Justin Langer. At 281/2, they had the perfect springboard to go well past our score and leave us batting for a day and a half to save the Test. This was not an appealing prospect against Shane Warne, who was chomping at the bit to bowl at us again after picking up six wickets first time around. In fact, our plight may have been much worse if Australia hadn't elected to go off for bad light twice during that time. They probably lost the best part of two sessions due to that decision, and that may have proved the difference at the end of the game. I could understand Ponting's thinking. It would have been difficult to bat in those dark conditions, and he risked losing the momentum his side had built up. In a must-win situation, you have to risk losing in order to win, and we will never know what would have happened if they had stayed out there.

As it was, they were forced to stay out in dark, gloomy conditions on the fourth day. Flintoff was a colossus, bowling throughout the entire morning session to pick up his second five-wicket haul in Test cricket. Hoggard gave it his all too, and Australia subsided from 281/2 to 367 all out. In reality, that inspired start to the fourth day probably meant that we had to bat for three sessions rather than four to save the game. With only a few minutes left in the day before the gloom descended one more, I was caught at bat-pad off Warne, probably playing too defensively. We were one down at the close, and we faced the prospect of batting for most of the last day to win the Ashes. I would play no further part.

The final day of the 2005 Ashes had everything. Warne was at his most competitive, wheeling away for most of the day, trying to find gaps in technique to exploit. McGrath was also back to his miserly best, dismissing Vaughan and Bell in consecutive deliveries to leave us standing on the edge of an abyss at 67/3. Pietersen survived the hat-trick ball, but didn't look too comfortable in the early stages of his innings. A potential catch off Warne clipped Gilchrist's glove on the way, so as to make it impossible for Hayden to catch it at slip. Also, he had an outrageous piece of fortune when he had scored just 11. Warne dropped a regulation chance at slip off Lee to give him a crucial lifeline.

His innings, though, was a complete masterpiece. He decided against defending his way to the finish line in favour of his preferred attacking style. When Lee dropped short he swatted him over square-leg for six. Instead of trying to nudge singles off Warne, he slog-swept him out of the park. From the dressing-room, it was agonising viewing. Whenever one of his audacious shots disappeared over the ropes there would be pandemonium, with people banging on tables and shouting, 'Shot, KP.' We would then look at each other and mouth the words, 'Calm down, for God's sake, we can't afford to lose a wicket now.' While he quite clearly felt in complete control of events, for us in the dressing-room it was a little like watching a horror movie. We knew that something horrible might happen any moment, and the temptation was to look away. But there was no way we could. It kept us all spellbound.

By the time we reached the tea break, we dared not say it, but we were just about there. KP had reached his first and surely the most brilliant hundred he will ever score for England, and we were 221/7, a lead of 227. It seemed unlikely that Australia would chase down a score in excess of 250, especially with less than 40 overs to go, and the number decreasing with every over we stayed out there. If we could bat another hour, the match was certainly won.

I think everyone knows that we did do exactly that. Pietersen went past 150, Giles got a half-century of his own and, despite eventually getting bowled out for 335, the players on both sides knew that the 2005 Ashes series was effectively over. There was a semi-farcical situation where the umpires forced us out on the field for a few overs, before the match was finally called off. The umpires went out on to the pitch to remove the bails. The Ashes were over, and after 16 long painful years, England held the urn again.

There are some things in life that should remain sacred, and the celebrations of the England cricket team on the night of our Ashes victory are one of those things. Needless to say they went on long and late, and from the look on the faces of everyone as we boarded the bus to Trafalgar Square the next morning, our celebration had done justice to the occasion.

For me, the highlight of the evening was not in the night spots of London in the small hours, but well before that, when we were still at The Oval. When Michael Vaughan came into the dressing-room to tell us that the umpires were calling the game off, absolute pandemonium broke loose. Guys, who had remained so calm under the most intense of pressure earlier in the day, were jumping around like lunatics. There was the giddy combination of singing, hugging and jumping that only the most intense of feelings can bring out spontaneously. We could not sit around for too long before going down to do the post-match presentation, and receive the urn. These were the moments that a generation of England cricketers had lived for but never achieved. Parading the Ashes around a packed Oval, receiving the congratulations and adulation of people who had become completely transfixed by our contest as the summer wore on, was the stuff of dreams, and was immensely satisfying.

It was when we got back in the dressing-room, though, that the enormity of what we had achieved finally sank in. I had brought some cigars that I had picked up on holiday in Cuba to the ground on the off chance of victory, and handed them out to everyone. We sat there as a team like none other. There was some excited chat, but for the most part we smoked, drank, and relived the previous seven weeks. As I looked around the room, I felt an enormous pride in my team-mates. We had been through so much together, put in so much effort, fought so many battles and ulti-mately answered so many questions. There was a bond between us that no one could break and, regardless of what happens to all of us in the rest of our careers, we will always be able to look each other in the eye, give a little wink, and have those memories to fall back on.

After a couple of hours, we forced ourselves out of the dressing-room, and to the Australian camp. They are a great bunch of guys, who love representing their country, and they took the defeat like true champions. We knew that they must have been hurting like hell, but they were still there to share in our triumph. An hour was spent reminiscing about the summer, before we got back to the hotel and headed for the bright lights of London town.

The following morning we all stumbled into the hotel foyer to be met by a press barrage. BBC, ITV and Sky all had crews filming live, and it was not good viewing. We were a rabble, unsure of what lay in store, and coming to terms with stinking headaches. We managed to stumble on to a bus for the short journey to the Lord Chancellor's house to get ready for the victory parade. It was a bizarre situation, and we were all a little concerned that it was going to be a massive flop. Who would come out to see a bunch of drunken cricketers? Footballers maybe, but not cricketers.

We could not have been more wrong. From the moment we boarded the open-topped bus, right through till we finally arrived at Lord's for a reception organised by Vodafone, we were cheered, congratulated and honoured by people who were still genuinely excited about what we had achieved. It was completely humbling stuff, and made us all appreciate how many people take an interest in what we do, and what an important part sport plays in making people feel good. Even in 10 Downing Street, members of staff lined up and applauded us as we made our way through the labyrinth that led to the garden. It made up for the lack of alcohol, and made us realise that not everyone involved in the government was doing it for purely political reasons.

It was incredibly well organised for a last-minute celebration, and I still get goosebumps when I see the pictures of us standing in Trafalgar Square with thousands, dancing and singing in red and white, looking on. It was a strange, magnificent day.

13

MUD, HEAT AND DUST

The end of the Ashes was like the end of term. Players who had eaten, slept, batted and bowled in each other's company for the best part of six months all went their separate ways. There were six weeks between those final absorbing scenes at The Oval and the date of our departure to the subcontinent, and each of us had to decide how best to approach our preparation for a gruelling winter of six Test matches and 12 one-day internationals in some of the most inhospitable cricketing conditions. It was clear that we all needed to be as fit as possible in order to compete for long periods in the humidity and heat of Pakistan and India, and some technical adjustments needed to be made also. Suddenly six weeks didn't seem like a long time, especially as we all needed at least two weeks completely away from cricket to let tired bodies recover, freshen up mentally, do some celebrating, and let the post-Ashes glow start to fade.

While I managed to arrive at the airport in early November feeling fully fit and prepared to go, I had plenty to think about as the plane took off destined for Dubai, and then Islamabad airport. Ruth was heavily pregnant, and due some time during the Third Test match, and it was horrible to think that she would have to go through all the difficulties and uncertainty of the last few weeks on her own. Also, I was going to a country I knew very little about. Unlike my team-mates, most of whom had been to Pakistan at some point with England age-group sides, I had never set foot in the country, and the stories that I had heard about the place were not overly complimentary. Old pros like Mike Gatting, as well as a couple of Middlesex players who had been on Under-19s tours there, seemed to have endless stories about dodgy hotels, mystery viruses and the need to be a certified alcoholic in order to get a drink. It didn't sound good, but we all knew that these were the sort of challenges we needed to overcome in order to build on the Ashes and attempt to dislodge Australia as the world's number one.

As we touched down in Islamabad, I suppose we had reason to believe that our arrival would be big news. Here were the Ashes champions coming to a cricket-mad country to take on the world's most talented, enigmatic and potentially devastating side. One look at the piles of humanitarian aid littering the runway, and the continuous ferrying of supplies by military helicopters told us that something far more important than cricket was taking place. That something was, of course, the after-effects of a massive earthquake which had killed close to 300,000 people in the remote mountainous area of the country and had left millions homeless. When you see disasters like this on your TV screen it looks horrible, and you may even spare a thought for those who are affected, but when you are in the country and feel the sorrow and despair of lives ruined and families mourning, the human side of the tragedy really hits home. Although everyone involved with the tour did as much as possible to make us feel at home, that sickening atmosphere was never far away.

The other major concern prior to going was that of security. Since the start of the so-called war on terror, and the London bombings of July 2005, the tour to Pakistan was always going to have security problems associated with it. It was extremely unlikely that anyone would target the England cricket team specifically, but it was always possible that we could get caught up in one of the many bombings that have gone on in Pakistan, especially in Karachi. New Zealand had to abort their tour of Pakistan in 2001 due to a bomb going off near their team hotel, and they were lucky that no one was inside at the time, so we knew that the threats were real. With an altered schedule that saw us staying in Karachi for only one night, we realised that us not going to Pakistan would be like a team not going to England because they might be bombed in London. The tour would go ahead with a presidential level of security which ended up being restrictive, and probably unnecessary, despite the best efforts of the private security team we used to co-ordinate local policemen.

I suppose the issues surrounding the tour, including the possibility of an Ashes hangover, make it seem that the trip was doomed from the start, but that was not the way we saw it at all. We were cock-a-hoop in a very impressive hotel in Islamabad, far from the hellish stories I had heard, we were enjoying each other's company and looking forward to the challenge of winning out in Pakistan. We prepared ourselves properly, doing as much work in the gym as I have ever done whilst playing for England, and even a poor warm-up performance against Pakistan A failed to dent our enthusiasm. We travelled to Multan, the venue of the First Test, still assured that we would be at our best once the match got under way.

The one telling blow we had prior to the match was Michael Vaughan injuring his knee. It meant he wasn't available to captain the side and Marcus Trescothick would have to deputise. He was expected to be out for only one match, and at the time no one would have dreamt that it would carry on throughout the tour, and eventually finish his tour in India without it even starting.

While Multan, a dusty town in the middle of nowhere, would not be top of my list of must-see tourist spots, the stadium there was new and impressive, and for four days of an absorbing Test match, we carried on from where we had left off against the Aussies. Their batsmen, Inzamam-ul-Haq apart, all seemed to struggle against the relentlessness of our seam attack, and their innings of 274 and 341 were both under par on a perfect batting track. Marcus Trescothick was magnificent in our first innings, scoring 193, and that effort left us chasing a modest target of 198 on the final day to win the game.

It was this run-chase that was to be the pivotal moment in the series. We should have chased down the runs comfortably, even though the wicket was encouraging the legspinner Danish Kaneria in particular. All we had to do was provide a decent base for our attacking middle order of Flintoff, Pietersen and Jones to finish off the job. Unfortunately, it didn't happen. Trescothick went early, Ian Bell and I weren't able to build on a 50 partnership, and our middle order was defeated as much by their own efforts to be positive as by the Pakistan bowlers. Despite a bit of a wagging of the tail, we went down by 22 runs. As we made our way back to the hotel we realised that we had wasted a great chance to take a series lead, and made life incredibly difficult for ourselves in the remaining two Test matches.

Looking back over what-if scenarios is never a particularly useful exercise in international sport, but I am certain that victory in that Test breathed new life into a Pakistan side who had been inconsistent at best over the previous year. Suddenly they believed they could beat us, and their pace bowlers, Shoaib Akhtar in particular, found a new spring to their step. Shoaib knew that they could make life uncomfortable for our batsmen with his extreme pace, and he was keen to prove a point to the Pakistan selectors and a cricketing public who were doubting his application.

As we dragged ourselves from the wasteland of Multan to the industrial heartland of Pakistan, Faisalabad, the reality of a tour to this part of the world set in. Although the hotel we were staying in was once again more than adequate, a combination of tight security and lack of opportunity meant it was tough to get out of the hotel. A trip to a local garment factory to get our hands on some cheap Ralph Lauren gear had to be aborted when most of the city turned up to watch us, and even the local market was a no-go area due to the logistical nightmare of organising a visit to it. So hour after hour was spent in hotel rooms, watching DVDs, and gradually this inactivity brought on a kind of lethargy that was hard to shake off.

The cricket should have been the ideal way to provide the entertainment we were looking for but, having started the Second Test by spending a day and a half in the field watching Pakistan rack up 462, it was clear that they were beginning to find our bowling easier to counteract on the low, slow surfaces. We replied strongly with Bell and Kevin Pietersen both getting hundreds, but being 1–0 down in the series meant that we could not afford just to play out draws; we needed to force the pace, and were unable to do it.

Inzamam played the conditions in the second innings incredibly well to score his second century of the match. He has the appearance, as he plods his way to the wicket, of a man who has to be forced out of bed in the morning, but this dopey exterior masks an incredibly organised mind and technique. On these wickets he gives the impression that he can hit any ball wherever he wants, but is also more than happy to play the percentage game. Throughout the tour we never really found a way to breach his defences, and he underlined what a quality player he is. Due to his hundred, Pakistan were able to declare with a lead of 285, leaving us with two sessions to bat. A major scare, when we slumped to 20/4, was averted by Pietersen, Flintoff and Geraint Jones, who saw us through to safety. We could no longer win the series, and were looking increasingly unlikely to register a victory unless we could improve our performance in the final Test.

For me, the night after the final day of the Second Test was my cue to get home for the birth of my son, Sam. The two Test matches had been largely unsuccessful, with scores of 9, 23, 13 and 0 to my name, and the lack of form was made even more frustrating by having to spend days in the field watching players knock up runs for fun. My natural game, which relies on using cross-batted shots to short-of-a-length balls, was clearly not working on these low-bouncing wickets, and having played the ball on to my stumps twice, I hadn't adjusted my game enough to be successful. It was my first real lean spell for England, and it was disappointing to have to get on the plane without having another attempt to get things right, but at the time I had different priorities.

I received quite a lot of negative press for leaving the tour with England struggling to go home for the birth of my son. If I had any doubts that I was doing the right thing when I arrived home, seeing his face when he was finally born (a week late) made me realise immediately that I had made the correct decision. I am extremely proud to be representing my country in a sport that I love playing. I know the importance of the England team, and I also know how many players are trying their utmost to get into the team. For me, though, my family does, and has to, take priority over what happens on the pitch. A person who spends his whole life eating, drinking, thinking and playing cricket ultimately ends up a sad lonely man when his career is over, and I know from experience that the right balance in your life can also help you perform on the pitch. I think Duncan Fletcher and the powers that be in the ECB also understand this and I am grateful for their support. I don't blame other players for opting to stay on tours in similar circumstances, but I couldn't have done it myself.

As it was, I was in the labour ward as England collapsed on the final day of the final Test to give Pakistan an unlikely 2–0 series victory. I don't think that this was a fair reflection of the series, and Pakistan were certainly helped by winning the first two tosses, but ultimately we performed below our best, and received a clear lesson that past performances guarantee you nothing in cricket.

The one-day series that followed also provided us with a couple of lessons. Despite winning the first game with a near-perfect batting performance in reaching 327, during the rest of the series we lost too many wickets too early, and were probably flattered by the final scoreline of 3–2. By the time we boarded the plane for the UK, we had played five ODIs in 11 days, we were exhausted after an incredibly busy 2005, and after two months in Pakistan, the thought of Christmas at home and a couple of months off was music to our ears.

There is no place in the world like India, and there is no place to play cricket like India. After two months spent recharging batteries, spending time with families, and analysing the defeats in Pakistan, we came together in early February 2006 ready and waiting to experience a tour like none other. Our journey was to take us from Nagpur in the centre of the country, through Chandigarh and Mumbai for the Test matches, before rushing through Delhi, Faridabad, Cochin, Goa, Guwahati, Jamshedpur and Indore for seven one-day internationals. It was to be a difficult schedule, playing in some of the hottest conditions imaginable, while relying on the vagaries of the Indian transport system to get us to remote venues but, much like the country, it was to be a tour full of opportunity. We could see this magnificent land in all its glory, and we had the possibility of beating the Indian team on home soil, something that very few had achieved.

After spending so much time inside hotels during the Pakistan tour, I was determined to get out as much as possible, sample some of the local food and culture, and only use the hotel restaurants if there was nowhere else to go. Fortunately, there were a few guys in the team who had similar thoughts to me, and from the moment we arrived in the magnificent Taj Hotel in Mumbai, the tour took on a very different flavour to the Pakistan leg.

I had been to Mumbai before, when attending the World Cricket Academy, a spin-bowling camp set up by a die-hard cricket fan, Sachin Bajaj, in 2002, but I was amazed by how much the city had changed in the intervening years. The hustle and bustle of the place is infectious. The road system is a chaotic mixture of taxis, bicycles, scooters and lorries, none of which appear to pay any attention to any sort of traffic regulations, and the city mirrors its road system. Brand new state-of-the-art business centres stand alongside derelict colonial buildings. Some of the most expensive real estate in the world overlooks a slum in which millions of poor city-dwellers live. It is a strange city of contradiction, and was the ideal place in which to start our tour.

The first week went entirely according to plan. Magnificent

practice facilities were accorded us by the Cricket Club of India at the Brabourne Stadium, and we acclimatised ourselves to the 35–40° heat with a comfortable victory over our first opponents. From there, however, things went rapidly downhill. We were already without Ashley Giles who was recovering from hip surgery and, in a crazy 48-hour period, we were to lose three more front-line players. Our captain suffered a recurrence of his knee injury and had to go home, our most experienced player, Marcus Trescothick, joined him on the plane with personal matters to attend to, and Simon Jones, potentially our most potent weapon on subcontinent wickets, broke down with a knee injury of his own. Before the tour had really started, it was over for three of our players, and we had the look of a team whose wheels were coming off. To add insult to the injuries, we were comfortably beaten by India A in our final warm-up game, and none of our batsmen looked in decent nick.

It is in moments of crisis that Duncan Fletcher is at his best. He is not prone to panic, and will quietly think through all the options at his disposal before coming up with a plan. The first part of the plan was to install Andrew Flintoff as captain. He had long been one of the most influential people in the dressing-room, a person who had a huge amount of respect from the rest of the team for his performances on the pitch, and he was the natural choice to take over in the absence of Vaughan and Trescothick. He rose to the challenge from the word go, and a huge amount of credit has to go to him for bringing a bunch of young, inexperienced players together and making us believe that we could beat India.

The second job Fletcher had to do was get some more players on the tour. Alastair Cook, Owais Shah and James Anderson all hurried over to join us from the A tour in the West Indies, and were all to make a mark at some point during our stay. The hardest task of all, however, was to get a side, without the services of four of its most experienced players, ready to take on the might of India, a team chosen from a billion people, a team full of living legends.

Fletcher was able to do this by preparing us thoroughly for the conditions we were likely to face. Although many people assume that the wickets in Pakistan and India are similar, they actually aren't. In Pakistan they have the look of rolled mud which has been baked dry. The wickets don't change much over the course of five days and that is why getting a victory there is so difficult. In India the wickets are a little more dusty. Towards the end of the game they are likely to aid the spinners, but because there is some grass on them, the seamers can get some help early on.

We went into the first game of the series with a nothing-to-lose mood among the boys. We had been written off by everyone due to our injury situation, and Cook had only just arrived from the Caribbean. He was going to be thrust straight into the action without any time to adjust to the conditions. If we performed badly and were beaten, it wouldn't be entirely unexpected, and in some ways that took the burden off us. We dominated the First Test match, putting India under the sort of pressure that they are unused to experiencing at home. Paul Collingwood proved the mainstay of our first innings of 393, with a magnificent knock of 134. He had finally established himself in the team in Pakistan, scoring 96 and 80 in Lahore, and everyone in the side was delighted as he reached his first Test century. He is the sort of hard-working and unselfish player that every side needs, and it gives everyone in the team a lift when someone like him does well. Cook also impressed in his first innings for England. Although he is only 21 years old his temperament saw him through the difficult first overs as an England player, and from then on he played with an authority that few youngsters could match, eventually being dismissed for 60. There is no doubt that he will be around for a while.

India were in real trouble in reply, slumping to 190/7, largely thanks to Matthew Hoggard's six wickets. It was a significant breakthrough for Hoggard in more ways than one. He had managed to unsettle the India top order with his nagging accuracy but, more importantly, he proved to everyone that he was able to adapt to conditions when the ball wasn't swinging. Too often in the past he has been written off as only being effective if there is movement through the air, but in completely inhospitable circumstances, he showed how much he has developed over the last couple of years. Monty Panesar also impressed on debut. He got the prized wicket of Sachin Tendulkar, and only went at 2 runs an over. He is not the most co-ordinated man in the field, but he seems to transform completely with a ball in his hand. His action is as pure as you can get as a spinner, and he rarely bowls a bad ball.

Our second innings went entirely according to plan. Cook rounded off a brilliant debut by getting a century, an outstanding feat against two of the world's best spinners, and Pietersen clubbed his way to 87 to help set up the declaration. We had an opportunity to draw first blood against India if we could get ten wickets on the final day.

In the end things didn't work out for us. Wasim Jaffer got a century, Rahul Dravid, the Indian captain, blunted our attack for five hours, and a late surge for victory put us under some pressure. The game ended honourably in a draw with India six wickets down, and we could hold our heads high. We had competed, and largely dominated an intriguing First Test, and you could feel the confidence growing in our young, inexperienced players. We could compete with India.

The venue for the Second Test was Chandigarh, an orderly, well-maintained city in the north of the country, where the temperatures were far less oppressive than the rest of India. It was the sort of place that should have suited us. The hotel was magnificent, serving just about any food you could want to international standards. There was plenty to do outside the hotel, with decent shops, and even a golf course, and we were being supported by an increasing number of England fans. It was ironic, therefore, that we slumped to a nine-wicket defeat, and were brought back down by earth by India's most consistent and under-valued performer, Anil Kumble.

While some of his colleagues are treated like film stars, featuring in adverts and having their faces splashed over billboards wherever you go, Kumble doesn't seem to court attention at all. Despite this, his record is second to none, having taken 500 Test wickets, with a staggering 32 five-wicket hauls. He bowls much quicker and flatter than most spinners, combining deadly accuracy with the ability to bowl a brilliant and deceptive googly. On the low-bounce wickets in India, you feel that every ball he bowls could potentially get you out lbw, and you have to be very careful about leaving any delivery, in case it is the dreaded variation ball. While Harbhajan Singh relies mainly on turn and bounce, Kumble's main weapon is the ability to skid the ball through, and he has to be played completely differently to his off-spinning team-mate. As a combination, they complement each other perfectly, and if you are to score runs against India, you have to come up with plans to score off both of them. It is not an easy task, and that is why so few teams do well out there.

Despite going 1–0 down in the series, spirits in the camp were still high. We knew that it was going to be a monumental task to come back and win the final Test, especially as the Mumbai wicket was famed for helping the spinners, but we knew that we had shown enough in both Tests to believe that we could do it. We were going to be cheered on by as many as 10,000 England supporters, which was an incredible number to be visiting the subcontinent, and we could take comfort from the fact that a few of India's senior players, including Tendulkar and Virender Sehwag had struggled for runs and looked vulnerable against the short ball.

The heat in Mumbai at the end of March was completely oppressive. India had never played a Test match there this late in the year, and I could see why. A combination of 40°C heat, energy-sapping humidity and a hot wind meant that batting for a long time was completely physically exhausting. I could only count my lucky stars that I was not a bowler. In conditions like that it was crucial to win the toss and grab the momentum of the game. Fortunately, Flintoff did that, and I played probably my most satisfying innings for England. I had felt more comfortable in the Indian conditions than I had in Pakistan, but for the first two Tests I had failed to convert promising starts. It was eating away at me, and I knew that I only had myself to blame. A few loose shots had contributed to my dismissals. In Mumbai, I made a conscious effort to wait for the bowlers to come to me. If they wanted to get me out, they would have to strive for my wicket, and in doing so would present me with scoring opportunities. After five Tests in the subcontinent, I finally learnt the key to success out there. Runs do not come from domination, but more from wearing down opposition bowlers. In the humidity and heat of the Wankhede Stadium, I scored my eighth Test hundred and laid a few Asian demons to rest along with it. At the other end my team-mate from Middlesex, Owais Shah, continued the new tradition of debutants getting runs by getting 88, and we reached a challenging total of 400.

Jimmy Anderson made a triumphant return to the side after a year in the wilderness in taking 4/40 to bowl India out for 279, giving us a first-innings lead of 121. Once again we were in the box seat and, with the wicket deteriorating and scoring becoming increasingly difficult, we knew that anything over 300 would be tough to chase. As it was, we only just achieved that target, by getting bowled out for 191, with Kumble and Harbhajan once more among the wickets. If we were going to bowl out India on the final day, it would take one of our spinners, Shaun Udal or Panesar, to bowl us to a famous victory.

The final day of that Third Test rates as highly as anything we achieved in the Ashes. India reached lunch only three wickets down, and it seemed as though the game was destined for a draw. Just before we returned to the field Flintoff took control of the sound system in the dressing-room and put on Johnny Cash's 'Ring of Fire'. The tune caught the moment and every member of the squad, including the coaching staff, bellowed it out. I don't think Flintoff expected the song to inspire us as it did but, within the space of 14 crazy overs, India lost seven wickets for 25 runs, and plummeted to defeat. Shaun Udal produced the spell of his life to take 4/14, and the ice-cold Kingfisher beers we drank in that crowded, sweltering dressing-room were as sweet as anything I've tasted. In the harshest of conditions, without half the side that played in the Ashes, we had won England's first Test match in India for 20 years and in doing so had drawn the series.

After five weeks of torturous conditions, after five days of extreme heat, exhaustion and nail-biting cricket, those of us going on to the one-day series had the grand total of one day of rest and recuperation before setting off on surely the most difficult schedule that any England team has faced. We had a chartered jet to take us to Jaipur, Delhi, Faridabad, Goa, Cochin, Guwahati, Jamshedpur and Indore and all in the space of three weeks. Although Goa and Cochin were popular tourist destinations, and Delhi was the nation's capital, the other venues were cities very much off the beaten track. Guwahati, in particular, was in a part of India to the east of Bangladesh that I didn't even know existed. They were tough, challenging times for an inexperienced one-day side against a well-drilled, battle-hardened Indian XI, and in near farcically hot conditions, there was only ever going to be one winner. The 5–1 scoreline was probably a fair reflection of the way the games went. Kevin Pietersen played exceptionally well for us, but we could not find enough consistency with the bat to put the Indians under pressure and paid the price.

The one memory that I will take back from that one-day series was in Jamshedpur. The temperature reached an unbearable 44°C, quick bowlers could not bowl spells of more than two overs, and it was impossible to drink enough fluid to replace the vital salts that were being lost in sweat. I batted for 30 overs, and had to join Matt Prior on a drip for half an hour to alleviate severe cramps. Our dressing-room was like a scene from *MASH*, and our support staff were stretched to the absolute limit in keeping everyone on the park. It was as close as I have ever been to seeing unplayable conditions due to heat, and yet we won the game by four wickets.

I had been asked to captain England in the previous game in Guwahati so that Flintoff could take a much deserved rest. My first day in charge could hardly be claimed a success. Overnight rain had saturated the outfield and my first decision as England captain, which was to abandon the match without a ball being bowled, resulted in a riot. It was therefore immensely satisfying for me to win my first full game in charge of the England team, and it emphatically proved the point that on our day we can beat any team in the world. What we lack is consistency, and we need to find that before the World Cup in 2007.

On 16 April, we finally boarded the plane for our fifteenth and last journey by air on the tour. We were destined for London Heathrow, and we had three weeks before the onset of another English summer and the visiting Sri Lankans. I was extremely pleased to be on my way home, but I had loved every minute of our Indian adventure. The madness of the country, the friendliness of the people, the popularity of the game of cricket, and the good nature of the members of the Indian cricket team all combined to make our trip truly memorable. Other parts of the world may be far easier to visit, but nothing that you see in any other part of the world can prepare you for what awaits in India.

14

SRI LANKAN CHALLENGE

After two weeks spent re-acquainting myself with the nice soft leather sofa in my front room, and the television remote control, it was time to start preparing for the fast-approaching three-Test series against Sri Lanka. The tour of India had been long and physically demanding but there is something reinvigorating about being in England in April. The sense of people coming out of hibernation after a winter stuck indoors and the wonderful smell of freshly cut grass make you realise that the arrival of summer, along with the cricket season, is imminent. For those of us fortunate enough to earn a living playing cricket it is an exciting time of the year. April, weather permitting, is the month when the first round of county matches are played. Before I broke in to the England side I went away to work at improving my game during the winter and my efforts were put to the test in April. It is a time of year when it feels right to start playing cricket.

Duncan Fletcher had asked those of us who had taken part in both the Test and one-day series in India to play in one match before the First Test against Sri Lanka at Lord's. Andrew Flintoff and Kevin Pietersen played in one-day games for their counties whilst I attempted to acclimatise in a four-day match for Middlesex against Hampshire at the Rose Bowl. The Rose Bowl, with its unpredictable pitch, is not an ideal place to find early season form but I drove down to Southampton with enthusiasm. I was excited about the coming season and looking forward to catching up with my Middlesex team-mates, of whom I am seeing less and less. Getting trapped in front by James Bruce for nought in the first over of the match did little to increase my affection for the venue, but a second innings score of 141 left me feeling confident as I returned to London.

Sri Lanka are a difficult side to defeat at home. Muttiah Muralitharan, Chaminda Vaas, Mahela Jayawardene and Kumar Sangakkara are world-class performers with outstanding career records but, as a side, they do not travel particularly well. The damp, cold, seamer-friendly conditions that prevail in April do not help players who are accustomed to playing on slow, low pitches in 40 degree heat. Buoyed by our Test victory over India in Bombay we, along with every other England supporter, were expecting a comfortable series victory. Pakistan, who arrived in July, were seen as the team that would provide us with a tough challenge.

Injury, unsurprisingly, dominated the build-up to the First Test. Michael Vaughan, Simon Jones, Ashley Giles and Steve Harmison, who had each returned home early from our winter tours, were no closer to being fit and James Anderson, who had finished the tour of India strongly, had been diagnosed with a stress fracture in his back. The one piece of good news concerned Marcus Trescothick. Trescothick had had a difficult winter and he was welcomed back into the dressing-room. It was great to walk out to bat with him once again at Lord's and he showed immense character by scoring an excellent 106 on the opening day of the series. Alastair Cook, on his home debut, impressed again with an accomplished 89 and the irrepressible Pietersen highlighted his class with a breathtaking 158.

Flintoff declared on the second day with England on 551/6 and in the 30 overs that remained Sri Lanka had been reduced to 91/6. Sajid Mahmood bowled fast and straight on his Test debut and by the close of play had the amazing figures of 3/9 in five overs. As we left the ground, people were predicting that the Test would be over before the FA Cup final in Cardiff, and we were already contemplating a celebratory round of golf on Sunday or Monday. But, as is so often the case in international cricket, when you take something for granted you come unstuck.

And we did. Matthew Hoggard took his two-hundredth Test wicket on the Saturday morning and Sri Lanka were asked to follow on. Then, when Hoggard bowled Jehan Mubarak in his fifth over of Sri Lanka's second innings, we all thought, 'Here we go,' but rather than witness the clatter of wickets we frustratingly spent two and a half days watching a defiant and skilful fight-back. Jayawardene, Sri Lanka's impressive captain, led the way with a magnificent 119, whilst six of his team-mates posted half-centuries. Jayawardene seems to enjoy batting at Lord's as much as I do – he has now scored a century in each of the two Tests he has played there.

Our inability to bowl Sri Lanka out for a second time was largely down to appalling slip catching. The number of chances we dropped varied from report to report but, whatever the total was, it was unacceptable. Various theories flew round. Derek Pringle, in the *Daily Telegraph*, thought it may have had something to do with our practice. Duncan Fletcher, who takes much of our slip-catching practice, is a left-handed batsman and Pringle suggested we were not getting enough practice against right-handed batsmen. Others said Lord's was a poor ground in which to pick up the ball, and some even blamed the slope – the theory being that your eyes weren't level when the ball came at you.

The slope theory might have some substance, because it is more difficult to judge height with a sloping ground, but the others were incorrect. I dropped my fair share of chances in the Test and I saw all of them clearly. What I did notice, though, was that each catch hit my hands a bit quicker than I had expected. This was probably down to the nature of the pitch. In India we had become used to the ball gripping and slowing down after it pitched but here, on a fresher, harder surface, the ball seemed to skid on. This meant that for the slip-catch chances we had, the ball came quick and low, and these are generally the hardest to take.

It is not the first time this has happened to England at Lord's and I imagine it won't be the last. Touring teams – Pakistan dropped several catches at Lord's in the First Test of their series – have struggled too, so there must be something unique about the place.

What I will say is that it is a nightmare if the team drops a couple of catches early in the match. The sight of a colleague shelling a catch sends a negative vibe through the slip cordon and everybody starts to get a bit jittery. I felt it after I dropped one in the slips and began to dread the ball coming to me, which is not a great state of mind to be in when it is your job to snaffle everything that comes your way. Our catching for the remainder of the series was excellent, so I suppose the best thing to do was to forget about it and move on.

We left Lord's frustrated, tired and disappointed with the draw. There were no post-mortems, and why should there be? Most of the cricket we had played was very good and we did not need to be told what we had done wrong. When we met at Edgbaston for the Second Test we did focus on our fielding a bit more, and in particular our slip catching, but the last thing a player needs to do is take baggage from the previous game into the next one.

Despite what happened at Lord's, we went into the Second Test still expecting to win the series 2–0.

Flintoff's welfare dominated the week between the Test matches. Initially it was the number of overs he bowled in the First Test that caused concern, and then it was his lifestyle off the pitch. Andrew carried a heavy workload at Lord's where he bowled 68.3 overs. It is not ideal for a fast bowler to bowl this many overs but it is unavoidable if he is your likeliest wicket-taker. People may look at this game and say it caused the recurrence of the ankle problem that ruled him out for the second half of the summer, but it is wrong to protect players in a Test match. Every Test you play in is important and you do what you can to win that game. The match situation dictates who bowls and if it results in a couple of players carrying a particularly heavy workload, then so be it.

Pietersen was the star of the Second Test, scoring a brilliant 142. His innings once again highlighted what a great player of spin bowling he is. The prospect of facing Shane Warne or Muttiah Muralitharan has turned many a batsman into a nervous wreck but Pietersen seems to relish the challenge of pitting his wits against them.

Pietersen has the confidence to take the game to these two. Most batsmen feel uneasy about coming down the wicket and hitting a spinner of their quality over the top. The fear of dancing down, swinging, missing and, embarrassingly, getting stumped tends to put players off, yet he consistently backs himself to hit the ball and clear the field. Pietersen also had the audacity to reverse sweep Muralitharan over cover-point for six. Middlesex legend has it that Jacques Kallis, the South African all-rounder, produced a similar stroke twice in a NatWest Trophy game at

Uxbridge, but Pietersen's was one of the most remarkable shots I have seen in Test cricket.

Sri Lanka played Lasith Malinga, a fast bowler with a unique low slingy action, in the Second Test and he took some getting used to. We knew he had an unorthodox action and before the series we had heard stories about the New Zealand batsmen asking the umpires to wear white rather than black trousers when they played against him. They had insisted that they were losing sight of the ball as it came down the wicket towards them. We expected Malinga to be a tearaway fast bowler who did not have a clue where the ball was going. During the tour, however, he proved that he was a lot better than that. Malinga, whose action had been developed playing beach cricket in Sri Lanka, provided me with a unique challenge because his low arm basically meant that he was bowling stump to stump. As a batsman, you try to use the angle at which the ball comes towards you to your advantage but his line of attack gave you nothing at all. This reduced my run-scoring options and it also made his short ball a difficult delivery to avoid. Malinga's bouncers caused Trescothick and Paul Collingwood problems, and they both displayed nasty bruises after failing to get their bodies out of the way. Malinga did not have a great deal of success in the Test series but he bowled very well in the one-dayers that followed.

Monty Panesar had by now become something of a cult hero. At Lord's cheers greeted his every deed and they were even more apparent at Edgbaston, where he dropped a couple of clangers. He knows that the cheers are both affectionate and ironic, and he is aware that he needs to improve areas of his game. To begin with the cheers seemed to affect his fielding, but the odd error should not distract people from the fact that he is a fine bowler. The batsmen of India, Sri Lanka and Pakistan are magnificent players of spin and they have all struggled to score runs freely against him, which is a very encouraging sign for both him and England. However, the real test for Monty will come in Australia, where the batsmen will attack him and the crowd is merciless.

Panesar claimed three scalps in our six-wicket victory at Edgbaston but Liam Plunkett, with six victims, was our most successful bowler. Plunkett is an exciting fast bowler. He is raw and young but he is maturing and learning fast. He has a great attitude and there is a lot for the coaches to work with.

The win, achieved within four days, gave us an extra day off between back-to-back Test matches and sent us up to Nottingham feeling as though we were back on course. We had dominated the first two Tests and expected to do the same in the third.

Critics will blame our batting in the second innings for the defeat at Trent Bridge but this is not the case. After dismissing the tourists for 231 in their first innings, England should have posted a huge score and taken a commanding lead. But, through a combination of good Sri Lankan cricket and disappointing England batting, we allowed them to level the series. The display placed us in the position we had been attempting to avoid all series – chasing runs against Muralitharan in the fourth innings of a game on a turning pitch.

Trescothick and I gave our reply a decent start by putting on 84 for the first wicket, but the task of reaching 325 on an inexplicably dry pitch was always going to be beyond us. Muralitharan was superb, taking 8/70 in the innings and 11/132 in the match. Batting against Murali is a huge challenge, but it is not the fact that he turns the ball so much that makes him such a handful, it is that he is so difficult to read.

All our batsmen, Pietersen included, were bamboozled at some stage of the series. The problem is that it only takes one ball to turn the other way to get you doubting what you are doing out there – and once you get in that position you are in trouble. Because Muralitharan turns the ball so much, he also makes you look bloody stupid when you do misread a delivery. With some spinners you might miss the ball by a couple of inches, but with him you miss it by two feet.

Muralitharan is hard to pick because he deliberately scrambles the seam. Most spinners attempt to pitch the ball on the seam because when the stitching comes into contact with the pitch, it increases the likelihood of the ball gripping on the surface and changing direction. A batsman, if he watches the ball closely, can see which way the ball is turning and therefore he can make an assumption that it is going to spin a certain way. But when a bowler scrambles the seam, it is very difficult to see which way the ball is rotating as it comes towards you and this makes it very hard to play every ball with confidence. Murali can get away with not hitting the seam because his unique action allows him to impart so much spin on the ball that it turns sharply no matter which part of it comes into contact with the pitch.

In an attempt to overcome this tactic I spent hours practising against Merlyn, a bowling machine that spins a cricket ball appreciably. I asked those who were feeding the balls into the machine to keep varying the way they spun so that I could become accustomed to watching the ball closely and making instant decisions. It helped, but Murali was still very hard to read when the ball lost its redness because then the seam becomes similar in colour to the rest of it.

Facing Muralitharan is a very different challenge from facing

Shane Warne. Warne likes to smother you. He likes to intimidate you with his body language and his presence before he even lets go of the ball. When you face Warne, even though you try to avoid it, you occasionally get drawn in to playing against the man as well as the ball.

Murali is not an intimidating figure but when he runs in to bowl you know you are facing a magician. He is a guy who has the ability to conjure up an incredible delivery that you may or may not be able to pick, and this makes him a very difficult bowler to face. Pietersen confidently came down the pitch, as usual, but the rest of us preferred to stay in our crease and wait for the bad ball to come along. Unfortunately, these deliveries do not come along often and it makes it very hard to put Murali under pressure. He hates conceding runs but a batsman has to take a risk if he wants to build a score. We can all learn something from the way Pietersen played him. You have to try to be positive but it is a Catch 22 situation.

After Trescothick fell Muralitharan, sniffing success, went through the gears and consumed us. The pitch was offering him help, he was in wonderful form, and I don't think any side in the world would have come through the ordeal successfully. Our disappointment in drawing a series we should have won was compounded by the sight of Andrew Flintoff limping around with a recurrence of the ankle injury he picked up in South Africa during the winter of 2004/05.

The injury, along with Flintoff being advised to rest for six weeks, meant that I was given the honour of captaining England during the five NatWest series one-day games against Sri Lanka. I had been invited to captain England in India when, with the seven-match series lost, Flintoff was given a rest. The first decision

265

I made while in charge – to abandon a match in Guwahati – resulted in a riot but England won one of the two games where we actually got on the field.

The circumstances were far from ideal but, nevertheless, the prospect of leading England at home excited me hugely. The series proved to be a baptism of fire for me and a miserable one for everyone else connected with the side, as we were thrashed 5–0. On the field England were poor all round. At the start of the series I suggested that if England's batsmen scored five centuries we would win it comfortably. Yet it was Sri Lanka, with six hundreds, who coasted home.

The role of a captain should not be underestimated because it is he who gets the team in the right frame of mind before they walk out to play. If the team walks out on to the pitch feeling good and confident, the players are more likely to perform well but, even so, a captain is only as good as his team. If your batsmen don't score runs and your bowlers fail to bowl where you want them to, it does not matter what you say before the game.

Captaining an international side, like batting and bowling at that level, is very different from captaining a county side. The spotlight is constantly on you and people are constantly question-ing what you do. Yet I maintain you have to be your own man. You have to follow your hunches and lead the side as you see fit. You cannot go around attempting to captain a side as someone else does. I will not attempt to captain a team in the way that Michael Vaughan or Andrew Flintoff would captain it. You are what you are and you have to be true to yourself, because that is what has got you in to this position in the first place.

Yet, despite the gloom, there were some positives to take out of the series. Throughout my period in charge I gained a very good understanding of what the job entails and what a captain should be trying to do in a one-day international. And, although I was a tired and dejected man at the end of the series, I did feel as though I was better for the experience, and I hope some of the new players we blooded during it feel the same way.

15

LOOKING AHEAD

The last eight months have not quite gone according to plan but the two and a half years I have spent with the England team have provided me with a lifetime of experiences. When I was scratching around at Durham University in the late 1990s I dreamt about playing for England but I did not have the slightest clue about where to start and how to get there. So to sit here now and contemplate how far I have come in such a short period of time is a very satisfying and humbling experience.

My Test career could not have got off to a better start. I scored a hundred on my debut at Lord's and played in an England team that won a record eight consecutive matches. Since that memorable day at the home of cricket I have scored nine further Test hundreds and two one-day centuries on three different continents, and I now find myself captaining the England team and beating Pakistan in a home series.

But the highlight of this period is, undoubtedly, the Ashes series of 2005. Even now, 12 months down the line, I still find it hard to believe that I played in those five unforgettable matches. The scenes at The Oval, and then at Trafalgar Square, where tens of thousands of people cheered us through the streets of London, will live with me forever. A generation of England players, a couple of whom I played with on my debut, never had this experience and I cannot believe how lucky I am to have been involved with such a good

England side and with so many good people so early in my career.

Batting against Shane Warne, Glenn McGrath and Muttiah Muralitharan in front of full houses at Lord's, and taking on Shoaib Akhtar, Shaun Pollock and Anil Kumble in their own back yard, has tested me to the limit but these challenges have provided me with experiences I will always cherish – as has the thrill of being able to watch Brian Lara, Sachin Tendulkar and Ricky Ponting bat at such close quarters. These are the players about whom cricket-lovers will talk affectionately in 50 years' time.

When a list of achievements grows, so do people's expectations and the challenge for me is to continue to improve, to keep setting myself new goals and to try to live up to them. There have been hundreds of cricketers who have come in to the game, made a sudden impact, and then slowly drifted away. The best players are the ones who perform to a consistently high level over a long period of time and I still have some way to go before I achieve this. Reaching these objectives will be far harder than establishing myself as a Test cricketer, which is what I have done so far. It is quite right that this should be so. It is this that keeps me motivated when I get up every morning, and I am looking forward to pushing and testing myself even harder over the coming years.

After winning consecutive Test series against the West Indies, New Zealand, West Indies, South Africa, Bangladesh and then Australia, people were beginning to expect England's run of victories to go on and on but, at some stage, there was bound to be a slight tapering off. However, you can view statistics how you want. You can look at England's recent results and say that we have won just one of our last four Test series or you can go back a bit farther and say that we have lost just one of our previous ten Test series. It is up to you.

Things have been more difficult since we regained the Ashes but this is largely down to a rotten run of luck with injury. The team that defeated Australia in the Fourth Test at Trent Bridge has yet to play together again. Some believe it never will, and at times we have been without five of our leading players.

These absences have, however, given other players the chance to show that they can perform at the highest level and most, if not all of them, have done very well. Paul Collingwood has scored two Test hundreds and shown what a determined and capable player he is. Alastair Cook, with two Test centuries as well, has made a wonderful start to his Test career. Owais Shah looked a class act in Bombay in his only Test appearance to date. Liam Plunkett and Sajid Mahmood show huge potential as young fast bowlers, and Monty Panesar appears to have the ability to go on and become one of England's best spinners. There are plenty of positives and, I believe, English cricket has many happy and successful days to look forward to.

ANDREW STRAUSS IN TEST CRICKET

Compiled by Victor Isaacs

Test Career Record

M	I	NO	Runs	HS	Avge	100s	50s
29	54	2	2353	147	42.25	9	6

1. v New Zealand at Lord's 20–24 May 2004 – won by 7 wickets
   Toss: New Zealand
   New Zealand 386 & 336 (M.H. Richardson 101); England 441 (A.J. Strauss 112)
   & 282-3 (N. Hussain 103*).

1st innings	c Richardson b Vettori	112
2nd innings	run out (Cairns)	83

   Match highlights:
   *Named Man of the Match; 15th player to score a century on debut for England
   and 80th in all; fourth player to score a century on debut at Lord's.*

2. v New Zealand at Headingley 3–7 June 2004 – won by 9 wickets
   Toss: England
   New Zealand 409 & 161; England 526 (M.E. Trescothick 132, G.O. Jones 100)
   & 45-1

1st innings	c Tuffey b Vettori	62
2nd innings	c Astle b Tuffey	10

3. v New Zealand at Trent Bridge 10–13 June 2004 – won by 4 wickets
   Toss: New Zealand
   New Zealand 384 (S.P. Fleming 117, S.B. Styris 108) & 218; England 319 (C.L.
   Cairns 5-79) & 284-6 (G.P. Thorpe 104*)

1st innings	c McCullum b Cairns	0
2nd innings	lbw b Cairns	6

4. v West Indies at Lord's 22–26 July 2004 – won by 210 runs
    Toss: West Indies
    England 568 (R.W.T. Key 221, A.J. Strauss 137, M.P. Vaughan 103) & 325-5 dec (M.P. Vaughan 101*); West Indies 416 (S. Chanderpaul 128*) & 267 (A.F. Giles 5-81)

1st innings	c Jacobs b Banks	137
2nd innings	c Sarwan b Collins	35

    Match highlights:
    Third player to score a century in his first two Lord's Test matches.

5. v West Indies at Edgbaston 29 July–1 August 2004 – won by 256 runs
    Toss: England
    England 566-9 dec (A. Flintoff 167, M.E. Trescothick 105) & 248 (M.E. Trescothick 107, C.H. Gayle 5-34); West Indies 336 (R.R. Sarwan 139) & 222 (A.F. Giles 5-57)

1st innings	c Jacobs b Lawson	24
2nd innings	c Jacobs b Lawson	5

6. v West Indies at Old Trafford 12–16 August 2004 – won by 7 wickets
    Toss: West Indies
    West Indies 395-9 dec & 165; England 330 (G.P. Thorpe 114, D.J. Bravo 6-55) & 231-3

1st innings	b Bravo	90
2nd innings	c Chanderpaul b Collins	12

7. v West Indies at The Oval 19–21 August 2004 – won by 10 wickets
    Toss: England
    England 470 & 4-0; West Indies 152 (S.J. Harmison 6-46) & 318 following on (C.H. Gayle 105)

1st innings	c Edwards b Lawson	14
2nd innings	not out	0

8. v South Africa at Port Elizabeth 17–21 December 2004 – won by 7 wickets
    Toss: South Africa
    South Africa 337 (H.H. Dippenaar 110) & 229; England 425 (A.J. Strauss 126) & 145-3

1st innings	c de Villiers b Pollock	126
2nd innings	not out	94

    Match highlights:
    Named Man of the Match; eighth consecutive victory – an England record; seventh player to score a century on debut in home and away Test matches.

9. v South Africa at Durban 26–30 December 2004 – match drawn
Toss: South Africa
England 139 & 570-7 dec (A.J. Strauss 136, M.E. Trescothick 132, G.P. Thorpe
118*); South Africa 332 (J.H. Kallis 162) & 290-8

| 1st innings | c Ntini b Boje | 25 |
| 2nd innings | c van Jaarsveld b Ntini | 136 |

10. v South Africa at Cape Town 2–6 January 2005 – lost by 196 runs
Toss: South Africa
South Africa 441 (J.H. Kallis 149) & 222-8 dec; England 163 (C.K. Langeveldt
5-46) & 304

| 1st innings | b Ntini | 45 |
| 2nd innings | lbw b Boje | 39 |

Match highlights:
*Reached 1000 Test runs during first innings score of 45; joint 17th fastest player to
reach that target (19 innings) and fourth-fastest Englishman (behind Sutcliffe,
Hutton and Hammond).*

11. v South Africa at Johannesburg 13–17 January 2005 – won by 77 runs
Toss: England
England 411-8 dec (A.J. Strauss 147) & 332-9 dec (M.E. Trescothick 180); South
Africa 419 (H.H. Gibbs 161, M.J. Hoggard 5-144) & 247 (M.J. Hoggard 7-61)

| 1st innings | c Kallis b Pollock | 147 |
| 2nd innings | c de Villiers b Ntini | 0 |

12. v South Africa at Centurion 21–25 January 2005 – match drawn
Toss: England
South Africa 247 & 296-6 dec (J.H. Kallis 136*, A.B. de Villiers 109); England
359 (A. Nel 6-81) & 73-4

| 1st innings | c Boucher b Nel | 44 |
| 2nd innings | c Kallis b Ntini | 0 |

Match highlights:
Named Man of the Series for his three centuries.

13. v Bangladesh at Lord's 26–27 May 2005 – won by an innings and 261 runs
Toss: England
Bangladesh 108 & 159; England 528-3 dec (M.E. Trescothick 194, M.P.
Vaughan 120)

| 1st innings | lbw b Mashrafe Mortaza | 69 |

14. v Bangladesh at Riverside 3–5 June 2005 – won by an innings and 27 runs
Toss: England
Bangladesh 104 (S.J. Harmison 5-38) & 316 (M.J. Hoggard 5-73); England
447-3 dec (I.R. Bell 162*, M.E. Trescothick 151)

1st innings	lbw b Mashrafe Mortaza	8

15. v Australia at Lord's 21–24 July 2005 – lost by 239 runs
Toss: Australia
Australia 190 (S.J. Harmison 5-38) & 384; England 155 (G.D. McGrath 5-53)
& 180

1st innings	c Warne b McGrath	2
2nd innings	c & b Lee	37

16. v Australia at Edgbaston 4–7 August 2005 – won by 2 runs
Toss: Australia
England 407 & 182 (S.K. Warne 6-46); Australia 308 & 279

1st innings	b Warne	48
2nd innings	b Warne	6

17. v Australia at Old Trafford 11–15 August 2005 – match drawn
Toss: England
England 444 (M.P. Vaughan 166) & 280-6 dec (A.J. Strauss 106, G.D. McGrath
5-115); Australia 302 (S.P. Jones 6-53) & 371-9 (R.T. Ponting 156)

1st innings	b Lee	6
2nd innings	c Martyn b McGrath	106

18. v Australia at Trent Bridge 25–28 August 2005 – won by 3 wickets
Toss: England
England 444 (A. Flintoff 102) & 129-7; Australia 218 (S.P. Jones 5-44) & 387

1st innings	c Hayden b Warne	35
2nd innings	c Clarke b Warne	23

19. v Australia at The Oval 8–12 September 2005 – match drawn
Toss: England
England 373 (A.J. Strauss 129, S.K. Warne 6-122) & 335 (K.P. Pietersen 158, S.K.
Warne 6-124); Australia 367 (J.L. Langer 105, M.L. Hayden 138, A. Flintoff
5-78) & 4-0

1st innings	c Katich b Warne	129
2nd innings	c Katich b Warne	1

20. v Pakistan at Multan 12–16 November 2005 – lost by 22 runs
Toss: Pakistan
Pakistan 274 & 341 (Salman Butt 122); England 418 (M.E. Trescothick 193) & 175

1st innings	lbw b Mohammad Sami	9
2nd innings	c Hasan Raza b Danish Kaneria	23

21. v Pakistan at Faisalabad 20–24 November 2005 – match drawn
Toss: Pakistan
Pakistan 462 (Inzamam-ul-Haq 109) & 268-9 dec (Inzamam-ul-Haq 100*);
England 446 (I.R. Bell 115, K.P. Pietersen 100) & 164-6

1st innings	b Naved-ul-Hasan	12
2nd innings	b Naved-ul-Hasan	0

22. v India at Nagpur 1–5 March 2006 – match drawn
Toss: England
England 393 (P.D. Collingwood 134*) & 297-3 dec (A.N. Cook 104*); India 323
(M.J. Hoggard 6-57) & 260-6 (W. Jaffer 100)

1st innings	c Laxman b Sreesanth	28
2nd innings	c Dhoni b Pathan	46

23. v India at Mohali 9–13 March 2006 – lost by 9 wickets
Toss: England
England 300 (A. Kumble 5-76) & 181; India 338 & 144-1

1st innings	c Dhoni b Pathan	18
2nd innings	c Dhoni b Kumble	13

24. v India at Mumbai 18–22 March 2006 – won by 212 runs
Toss: India
England 400 (A.J. Strauss 128) & 191; India 279 & 100 (S.D. Udal 4-14)

1st innings	c Dhoni b Harbhajan Singh	128
2nd innings	c Dhoni b Patel	4

25. v Sri Lanka at Lord's 11–15 May 2006 – match drawn
Toss: England
England 551-6 dec (K.P. Pietersen 158, M.E. Trescothick 106); Sri Lanka 192 &
537-9 following on (D.P.M.D. Jayawardene 119)

1st innings	c Jayawardene b Muralitharan	48

Match highlights:
*Reached 2000 Test runs during his first innings score of 48; 10th fastest
Englishman to achieve this feat (47 innings).*

26. v Sri Lanka at Edgbaston 25–28 May 2006 – won by 6 wickets
Toss: Sri Lanka
Sri Lanka 141 & 231 (M.G. Vandort 105); England 295 (K.P. Pietersen 142, M. Muralitharan 6-86) & 81-4

| 1st innings | run out (Samaraweera) | 30 |
| 2nd innings | c Jayawardene b Muralitharan | 16 |

27. v Sri Lanka at Trent Bridge 2–5 June 2006 – lost by 134 runs
Toss: Sri Lanka
Sri Lanka 231 & 322 (M.S. Panesar 5-78); England 229 & 190 (M. Muralitharan 8-70)

| 1st innings | b Vaas | 7 |
| 2nd innings | c Jayawardene b Muralitharan | 55 |

28. v Pakistan at Lord's 13–17 July 2006 – match drawn
Toss: England
England 528-9 dec (P.D. Collingwood 186, A.N. Cook 105, I.R. Bell 100*) & 296-8 dec (A.J. Strauss 128); Pakistan 445 (Mohammad Yousuf 202) & 214-4

| 1st innings | lbw b Abdul Razzaq | 30 |
| 2nd innings | c Imran Farhat b Danish Kaneria | 128 |

Match highlights:
Test captain for the first time, the 77th Test captain for England; his 128 was highest score by an England captain on debut.

29. v Pakistan at Old Trafford 27–29 July 2006 – won by an innings and 120 runs
Toss: Pakistan
Pakistan 119 (S.J. Harmison 6-19) & 222 (S.J. Harmison 5-57, M.S. Panesar 5-72); England 461-9 dec (A.N. Cook 127, I.R. Bell 106*)

| 1st innings | c Kamran Akmal b Abdul Razzaq | 42 |

Match highlights:
England captain.

ANDREW STRAUSS IN ONE-DAY INTERNATIONAL CRICKET

Compiled by Victor Isaacs

ODI Record

M	I	NO	Runs	HS	Avge	100s	50s
56	56	7	1682	152	35.04	2	9

1. v Sri Lanka at Dambulla 18 November 2003 – lost by 10 wickets
   Toss: England
   England 88 (46.1 overs); Sri Lanka 89-0 (13.5 overs)

   c and b K.A.D.M. Fernando   3

2. v West Indies at Georgetown 18 April 2004 – won by 2 wickets
   Toss: England
   West Indies 156-5 (30 overs) (S. Chanderpaul 84); England 157-8 (29.3 overs)

   b D.J. Bravo   29

3. v West Indies at Port-of-Spain 24 April 2004 – no result
   Toss: West Indies
   West Indies 57-2 (16 overs); England did not bat

4. v West Indies at Gros Islet 1 May 2004 – lost by 5 wickets
   Toss: West Indies
   England 281-8 (50 overs) (M.E. Trescothick 130, A. Flintoff 59); West Indies 284-5 (48 overs) (R.R. Sarwan 73*)

   b M. Dillon   10

5. v West Indies at Gros Islet 2 May 2004 – lost by 4 wickets
   Toss: West Indies
   England 280-8 (50 overs) (M.P. Vaughan 67, A.J. Strauss 67); West Indies 282-6 (47.1 overs) (S. Chanderpaul 63, B.C. Lara 57)

   lbw b C.H. Gayle   67

6. v West Indies at Bridgetown 5 May 2004 – won by 5 wickets
    Toss: England
    West Indies 261-6 (50 overs) (R.R. Sarwan 104*); England 262-5 (47.2 overs)
    (M.E. Trescothick 82, A.J. Strauss 66)

    b I.D.R. Bradshaw   66

7. v West Indies at Trent Bridge 27 June 2004 – lost by 7 wickets
    Toss: West Indies
    England 147 (38.2 overs); West Indies 148-3 (32.2 overs) (C.H. Gayle 60*)

    c R.D. Jacobs b D.J. Bravo   43

8. v New Zealand at Riverside 29 June 2004 – lost by 7 wickets
    Toss: New Zealand
    England 101 (32.5 overs) (J.E.C. Franklin 5-42); New Zealand 103-3 (17.2
    overs)

    c J.D.P. Oram b J.E.C. Franklin   8

9. v West Indies at Headingley 1 July 2004 – won by 7 wickets
    Toss: England
    West Indies 159 (40.1 overs); England 160-3 (22 overs) (M.E. Trescothick 55)

    not out   44

10. v New Zealand at Bristol 4 July 2004 – lost by 6 wickets
    Toss: New Zealand
    England 237-7 (50 overs) (A. Flintoff 106, A.J. Strauss 61); New Zealand 241-4
    (47.2 overs) (S.P. Fleming 99, H.J.H. Marshall 55, N.J. Astle 53)

    c N.J. Astle b I.G. Butler   61

11. v West Indies at Lord's 6 July 2004 – lost by 7 wickets
    Toss: West Indies
    England 237-7 (50 overs) (A. Flintoff 123, A.J. Strauss 100); West Indies 286-3
    (49.1 overs) (C.H. Gayle 132*, R.R. Sarwan 89)

    c D.J. Bravo b C.H. Gayle   100

12. v India at Trent Bridge 1 September 2004 – won by 7 wickets
    Toss: England
    India 170 (43.5 overs) (M. Kaif 50); England 171-3 (32.2 overs) (V.S. Solanki
    52)

    not out   41

13. v India at The Oval 3 September 2004 – won by 70 runs
Toss: India
England 307-5 (A. Flintoff 99, P.D. Collingwood 79*); India 237 (46.3 overs)
(M. Kaif 51, D. Gough 4-50)

c S.C. Ganguly b V. Sehwag   2

14. v India at Lord's 5 September 2004 – lost by 23 runs
Toss: India
India 204 (49.3 overs) (S.C. Ganguly 90, R. Dravid 52, S.J. Harmison 4-22);
England 181 (48.2 overs) (M.P. Vaughan 74)

lbw b I.K. Pathan   2

15. v Zimbabwe at Edgbaston 10 September 2004 – won by 152 runs
Toss: Zimbabwe
England 299-7 (50 overs) (P.D. Collingwood 80*, V.S. Solanki 62); Zimbabwe
147 (39 overs)

c T. Taibu b E.C. Rainsford   25

16. v Sri Lanka at Rose Bowl 17 and 18 September 2004 – won by 49 runs (D/L)
Toss: Sri Lanka
England 251-7 (50 overs) (A. Flintoff 104, M.E. Trescothick 66); Sri Lanka
95-5 (24 overs)

run out (M.F. Maharoof)   7

17. v Australia at Edgbaston 21 September 2004 – won by 6 wickets
Toss: England
Australia 259-9 (50 overs) (D.R. Martyn 65); England 262-4 (46.3 overs) (M.P.
Vaughan 86, M.E. Trescothick 81, A.J. Strauss 52*)

not out   52

18. v West Indies at The Oval 25 September 2004 – lost by 2 wickets
Toss: West Indies
England 217 (49.4 overs) (M.E. Trescothick 104); West Indies 218-8 (48.5 overs)

run out (D.J. Bravo)   18

19. v Zimbabwe at Harare 28 November 2004 – won by 5 wickets
Toss: England
Zimbabwe 195 (49.3 overs) (E. Chigumbura 52); England 197-5 (47.4 overs)
(I.R. Bell 75, M.P. Vaughan 56)

c and b S. Matsikenyeri   8

20. v Zimbabwe at Harare 1 December 2004 – won by 161 runs
Toss: England
England 263-6 (50 overs) (K.P. Pietersen 77*, G.O. Jones 66); Zimbabwe 102
(36 overs) (A.G. Wharf 4-24)

b G.M. Ewing   33

21. v Zimbabwe at Bulawayo 4 December 2004 – won by 8 wickets
Toss: Zimbabwe
England 238-7 (50 overs) (S. Matsikenyeri 73, D.D. Ebrahim 65); England
239-2 (43.1 overs) (V.S. Solanki 100, M.P. Vaughan 54*, I.R. Bell 53)

not out   22

22. v Zimbabwe at Bulawayo 5 December 2004 – won by 74 runs
Toss: England
England 261-6 (50 overs) (M.P. Vaughan 90*, G.O. Jones 80); Zimbabwe 187
(48.4 overs) (H. Masakadza 66, D. Gough 4-34)

c E. Chigumbura b S. Matsikenyeri   17

23. v South Africa at Johannesburg 30 January 2005 – won by 26 runs (D/L)
Toss: England
South Africa 175-9 (50 overs); England 103-3 (25.1 overs)

c J.M. Kemp b A. Nel   15

24. v South Africa at Bloemfontein 2 February 2005 – match tied
Toss: South Africa
England 270-5 (50 overs) (K.P. Pietersen 108*); South Africa 270-8 (50 overs)
(H.H. Gibbs 78, J.H. Kallis 63)

c M.V. Boucher b A.J. Hall   2

25. v South Africa at Port Elizabeth 4 February 2005 – lost by 3 wickets
Toss: England
England 267-8 (50 overs) (V.S. Solanki 66); South Africa 270-7 (49.1 overs)
(G.C. Smith 105, H.H. Gibbs 50)

c A.G. Prince b S.M. Pollock   35

26. v South Africa at Cape Town 6 February 2005 – lost by 108 runs
Toss: England
South Africa 291-5 (50 overs) (H.H. Gibbs 100, J.H. Kallis 71, J.M. Kemp 57);
England 183 (41.2 overs) (K.P. Pietersen 75)

c A.G. Prince b A. Nel   17

27. v South Africa at East London 9 February 2005 – lost by 7 runs
Toss: South Africa
South Africa 311-7 (50 overs) (G.C. Smith 115*, J.M. Kemp 80); England 304-8
(50 overs) (K.P. Pietersen 100*, M.P. Vaughan 70)

run out (M.V. Boucher)   20

28. v South Africa at Durban 11 February 2005 – no result
Toss: South Africa
South Africa 211 (46.3 overs) (H.H. Gibbs 118); England 7-2 (3.4 overs)

not out   0

29. v South Africa at Centurion 13 February 2005 – lost by 3 wickets
Toss: South Africa
England 240 (49.5 overs) (K.P. Pietersen 116); South Africa 241-7 (49 overs)
(A.G. Prince 62*)

c M.V. Boucher b A. Nel   15

30. v Bangladesh at The Oval 16 June 2005 – won by 10 wickets
Toss: England
Bangladesh 190 (45.2 overs) (Aftab Ahmed 51, S.J. Harmison 4-39); England
192-0 (24.5 overs) (M.E. Trescothick 100*, A.J. Strauss 82*)

not out   82

31. v Australia at Bristol 19 June 2005 – won by 3 wickets
Toss: Australia
Australia 252-9 (50 overs) (M.E.K. Hussey 84, S.J. Harmison 5-33); England
253-7 (47.3 overs) (K.P. Pietersen 91*, M.P. Vaughan 57)

b G.D. McGrath   16

32. v Bangladesh at Trent Bridge 21 June 2005 – won by 168 runs
Toss: England
England 391-4 (50 overs) (A.J. Strauss 152, P.D. Collingwood 112*, M.E.
Trescothick 85); Bangladesh 223 (45.2 overs) (Mohammad Ashraful 94, Javed
Omar 59, P.D. Collingwood 6-31, C.T. Tremlett 4-32)

lbw b Nazmul Hossain   152

Match highlights:
Reached 1000 runs (31 innings)

33. v Australia at Riverside 23 June 2005 – lost by 57 runs
Toss: England
Australia 266-5 (50 overs) (A. Symonds 73, D.R. Martyn 68*); England 209-9 (50 overs)

b B. Lee   3

34. v Bangladesh at Headingley 26 June 2005 – won by 5 wickets
Toss: Bangladesh
Bangladesh 208-7 (50 overs) (Javed Omar 81, A. Flintoff 4-29); England 209-5 (38.5 overs) (A.J. Strauss 98)

b Manjural Islam Rana   98

Match highlights:
Named Man of the Match for first time in One-Day Internationals

35. v Australia at Edgbaston 28 June 2005 – no result
Toss: Australia
Australia 261-9 (50 overs) (A. Symonds 74); England 37-1 (6 overs)

c J.N. Gillespie b G.D. McGrath   25

36. v Australia at Lord's 2 July 2005 – match tied
Toss: England
Australia 196 (48.5 overs) (M.E.K. Hussey 62*), England 196-9 (50 overs) (G.O. Jones 71, P.D. Collingwood 53)

b B. Lee   2

37. v Australia at Headingley 7 July 2005 – won by 9 wickets
Toss: England
Australia 219-7 (50 overs) (P.D. Collingwood 4-34); England 221-1 (46 overs) (M.E. Trescothick 104*, M.P. Vaughan 59*)

c A.C. Gilchrist b G.B. Hogg   41

38. v Australia at Lord's 10 July 2005 – lost by 7 wickets
Toss: Australia
England 223-8 (50 overs) (A. Flintoff 87, B. Lee 5-41), Australia 224-3 (44.2 overs) (R.T. Ponting 111)

b M.S. Kasprowicz   11

39. v Australia at The Oval 12 July 2005 – lost by 8 wickets
Toss: Australia
England 228-7 (50 overs) (K.P. Pietersen 74, V.S. Solanki 53*); Australia 229-2 (34.5 overs) (A.C. Gilchrist 121*)

c A.C. Gilchrist b M.S. Kasprowicz   36

40. v Pakistan at Lahore 10 December 2005 – won by 42 runs
Toss: England
England 327-4 (50 overs) (A.J. Strauss 94, A. Flintoff 72*, K.P. Pietersen 56);
Pakistan 285 (46.5 overs) (Salman Butt 67, Younis Khan 60, Mohammad
Yousuf 59, Shoaib Malik 50)

c Salman Butt b Danish Kaneria   94

Match highlights:
Named Man of the Match

41. v Pakistan at Lahore 12 December 2005 – lost by 7 wickets
Toss: England
England 230 (48.4 overs) (L.E. Plunkett 56, Shoaib Akhtar 5-53); Pakistan 231-
3 (44 overs) (Kamran Akmal 102)

c Kamran Akmal b Shoaib Akhtar   0

42. v Pakistan at Karachi 15 December 2005 – lost by 165 runs
Toss: England
Pakistan 353-6 (50 overs) (Kamran Akmal 109, Mohammad Yousuf 68, Abdul
Razzaq 51*); England 188 (42 overs)

lbw b Mohammad Sami   23

43. v Pakistan at Rawalpindi 19 December 2005 – lost by 13 runs
Toss: Pakistan
Pakistan 210 (47.2 overs) (Inzamam-ul-Haq 81*); England 197 (48.1 overs)

lbw b Naved-ul-Hasan   0

44. v Pakistan at Rawalpindi 21 December 2005 – won by 6 runs
Toss: England
England 206-9 (50 overs); Pakistan 200-9 (50 overs) (Yasir Hameed 57,
Mohammad Yousuf 54, J.M. Anderson 4-48)

st Kamran Akmal b Arshad Khan   26

45. v India at Delhi 28 March 2006 – lost by 39 runs
Toss: England
India 203 (46.4 overs) (Kabir Ali 4-45); England 164 (38.1 overs) (Harbhajan
Singh 5-31)

c M.S. Dhoni b I.K. Pathan   0

46. v India at Faridabad 31 March 2006 – lost by 4 wickets
Toss: England
England 226 (49.5 overs) (K.P. Pietersen 71, A.J. Strauss 61); India 230-6 (49 overs) (S.K. Raina 81*)

b R.R. Powar   61

47. v India at Goa 3 April 2006 – lost by 49 runs
Toss: India
India 294-6 (50 overs) (Yuvraj Singh 103, S.K. Raina 61); England 245 (48.5 overs) (P.D. Collingwood 93, I.K. Pathan 4-51)

c M.S. Dhoni b I.K. Pathan   7

48. v India at Cochin 6 April 2006 – lost by 4 wickets
Toss: England
England 237 (48.4 overs) (K.P. Pietersen 77); India 238-6 (47.2 overs) (R. Dravid 65)

lbw b I.K. Pathan   7

49. v India at Jamshedpur 12 April 2006 – won by 5 wickets
Toss: India
India 223 (48 overs) (M.S. Dhoni 96, R.R. Powar 54); England 227-5 (42.4 overs) (A.J. Strauss 74*)

retired hurt   74

Match highlights:
First match as England captain; named Man of the Match; retired hurt at 74, suffering from exhaustion.

50. v India at Indore 15 April 2006 – lost by 7 wickets
Toss: India
England 288 (50 overs) (K.P. Pietersen 64, P.D. Collingwood 64, G.O. Jones 53, S. Sreesanth 6-55); India 289-3 (49.1 overs) (A.R. Uthappa 86, R. Dravid 69, Yuvraj Singh 63*, S.K. Raina 53)

c K.K.D. Karthik b S. Sreesanth   25

Match highlights:
England captain.

51. v Ireland at Belfast 13 June 2006 – won by 38 runs
Toss: England
England 301-7 (50 overs) (M.E. Trescothick 113, I.R. Bell 80); Ireland 263-9 (50 overs) (A.C. Botha 52)

c A.C. Botha b K.J. O'Brien   4

Match highlights:
England captain.

52.   v Sri Lanka at Lord's 17 June 2006 – lost by 20 runs
Toss: England
Sri Lanka 257-9 (50 overs) (W.U. Tharanga 120); England 237-9 (50 overs) (M.E. Trescothick 67, J.W.M. Dalrymple 67)

c K.C. Sangakkara b C.R.D. Fernando   12

Match highlights:
England captain.

53.   v Sri Lanka at The Oval 20 June 2006
Toss: Sri Lanka
Sri Lanka 319-8 (50 overs) (S.T. Jayasuriya 122, D.P.M.D. Jayawardene 66, K.C. Sangakkara 51); England 273 (46.4 overs) (K.P. Pietersen 73, P.D. Collingwood 56)

c Muralitharan b Maharoof   18

Match highlights:
England captain.

54.   v Sri Lanka at Riverside 24 June 2006 – lost by 8 wickets
Toss: England
England 261-7 (50 overs) (I.R. Bell 77); Sri Lanka 265-2 (42.2 overs) (D.P.M.D. Jayawardene 126*, K.C. Sangakkara 58)

lbw b C. Vaas   32

Match highlights:
England captain.

55.   v Sri Lanka at Old Trafford 28 June 2006 – lost by 33 runs
Toss: Sri Lanka
Sri Lanka 318-7 (50 overs) (D.P.M.D. Jayawardene 100, W.U. Tharanga 60, M.F. Maharoof 58*); England 285 (48.4 overs) (A.J. Strauss 45)

c K.C. Sangakkara b Dilshan   45

Match highlights:
England captain.

56. v Sri Lanka at Headingley 1 July 2006 – lost by 8 wickets
Toss: England
England 321-7 (50 overs) (M.E. Trescothick 121, S.L. Malinga 4-44); Sri Lanka
324-2 (37.3 overs) (S.T. Jayasuriya 152, W.U. Tharanga 109)

c K.C. Sangakkara b S.L. Malinga   26

Match highlights:
England captain.

Full Career Records:

First-class (up to 2nd Test at Old Trafford v Pakistan)

Mat	Inns	NO	Runs	HS	Avge	100	50	Ct
119	211	12	8300	176	41.70	21	36	87

List-A (Limited Overs)

Mat	Inns	NO	Runs	HS	Avge	100	50	Ct
157	150	12	4188	152	30.34	4	27	36

INDEX